The Dollar and National Security

The Dollar and National Security

The Monetary Component of Hard Power

Paul R. Viotti

Stanford Security Studies

An Imprint of Stanford University Press

Stanford, California

Stanford University Press
Stanford, California

Library of Congress Cataloging-in-Publication Data

Viotti, Paul R., author
  The dollar and national security : the monetary component of hard power / Paul R. Viotti.
      pages cm.
  Includes bibliographical references and index.
  ISBN 978-0-8047-9113-7 (cloth : alk. paper) — ISBN 978-0-8047-9225-7 (pbk. : alk. paper)
  1. National security—Economic aspects—United States—History. 2. Foreign
exchange—United States—History. 3. Monetary policy—United States—
History. 4. Dollar, American—History. 5. National security—Economic aspects—
Europe—History. 6. Foreign exchange—Europe—History. 7. Monetary policy—
Europe—History.   I. Title.

  HC110.D4V56 2014
  355'.033073—dc23   2014010073

ISBN 978-0-8047-9230-1 (electronic)

Typeset at Stanford University Press in 10/14 Minion

Special discounts for bulk quantities of Stanford Security Studies are available to
corporations, professional associations, and other organizations. For details and
discount information, contact the special sales department of Stanford University Press.
Tel: (650) 736-1782, Fax: (650) 736-1784

To JOHN GERARD RUGGIE
for the conceptual insights he shared
and the support he gave me and
fellow doctoral students at Cal decades ago,
which are as meaningful now as they were then.

CONTENTS

Tables

Acknowledgments

There are many to whom I'm indebted over many years of research on this project. Foremost among them for their direct impact on my work decades ago at Cal Berkeley are the late Ernst B. Haas and Kenneth N. Waltz—the dialectic in their thinking challenging my understandings of international relations and the economic component within IR; John G. Ruggie, to whom this volume is dedicated; and Richard Norgaard, who read earlier versions and commented on the economics side of international political economy.

For the common interest we share in the security implications of globalization, I refer to my friend and colleague at the University of Denver (DU), David Goldfischer. I've relied on scholarly input from the economics side from three other friends and colleagues at DU—Haider Khan, Kishore Kulkarni, and George deMartino. Other friends and colleagues who have offered their suggestions—as well as their encouragement—include my decades-long friends Mark Kauppi and Dan Caldwell, John A. (Jay) Williams, Barry Hughes, Tom Farer, Alan Parrington, Warren Miller, Curtis Cook, and Brent Shapiro.

Phil Grub and Siegfried Garbuny at the George Washington University influenced my first work on this topic in the early 1970s. Editors with whom I've worked closely, benefiting greatly from their inputs, include Geoffrey Burn, James Holt, and the late Henry Tom, with whom I also shared a Honolulu identity. Kudos also are due to my graduate research associates at the University of Denver, particularly Eric de Campos, Daniel Green, Nathan Vasher, Robert Shelala, Carina Solmirano, and Chris Saeger. Finally, my son, Paul R. Viotti, Jr., very generously took time to review the manuscript and make important suggestions drawn from his own work and study of political economy. He also gets credit for the idea of starting the book with a hypothetical scenario that underscores the importance to national and international security of the issues before us. Having acknowledged all of these constructive influences on my work, I accept full responsibility for any errors the reader may find in this volume.

Preface

The volume and quality of resources mobilized for use in foreign affairs depends on two factors: first, the productive capacity and wealth of the country, i.e., manpower, capital, and land, and second, the share of these resources, or their outputs, allocated to foreign policy.

—Klaus Knorr

The discovery that banks could . . . create money came very early in the development of banking. . . . The process by which banks create money is so simple that the mind is repelled. Where something so important is involved, a deeper mystery seems only decent.

—John Kenneth Galbraith

SCENARIO

It has been the best of times. Now it seems the worst of times. Several months of political wrangling have been ongoing in Washington—legislative calls by a powerful minority in the House and Senate for even deeper budget cuts, coupled with a threat to block any effort to raise the national debt ceiling. These threats to shut government down or force default on government obligations have spooked the markets, already resulting in another rating downgrade for U.S. Treasuries.

The crisis begins with a two-pronged attack on the New York Stock Exchange (NYSE). The first shock begins innocuously enough with a coordinated phishing attack at 11:30 a.m.—hacker e-mails mimicking different offices in the New York Federal Reserve Bank that, because of their apparent identity, get ready access. These are not ordinary hackers with only short-term purposes in mind. No, the hackers are part of an insurgent group that wants to bring down American capital and, with it, the prominent position the U.S. dollar still enjoys in the global economy.

The phishers now have unfettered access to the NYSE secure server. Implanting malicious software, the phishers are not interested in downloading NYSE and corporate data. They want to delete information on record, destroying the massive archives of current past data in the NYSE server's memory. The phishers have also activated a botnet—tens of thousands of computers linked by the phishing attack—that overwhelms the NYSE server, causing it to freeze and then crash completely.

The NYSE is paralyzed and in complete turmoil. Panic erupts, spreading to other exchanges in the global market. Stock prices are down at least 20 percent worldwide—some more, others a few points less. The NYSE closes at noon, but since the server is down there is no way to communicate that through normal electronic channels to trading firms with seats on the exchange, not to mention investors who continue trying to place buy and sell orders. Television, radio, private e-mails, texts, phone calls, and social media are the principal outlets for communicating with trading houses and investors. If that were not enough, just as traders are clearing from the floor of the stock exchange, a high-explosive car bomb detonates in front of the exchange, killing pedestrians and bystanders and severely damaging the building's façade.

This two-pronged attack—combining the impact of cyber and high explosives—has devastating effects. Stock markets take a dive worldwide as people try to liquidate their assets. When the attack is understood as having been directed principally against the United States, where most damage was done, foreign markets gradually recover. The NYSE and other U.S. stock exchanges remain closed. There is a run, mostly on American banks. The president intervenes and, using Roosevelt's Depression-era precedent, declares a bank "holiday"—effectively closing the banks and other financial institutions until order can be restored to capital markets.

Notwithstanding market interventions by European, Japanese, Chinese, and other treasuries and central banks, market forces overwhelm their capabilities and genuine, well-intended, collaborative efforts to hold the dollar's position. These events undermine confidence in the U.S. economy and bring the dollar down to half its value vis-à-vis other major currencies. Unable to rely on the dollar for daily transactions—not to mention its loss as a store of value—corporate America is in disarray both at home and abroad.

OPEC countries quickly shift to euro-pricing of oil, promising they also will accept dollars once stability returns to currency markets. Meanwhile, the U.S. Treasury reluctantly imposes exchange controls, trying to stem the flood of depreciated dollars into already swamped global currency markets. Airlines have reduced international flights and shipping companies are holding many ships in port as they work to ensure necessary financing.

To keep international commerce from declining precipitously, a joint National Security Council (NSC) task force including representatives from the Treasury, the Federal Reserve, and Commerce and State departments meets to explore the feasibility of special trading arrangements organized regionally—Latin

America, Europe, Asia, and the Pacific. Bilateral arrangements will be sought to sustain trade with other countries in central and south Asia, the Middle East, and Africa.

To keep U.S. national security commitments abroad, the State and Defense departments (coordinating with Treasury and the Federal Reserve) get key allies to agree as a stopgap measure to facilitate U.S. government expenditures in local currency purchased from their respective central banks at 90 percent of the precrisis, dollar-euro or dollar-yen exchange rates. Nevertheless, talk in the Congress turns quickly to bringing American forces home from overseas deployments. Following an NSC meeting, the administration counters that bringing the fleet back to home ports, coupled with precipitous withdrawal from Japanese, South Korean, central Asian, Middle East, and European bases, would destabilize these regions and thus undermine American national security.

Could this happen? How realistic is this scenario? What are the adverse security and other implications of such a calamity? Could the euro or other key currencies face the same fate? Would worldwide depression be the outcome in any event? How dependent is maintaining national security on multilateral, collaborative actions that sustain the global monetary regime and the viability of currencies within it?

This book is about money and security. Defense establishments and the armed forces they organize, train, equip, and deploy depend upon the security of capital and capital flows that have become increasingly globalized. Military capabilities thus are closely tied not only to the size of the economic base from which they are drawn but also to the viability of global convertibility and exchange arrangements. We miss at our peril the potential for disruption of capital flows that can undermine U.S. economic security as well as the ability both to deploy military units, sustaining their operations worldwide, and to maintain the network of U.S. diplomatic missions and the programs they administer abroad.

Economic, military, and other capabilities do not exist in a vacuum as if they were objective realities "out there." Yes, a currency's (like the dollar's) exchange value is a function of supply and demand, but these are essentially *subjective* judgments in markets about its relative worth in relation to other currencies. Although mass publics at home and abroad have a stake in these technical matters, the interests and interpretive understandings held by policy elites matter most—in particular those among the *owners or managers of capital* (or OMC), who focus on international finance and the international monetary regimes that sustain global commerce and their capital positions.

Included in their ranks are the finance ministers, central bankers, private-sector bankers, and others who own or manage large concentrations of capital—the decisive factor of production in the present world economy. Their judgments—especially those held by monetary officials who manage global capital flows—are heavily influenced by subjective appraisals of a country's economic base and growth potential relative to other national economies. Also influential are the rules or accepted norms of the international monetary regime within which the currency operates (and which they and those among the transnational OMC who preceded them have constructed).

References in this volume to the owners or managers of capital that appear throughout this volume are an empirically grounded shorthand for net creditors, mainly those institutions or individuals with large capital holdings as well as those who may be less wealthy personally but manage capital held by others in relation to the capital flows that now occur globally. They are identifiable as real people. The category includes individuals in their private capacity or in their governmental or non-governmental roles in corporations, banks, and other groups. In our treatment of the relation between the dollar and national security in this book, however, our focus is primarily on banking and treasury officials (and those who advise or influence them)—all policy elites or experts who manage capital for central banks and governmental treasuries or finance ministries.

Because they deal with so important a factor of production as capital, especially its monetary representation, their decisions and actions are inherently political—as, indeed, most important and often contentious things are (or quickly become)! Just because the owners and managers of capital are an identifiable category does not mean that they are of one mind or that they always see their interests the same way.

Conflicts, formation of coalitions and countercoalitions among capital owners and managers, decisions (and the authority to make them) are the stuff of politics, whether one is acting domestically or globally. Authoritative choice about the dollar, its relation to other currencies, and the economy on which the currency is based are what matter to us here. Both mass publics and capital elites matter in financial and other markets, but on monetary policy decisions our focus is on the financial segment constituted by bankers (particularly central bankers) and Treasury officials.

Economic and national security is the objective we explore in the pages that follow, explicitly underscoring *cooperative security* as the most propitious means to that end. The Introduction, on Money and Security, sets the stage conceptually for what follows on the U.S. dollar, security, and monetary exchange. Subsequent chapters provide an historical narrative that underscores what is often overlooked—how *security* and *money* are inextricably linked. Most commentaries on international monetary matters focus on the implications for trade, investment, and economic growth of exchange-rate changes and the overall stability of a currency. Although these are an important part of economic security, few accounts take up how security in the broader sense can be advantaged or set back.

PART ONE: THE EUROPEAN CENTER—
STERLING, THE DOLLAR, AND SECURITY BEFORE WORLD WAR II

The first part of the book takes up national and global security in relation to monetary exchange in the late nineteenth century, before and during World War I, and the interwar period that followed. We begin this story in Chapter One ("Money, Empire, and Prewar Security") with current challenges in the European Union, but quickly flash back to the nineteenth century when Britain depended on the global acceptance of sterling (the pound, defined as equal to a fixed quantity of gold) for securing its worldwide empire, upon which, figuratively, "the sun never set." Indeed, globes well into the last half of the twentieth century standardized with pale rose color those parts of residual empire and commonwealth.

The chapter chronicles the years leading up to World War I. Then, as now, intervention by central and private banks and other financiers among the owners or managers of capital was key to maintaining international liquidity—an essential component of security in the late-nineteenth- and early-twentieth-century years before the outbreak of war in 1914.

In monetary finance things were never left purely to market forces then any more than they are today. Faced with crises, banks "too large to fail" now turn to governmental authorities for assistance, the latter understanding that allowing massive failures in the banking sector with spillover to the entire economy is contrary to the national interest. Notwithstanding laissez-faire, liberal sentiments in the ideological rhetoric of the day, economic- and military-security stakes were (and are) too high for the OMC to leave national currencies entirely at risk to market forces beyond their control. *Plus ça change, plus c'est la même chose.*

The money and security story continues in Chapter Two ("Wartime Security and Monetary Exchange in the Great War"). During the "Great War" the Allies and the Central Powers refashioned their monetary regimes to sustain their war efforts. The warring parties also shared an interest in securing currency exchange between the rival camps. Even in the midst of world war, the adversaries found ways to exchange each other's currencies, particularly on the neutral ground offered by Swiss and Dutch banks. Access to an enemy's currency for intelligence, espionage, or other purposes was a sideline activity, but one in which both sides had a vested interest.

World War I devastated European countries—both the defeated and the "victorious," the latter left with substantial war debts owed in particular to the United States. It also marked the beginning of the end of the British Empire, though few understood this at the time. It would take a depression, World War II, and its aftermath to bleed Britain's global capital position still further.

Chapter Three ("Restoring Sterling, Commerce, and Security after World War I") addresses the immediate task after the war ended in 1918: to return, if possible, to what was understood as normalcy—restoring the sterling-gold exchange standard as foundation for global commerce and for the security of Britain and its global-imperial position. British and American central bankers worked collaboratively to make this happen, the dollar linked to sterling, the latter remaining the global benchmark.

Monetary collaboration between Britain and the United States was the foundation for cooperative security efforts between the two in the immediate postwar years. Understandings among capital owners or managers in and out of government over their commercial and security interests inspired the effort to restore the pre-1914 gold-exchange standard as the cornerstone of a new international monetary regime.

PART TWO: THE UNITED STATES MOVES TO THE CENTER: DOLLAR PRIMACY AND AMERICAN NATIONAL SECURITY

Part Two of the book continues the monetary-security story, chronicling the dollar's rise to preeminence from World War II to present-day challenges. Indeed, the dollar has played an instrumental role in American economic and national security over the past seven decades, the euro joining it in center stage in the first years of the new century.

Efforts in the 1920s to restore security and stabilize international monetary exchange so essential to international commerce ran amok when the stock market crashed in 1929 and a decade of economic depression began. Cooperative security on monetary matters fell apart during the 1930s, which we discuss in Chapter Four ("Money and Cooperative Security, the Interwar Years, and World War II"). So weakened was its capital position during the 1930s (the Great Depression years), Britain was unable to sustain its international monetary leadership and the U.S. proved unwilling at the time to assume the role.

Competitive devaluations, raising import tariffs, and other "beggar thy neighbor" policies became the illiberal order of the day. Given an arms race between Germany and both Britain (challenging its naval supremacy) and France (threatening its ground forces) and other factors, the monetary world again divided into two opposing currency blocs between the Allies and the Axis powers. As in World War I, wartime monetary exchange was conducted not only within the two camps organized as opposing alliances, similar to the Great War, but also between them—Switzerland again a major neutral venue for such transactions. The Netherlands, occupied by Germany in World War II, no longer played the significant monetary role it had in World War I.

Officials at the international conference held in 1944 at Bretton Woods, New Hampshire, forged a political consensus to restore relatively fixed exchange rates in a new dollar-gold exchange regime. American preferences prevailed at this gathering of governmental and other capital-management experts one year before the end of the war. Now having the world's strongest capital position, U.S. officials finally took the torch of global monetary leadership from Britain, the dollar effectively displacing sterling in the new dollar-gold exchange regime.

In the minds of U.S. negotiators, it was in the U.S. (and capital) interest to do so. Given postwar opportunities (and the global responsibilities U.S. officials had assumed), the dollar as the universally accepted key currency and reserve asset allowed American decision-makers to make the substantial outlays necessary to finance the country's economic and national security objectives abroad. Even oil became priced in dollars as principal unit of account, a singular U.S. advantage in the conduct of its foreign and national security policy abroad, particularly military deployments that depend so heavily on access to energy sources.

We examine security in relation to the Bretton Woods relatively fixed exchange-rate regime (1946–71) in Chapter Five ("Cold War and the Bretton Woods Years") and, in Chapter Six ("Sustaining Dollar Primacy—From Bretton Woods to Managed Flexibility"), the present-day exchange-rate regime of managed flexibility that succeeded it. Dollar supremacy has marked the post–World War II period, but others sought alternatives. Frustrated by post–Bretton Woods exchange-rate turbulence in the 1970s, policy elites in European Union countries coalesced in constructing a European monetary system of closely co-ordinated exchange rates. These arrangements ultimately led to the establishment of a European Central Bank (ECB) and emergence of the euro at the beginning of the new millennium as an alternative key currency and reserve asset alongside the dollar.

The United States, the European Union, and other countries with currencies accepted not only in payment of obligations but also held as reserves by others enjoy greater freedom in the conduct of their foreign and national security policies. We discuss in Chapter Seven ("The Dollar, the Euro, and Cooperative Security") the development of the euro in relation to the dollar and the promotion of cooperative security. As with Americans, Europeans now are much less constrained in the outlays they make abroad than they would have been had the euro not come on stage and the Bretton Woods regime of relatively fixed exchange rates not yielded to one in which they fluctuate in relation to market forces moderated by treasury and central bank interventions.

Particularly when outlays are of massive scale, financing military and other government expenditures, however necessary they may seem, quickly becomes problematic if actions are taken unilaterally in the absence of a consensus or support base among policy elites in other countries. Cooperative measures from political and monetary authorities in other countries likely will be more forthcoming when, and if, efforts taken beforehand to develop a broad multilateral consensus have met with some success.

Policy elites among capital managers, particularly treasury or finance ministers and central bankers, understand and know how to serve individual and shared commercial and security interests. Perceived individual and collective interests are the key drivers toward building the kind of durable consensus necessary to sustain the external financing of American foreign and national security policy. The same is true, of course, as decision-makers in European Union countries, China, Japan, Russia, India, Brazil, or other countries assume an even larger policy presence in global commerce, monetary, and security matters in the coming decades.

The international monetary story we relate in the pages that follow is familiar to readers of economic history. What is new in this telling, however, is its grounding in economic and national security. It is not just a matter of how international monetary arrangements affect global trade and investment essential to economic security but also how they relate to the conduct of foreign and national security policies, especially the very expensive deployment and use of armed forces. It is this monetary component of hard power that is our focal point and that we address in the Conclusion.

The Dollar and National Security

Introduction: Money and Security

Few persons will be so visionary as seriously to contend that military forces ought not to be raised to quell a rebellion or resist an invasion. . . . Under a vigorous national government, the natural strength and resources of the country, directed to a common interest, would baffle all the combinations of European jealousy to restrain our growth. This situation would even take away the motive to such combinations, by inducing an impracticability of success. An active commerce, an extensive navigation, and a flourishing marine would then be the offspring of moral and physical necessity. . . .

Commerce is . . . the most productive source of national wealth. . . . Promoting the introduction and circulation of the precious metals [that is, money], those darling objects of human avarice and enterprise . . . serves to vivify and invigorate the channels of industry, and to make them flow with greater activity and copiousness. . . . Commerce . . . must of necessity render the payment of taxes easier, and facilitate the requisite supplies to the treasury. . . . A nation cannot long exist without revenues. . . . The necessities of the State . . . must be satisfied in some mode or other. . . . Unless all the sources of revenue are open to its demands, the finances of the community . . . cannot be put into a situation consistent with its respectability or its security. . . .

—Alexander Hamilton (later Secretary of the Treasury),
Federalist 25, 11, and 12 (1787)

The appropriation of vast sums of money and a well-coordinated executive direction of our defense efforts are not in themselves enough. Guns, planes, ships and many other things have to be built in the factories and arsenals of America. . . . I want to make it clear that it is the purpose of the nation to build now with all possible speed every machine, every arsenal, every factory that we need to manufacture our defense materiel.. . . We must be the great arsenal of democracy. . . .

—Franklin Delano Roosevelt (Fireside Chat, December 1940)

Security and the exchange of money are the subject of this book. Monetary matters are not just foundational to the "real" economy of domestic and international commerce, but also core to national and international security. Money and the economy are the means by which militaries are built and deployed operationally. They are also ends in themselves that we try to secure. Indeed, economy, money, and security are inextricably linked as both means and ends. We draw analytic distinctions among them, but empirically they are inseparable.

In these introductory remarks we set the stage conceptually for the chapters that follow with sections on (1) money and security as social constructions accommodating national interests with subsections on security and economy, cooperative security and money, and managing exchange rates; (2) ideas and power, examining economic security, the globalization of capital, and the elites or individuals who *own* or *manage* it—referred to here as the OMC, the owners or managers of capital; (3) the monetary component of U.S. foreign and national security policy—the privileges and costs of maintaining reserve currencies and how the U.S. dollar relates to European and Asian currencies, with particular attention to the Chinese case; and (4) international monetary regime change, U.S. commerce, and national security served by a greater propensity toward multilateralism.

THE SOCIAL CONSTRUCTION OF MONEY AND SECURITY

Money is a social construction.[1] So are the rules for its exchange. We use money to measure value by setting prices or estimating worth, which in turn allows us to buy and sell, import and export, save, invest, and reap the rewards or suffer the losses from such activities. As such, money is socially constructed to provide a unit of account and store of value as well as a medium of exchange—a claim on goods and services both domestically and internationally.

Whether for consumption, saving, or investment, we engage in these activities as individuals or in firms and other groups. So do governments. Commerce—the exchange of money, goods, and services as well as the norms we set and rules we make for its conduct in the markets we construct—is not just a private, nongovernmental domain. Governments and their agents—treasury officials and central bankers in monetary matters as managers of "sovereign" or state capital,[2] foreign ministers and defense officials, military personnel, police, intelligence agents, and the like—are full participants, some playing decisive roles.

Security is also a social construction, although one not so easily achieved. Leaders of some states may seek gains through the use of armed force. Others genuinely may seek to avoid war, but following the age-old maxim *si vis pacem, para bellum*—avoiding war through military preparedness—still costs enormous sums. This defense spending has to be financed, capital drawn from national resources through taxation or borrowed either domestically or from abroad.

Spending more on "defense" often leads others to spend more as well, thus precluding all parties from registering real gains in security. Arms competition may itself contribute to the outbreak of war. Notwithstanding this security dilemma,[3] military spending continues to consume extraordinary amounts of national product. Moreover, threats that motivate this spending come not only from other states but also from nonstate actors that engage in terrorism, insurgency, guerrilla warfare, or other forms of political violence.

Defense establishments and the armed forces they organize, finance, train, equip, and deploy depend upon the security of capital and capital flows that have become increasingly globalized.[4] Military capabilities are closely tied not only to the size of the economic base from which they are drawn but also to the viability of global convertibility and exchange arrangements. U.S. policymakers miss at their peril the potential for disruption of capital flows that can undermine U.S. economic security,[5] as well as the ability to maintain and deploy military units abroad.

Players in currency and other markets now face cyber threats that further undermine confidence in the security of capital and the financial institutions constructed to sustain both its value and its utility in national and international commerce. Attacks on private-sector and central banks are every much a threat to national and international security as are the more conventional threats states and societies face from the use of armed force. "Warriors" on the monetary front thus understand viscerally the amazingly complex set of challenges or outright threats from both state and nonstate actors.

In this volume we identify this historic but often overlooked linkage between security and international monetary arrangements that protects domestic stakes in international commerce and helps finance expenditures for foreign policy and national security purposes. Constructing, maintaining, adapting, or transforming these international monetary arrangements or *regimes*—the rules that govern international monetary exchange—is part of a highly complex, often highly charged political process.[6]

Security also shares with international monetary regimes this complexity and political connection, but has proven to be the far more elusive construct. It seems always beyond our grasp, whether defined more traditionally in the balance between war and peace among states or, as many now do, in terms of human rights and socioeconomic well-being. What security means (much less how it is to be achieved) seems daunting in a world still defined as the domain of states claiming rights to act independently by virtue of their sovereignty and in which nonstate actors also pose threats across national borders.

Given their importance to so many parties with diverse understandings of the interests at stake, both economy and security quickly enter the domain of politics. If, as is often said, war is too important to be left to the generals, so it is that money and commerce cannot be left just to economists, the owners and managers of capital, or others engaged in business or government pursuits! We need to grasp the threads that tie international monetary relations with security concerns, understanding them jointly as essentially political matters.

SECURITY AND ECONOMY

U.S. foreign and national security policy-makers depend to a greater degree than even they sometimes realize upon the purchasing power and continued acceptance of the dollar, which they use around the clock to finance military and other governmental expenditures abroad. Indeed, American policy-makers have faced fewer of the financial or monetary constraints that limit the foreign and security policies pursued by policy elites in other countries. Even oil is priced in dollars. This privileged position is due, of course, to the size and strength of the U.S. economy and, as a result, the dollar's standing since World War II as a principal reserve asset held by foreign finance ministries and central banks. Although the euro has assumed an ever-larger global role, the dollar is still the key currency used internationally as means of payment by those engaged in commercial, governmental, and other transactions. The dollar remains not only the most commonly used means to finance transactions globally—investing, buying and selling, importing and exporting—but also the unit of account in pricing and contracting.

The euro has joined the dollar in these reserve-asset and key-currency roles.[7] Although some predicted that the euro would challenge the dollar's preeminence, in fact thus far it has been more the partner than the competitor—as was the case earlier for the German mark, French franc, and Japanese yen—currencies from countries closely tied by shared interests with the United States commercially as well as for their collective defense and security. Notwithstanding predictions of its demise, the euro has weathered financial crises, particularly those occurring among Mediterranean countries within the eurozone. Unlike the United States, which has national monetary and fiscal policies centralized at the federal level, European Union countries coordinate national monetary policies within a common central bank but still have separate fiscal policies.

These policy asymmetries among the participating eurozone states and the adverse political impact of remedies agreed or effectively imposed on member states are ongoing challenges to European unity. Moreover, some EU members—notably Britain—have not adopted the euro, preferring instead to maintain their national currencies. Politics in the United Kingdom have led it to vacillate across the decades between a European and a transatlantic identity, the latter augmented by commonwealth ties that are the residuum of empire lost.

The Japanese yen—as with other national currencies—does not have the standing in world markets the dollar has enjoyed. Nor is it in sufficient supply to assume a role coequal with the dollar as key currency for international exchange. The same is true for the Chinese yuan (the renminbi or RMB) and other rising currencies that, although their presence has grown substantially, still have a relatively smaller presence globally.[8] Indeed, their monetary authorities still find it in their interest to maintain present arrangements for the exchange of their currencies with the dollar—the euro now joining it in center stage as well.

We depart in this book from the conventional script that tells the international monetary story only in relation to international trade, investment, and other forms of commerce. Our focus here, then, is not just on money and economy—important as they are—but also on security. In this regard, money, exchange rates, and rules for currency exchange are social constructions integral to essentially political processes and grounded in both commercial and security interests. It is this relation between security and international monetary relations that most other accounts overlook.

Security and economy are clearly intertwined.[9] Economic objectives—sustaining domestic economies, international commerce and monetary arrangements—rest on a security rationale. Moreover, foreign and national security policies pursued by decision-makers in the United States and other countries also depend on the economic and military capabilities (the "hard" power) they have (and others see them as possessing).[10] Indeed, military capabilities—the obverse side of the economic, hard-power coin—depend fundamentally on the capacity of the economic base and the willingness of policy-makers to allocate necessary resources to organize, train, equip and deploy armed forces. Government purchases—whether for nonmilitary purposes or for military deployments abroad—cannot take place or be sustained without international acceptance of the national currencies they use to finance these foreign policy outlays.

Our focus in these pages, then, is on the international monetary component of hard power. We take up exchange rates—in effect the price for which a currency can be bought or sold—and the norms and rules by which currencies are traded. As noted above, the relative value and acceptance of national currencies reflect understandings in markets and among monetary officials about the strength or weakness of the economies that underlie them. Whether commercial or governmental expenditures are made in one or another key currency and whether that currency is held as part of a country's reserves matter, as do changes in exchange rates that directly affect purchasing power, whether for private or governmental purposes. Obviously not just technical matters left to specialists, these important, often contentious, matters quickly become political.

COOPERATIVE SECURITY AND MONEY

As we review the historical record, we find substantial evidence of collaboration among governments, particularly their treasury or finance ministry officials and central bankers—the latter in the United States, United Kingdom, and other countries performing quasi-governmental roles that still reflect their private-sector origins. Maintaining international monetary arrangements or regimes, influencing currency exchange rates, and sustaining the international flow of capital require various forms of multilateral collaboration. These are essentially political processes—coordinating central bank interventions in currency markets, setting or influencing interest rates that affect international capital flows, extending credit to central banks and other financial institutions, or meeting to adapt or change the regime by which money is exchanged.

This is really *cooperative security*, although the term is usually not applied to international monetary matters.[11] We do so here on two grounds. First, the security of a currency—maintaining its acceptance as medium of exchange, unit of account, and store of value—has significant implications for trade, investment, and government expenditures for foreign policy and national security purposes. Second, this monetary security cannot be provided unilaterally. It depends on constructive engagement by governments and their monetary officials—the *managers* of capital—finding interest-based grounds for cooperative, often collaborative, measures that fit collectively under the rubric of cooperative security.

The concept of achieving security through cooperative, not just competitive, means has been applied in the post–Cold War period primarily to military contexts, as in the pursuit of arms control or confidence- and security-building measures among states. It has also been a means by which states deal cooperatively with terrorist or other asymmetric threats posed by nonstate actors or "failed" states often torn by civil war or intercommunal strife. We extend the concept in this volume to international monetary politics in which the key players are the international managers of capital, principally central bankers and treasury or finance ministry officials, their representatives, and the staffs that support them.

Their cooperative security, collective task is to maintain the stability of an international monetary regime in which both state and nonstate actors are free to exchange their currencies to finance both governmental and nongovernmental purchases and sales, imports and exports, capital investments, and other commercial transactions. Although we readily recognize their contribution to sustaining the global commerce of private-sector banks, corporations, other firms, and individuals, we focus in this volume on the often-overlooked security dependence by the United States and other state actors that rely on the international monetary regime to finance official purchases in support of the foreign and security policy actions they conduct abroad.

Failure to cooperate monetarily (as in the early 1930s during the Great Depression, when governments turned inward, devaluing their currencies competitively to discourage imports and promote their exports) tends to reduce the volume of trade, impede international capital flows, and have adverse implications for both economic and national security—conflicts that may result in war. At least that was the experience in the lead-up to World War II.

As the historical record makes clear, however, even the late-nineteenth- and early-twentieth-century gold standards required cooperative or collaborative measures to make them work. The alleged automaticity of gold standards also proves to be the stuff of myth or legend—widely believed by many then and some now, but not really so. In fact, as managers of capital, central bankers coordinated interest rates, garnered official currency deposits held as reserves, and took other measures in tandem with their counterparts to secure their currencies—sustaining their acceptance as legal tender for payments and their convertibility to gold (or silver) and other currencies for use internationally.

MANAGING EXCHANGE RATES—
ACCOMMODATING NATIONAL INTERESTS

High levels of collaboration by treasury officials and central bankers were also necessary to sustain fixed exchange rates in peacetime and during two twentieth-century world wars. Formal adjustments were required from time to time—either revaluing a particular currency upward or devaluing it. As in earlier periods, efforts were made to avoid these diverse effects by fixing or keeping exchange rates relatively constant. The Bank of England was de facto manager of the nineteenth- and early-twentieth-century gold exchange standard in which sterling was principal reserve currency. In the post–World War II Bretton Woods regime, the dollar served this function—governments or their central banks able to hold dollars as reserves or, until 1971, exchange them for gold at $35 per ounce.

The move to a floating-rate regime in the 1970s did not remove the need for treasury and central-banking collaboration. Favoring an idealized or "pure" float, some said such interventions no longer would be necessary. Global markets would be self-adjusting—currencies finding their "natural" or equilibrium exchange rates. In fact, whatever the theoretical merits of the claim, economic, security, and other domestic stakes in exchange rates remained so high that the international monetary regime quickly became, at best, one of "managed" flexibility. Moreover, avoiding the adverse experience of the 1930s required some degree of coordination to avoid the competitive devaluations and other measures in search of trade advantage that disrupted global commerce. Critics in any event dubbed it a "dirty" float—their way of describing government or central bank intervention in (or efforts to manage) currency markets.

To a greater degree than those in other economic sectors, central bankers understand and, for the most part, accept the need from time to time to intervene in financial markets. During the more than four decades of a managed-flexibility international monetary regime, treasury or finance ministry officials and central bankers have developed collaborative norms legitimizing these interventions. Laissez-faire liberal ideological arguments aside, leaving currency values entirely to the market in practice continues to be a political nonstarter. Whatever their rhetoric, governments tend not to leave things entirely to the market. The stakes for them typically are too high for laissez faire. For them, money is too important simply to be left to markets.

Continental Europeans in particular—displeased with the adverse effects on regional trade and investment stemming from exchange rate turbulence—began efforts in the 1970s initially to reduce fluctuations and later to fix their own exchange rates in a European Monetary System (EMS). The EMS became the basis, a quarter of a century later, for the emergence of the euro—its exchange value ultimately set in a managed float vis-à-vis the dollar and other currencies outside the euro area. To Europeans "management" meant providing stability to exchange rates—avoiding large swings in favor of smaller adjustments related to market supply and demand for particular currencies.

Stability within the euro zone (or euro currency area) requires coordination of national monetary policies within the European Central Bank (ECB) but, as noted above, this also depends on coordination of fiscal (tax, spend, and borrowing) policies—country-by-country expenditures not exceeding revenues beyond agreed limits. Not surprisingly, this macroeconomic coordination of both fiscal and monetary policies and national (or "sovereign") debt across the participating European countries has proven difficult, particularly given different national levels of development and political priorities.

Germany and other countries with relatively strong economies see themselves as shouldering a heavy burden—paying a high price to sustain the euro positions of weaker economies. "Bailouts"—loaning capital to Greece and Spain beginning in 2010—underscored the economic asymmetries that make sustaining the euro politically difficult. Indeed, the divergence in macroeconomic policy—some pursuing more expansionary fiscal policies than others—has contributed not only to the need for monetary adjustments within the euro zone but also to substantial swings in the exchange value of the euro vis-à-vis the dollar and other currencies.

IDEAS AND POWER

Ideas grounded in interests matter, as do the capabilities or power mustered to advance them in the construction of international monetary regimes. Economic and military capabilities are what Joseph Nye identifies as the bases of *hard power*, which he contrasts to the *soft* component that rests on the values and cultural understandings as well as diplomatic, bureaucratic, and other capabilities that lead others to follow.

When we unpack the international monetary component of "hard" power in Nye's formulation, we find that it also rests on rather "soft" interpretive judgments that go into the construction of money and the modalities of its exchange. How we organize the transfer and exchange of currencies—the rules we set forth and the institutions we create to facilitate this process—depends as well on the understandings that serve interests held by those in a position to construct, maintain, adapt, or transform these regimes. Correct or not, what matters are the *understandings* of interest held by those among the owners or managers of capital and others who also engage in day-to-day market transactions.

Our focus here is on the economic, particularly the monetary, component of "hard" power that not only drives military capabilities but also has implications for various forms of "soft" power. Although often overlooked, what becomes apparent is a dependent relation of the military on the economic component of "hard" power. Militaries cannot exist, much less operate, apart from the economic base that sustains them. Indeed, the size and quality of the armed forces that political and military leaders in a country are able to organize, finance, train, equip, and deploy are a function of the aggregate size and level of development of the domestic economy.

Moreover, soft-power capabilities are also linked to the magnitude of hard-power assets. Put another way, soft-power potential is substantially diminished in the absence of hard-power underpinnings. Quite apart from the quality of their ideas or other professional attributes, officials from countries possessing substantial military or economic, hard-power capabilities are usually taken more seriously in global markets and international organizations than those from smaller countries lacking these hard-power assets. The soft power that officials are able to exercise, then, is directly related to shared understandings other parties have of their hard-power assets.

Stated more formally, this distinction in Joseph Nye's account between "hard" (military and economic) and "soft" power leads us to explore how these components are related: (1) the dependent relation of the military on the economic component of hard power; and (2) the dependent relation of soft power on both economic and military capabilities that constitute this hard power. Military capabilities depend upon the strength of the underlying economy that provides the human and physical resources that can be allocated to military purposes. The soft power Joseph Nye describes is substantially diminished in the absence of hard power underpinnings.

Although we may draw analytical distinctions between hard and soft power, empirically these factors are always a function of *interpretive understandings* held by elites and mass publics both at home and abroad. Thus, economic, military, and "soft power" capabilities do not exist in a vacuum, as if they were objective realities "out there." Yes, a currency's (like the dollar's) exchange value is a function of supply and demand, but these are themselves subjective judgments in markets about its relative worth in relation to other currencies. These judgments are heavily influenced as well by subjective appraisals of a country's economic base—its magnitude and growth potential relative to other national economies. Also influential are the rules or accepted norms of the international monetary regime within which the currency operates.

The focus, then, is on which ideas serve whose interests, the relative capabilities—measured in large part by the capital base or productive capacity of the players (both state and nonstate actors) that empower or constrain the actions of their officials or representatives. In this regard, it is a mistake to reduce power or relative power merely to military capabilities, which themselves depend so heavily upon the capital base or productive capacity in a society—what Adam Smith called the wealth of nations.

Viewed in the aggregate, then, the economy is the foundational measure of a state's overall capabilities or power—economy understood broadly not just in terms of access to capital and natural resources but also in human-resource terms (the education, skills, and the ideas or values people hold related to savings and investment). These are essential to production and all forms of commerce and other social activities in and outside of governments pursued by both international and nongovernmental organizations. Of particular interest to us here, however, is that these are essential components that facilitate or constrain the size and overall capabilities of the armed forces political and military leaders are able to assemble. Understandings held by policy elites of the relative distribution of these capabilities profoundly influence the scope or range of alternatives from which policy-makers are free to choose.

ECONOMIC SECURITY, THE GLOBALIZATION OF CAPITAL OWNERS AND MANAGERS

Economic security matters to states and people in their societies. Indeed, security is not just a project for military, police, and paramilitary forces to attend, but also relates to capital and the stakes societies and their populations have in the value of their properties, investment, trade, the currencies they exchange, and other forms of commerce. The armed forces a country can raise, maintain, and deploy in combat, as noted above, also depend upon a society's capital base—the economy's productive capacity.

Functioning of the economy as a whole and the economic well-being of peoples nationally and in global society depend on security—maintenance of the security that facilitates and sustains all forms of commerce. Access to human and natural resources is an essential element of economic security, and this access depends upon the global flow of capital. Maintaining these capital flows that enable and facilitate the regional and global movement of labor and natural resources is a core security task for states as well as international and nongovernmental organizations (to include business firms) operating in a globalized economy.

Security calculations affect (and are affected by) international monetary regimes—the ways and means of managing capital flows in war and peace. The dollar, euro, and other currencies that play so important a role in the present-day global economy face substantial threats or challenges in global markets, particularly as officials who seek a balance between their domestic and international priorities confront market forces they may influence, but are essentially beyond their direct control. Economic and military security depends, in part, on successful use of the ways and means taken to sustain a currency's position within the international monetary regime.

Ideas or norms in the applied form of common practices and institutionalized rules (and the international organizations and practices in which these rules typically are embedded) facilitate international monetary exchange. These capital flows are essential to buying and selling, importing and exporting, investing, and realizing returns from all of these activities. Governments and their foreign policy and military establishments depend on the value and acceptance of their national currencies to finance the purchases they make abroad. It is the ideational component embedded in monetary-exchange rules, however, that defines the policy space in the construction, maintenance, adaptation, or transformation of international monetary regimes. Integral to the viability of capital and global capital flows are the adaptations or changes made from time to time in and to the regime itself.

Experts matter in these processes, particularly given the technical complexity of the subject matter. These "experts" are diverse, but crosscutting or overlapping elite groups are composed of central bankers, finance ministry or treasury officials, economists, and other academics. Of these, central bankers constitute what Peter Haas refers to as an *epistemic community*—"a network of professionals with recognized expertise and competence in a particular domain and an authoritative claim to policy-relevant knowledge within that domain or issue-area."[12]

They and treasury officials—at home and abroad—are an extraordinarily important part of those who own or manage capital worldwide. The principal agents of economic globalization are found among them in government, banking, the corporate sphere, and elsewhere in the private sector. These "managers" or "owners" of capital vary substantially in personal wealth and the incomes they earn. Quite apart from these considerations, however, they are the ones who are the principal players in global markets, who buy and sell, import and export, invest, and reap the rewards (or suffer losses) from the large capital holdings they manage or own. Some have governmental or quasi-governmental authority (treasury officials and central bankers respectively). Others do not (banking and corporate officials, investors, and other capital owners), but all have a stake in what governments do (or do not do), which has direct impact on their capital positions. Finding ways to influence those in authority to make decisions compatible with their understandings of public or private interests makes these economic matters essentially political. Put succinctly, these *politics deal with authoritative choice and the actions taken to implement decisions made.*

To a far greater degree than treasury officials who usually owe their positions to political appointment of relatively shorter duration,[13] central bankers have developed and expanded their "community" substantially through their multiple networks, established particularly during and since the founding in 1930 of the Bank for International Settlements (BIS). The BIS has provided a venue where they have met regularly in Basel and other institutional settings for more than eight decades. Most European members now communicate routinely as well within the ECB in Frankfurt.[14] A consensus among these "experts" on the ways and means of managing domestic and global monetary matters sustains existing arrangements or adapts them to changing circumstances, thus helping maintain a given international monetary regime. A shift in this ideational consensus can lead to (or legitimize) transformation from one set of rules to another, thus altering the way in which money is exchanged globally.

Such a shift in ideas or understandings may be a reaction to changes in circumstances (as in the outbreak of two world wars in the twentieth century) or may reflect new calculations on how better to serve the interests articulated by the relevant players, the officials of both states and nonstate actors that cross and crisscross state boundaries in an increasingly global, capitalist world economy. Not surprisingly, ideas grounded in the interests of capital-rich states and those they represent, particularly the capital owners or managers, have greater sway in these constructions. Relative capabilities or power does matter in the political determinations of which ideas become embedded in the rules, institutions, and resultant processes of the international monetary regime. Indeed, ideas grounded in interests (and driven by the relative capabilities or power as means) are the driving forces that matter in the construction, maintenance, adaptation, or transformation of international monetary regimes.

THE MONETARY COMPONENT OF
U.S. FOREIGN AND NATIONAL SECURITY POLICY

Money and the rules associated with its exchange, then, are the social constructions that enable or constrain the conduct of American foreign policy to include global deployments of military forces. Other finance ministries and their central banks more readily accept foreign currencies when their own security interests are at stake, as in the dollar's standing among NATO members and U.S. allies in Japan and South Korea—all of whom have depended on U.S. contributions to their security, particularly during the Cold War years. Similarly, Saudi Arabia depends upon a U.S. security guarantee and not only accepts dollars as a substantial part of its reserves, but also leads other petroleum exporters to price oil in dollars while, at the same time, ensuring that ample supplies of the commodity are available to global markets. For its part, China's interest in sustaining export markets and capital investment from abroad leads it to accept and accumulate as reserves not only dollars and yen, but also the euro.

The policy elites of major powers—politically connected central bankers and finance ministry or treasury officials—are the managers of capital, the principal drivers who construct the rules of the international monetary game, enabled as they are by (1) their technical expertise; (2) the economic, military, and other capabilities available to them; and (3) the international networks of which they are a part. What motivates them primarily is their interest in preserving their freedom of action or improving their relative positions nationally in the global pecking order as they manage the monetary component of their domestic economies. Consensus on norms or "best practices" developed within the central-banking, knowledge-based epistemic community also frames the choices they are likely to make. Policy elites of lesser powers have to plead their cause or make their case to those who hold the strings and are willing to listen or, alternatively, to those who can represent their position in the inner political decision-making circles of national governments and international organizations.

By design, international monetary regimes serve the interests (to include enlightened self-interests) of those who construct and maintain them. Ideas grounded in these interests drive the architecture of these regime constructions and legitimate efforts to maintain or adapt them to changing circumstances. Because sustaining transnational capital flows is so central to global and national economies, maintaining these regimes is itself an important security task for governments (particularly treasury officials and central bankers), their financial institutions, and international and nongovernmental organizations that participate in these capital-management processes.

THE PRIVILEGES AND COSTS OF
MAINTAINING RESERVE CURRENCIES

French president Charles de Gaulle famously complained at a February 4, 1965, press conference about what he described as an exclusive, extraordinary, or exorbitant privilege the United States enjoyed at the time[15]—"this signal privilege, this signal advantage," as he put it. American policy-makers had greater freedom of action and did not face the same monetary discipline as their counterparts in France and other countries. His remedy was a return to gold—"an indisputable monetary base, and one that does not bear the mark of any particular country. In truth, one does not see how one could really have any standard criterion other than gold."

Quite apart from de Gaulle's preference in the 1960s for a gold-based exchange standard, he correctly identified how the conduct of American foreign and national security policy depends to a greater degree than usually recognized on the viability of the U.S. currency—its acceptance not only in commercial markets, but also by treasury officials and central bankers abroad in payment for governmental obligations. A distant echo of this Gaullist complaint could be heard more than half a century later in March 2010 when former French president Nicholas Sarkozy, calling for European-American collaboration in "inventing the rules for the economy of tomorrow," asked whether a single country (the United States) and its currency (the dollar) should occupy so dominant a role in present-day global commerce.

In this regard, the widely recognized size and strength of the American economy that underlie the dollar's position remain foundational to global commerce. Since World War II—when, in the early postwar years U.S. GDP was half of the world's total—the dollar has served as the world's principal reserve currency (in which, as noted, oil and many other goods and services also are priced or contracted). After an initial dollar "shortage" in the late 1940s and 1950s,[16] sustained balance-of-payments deficits have kept the dollar in more than ample supply.

Key currencies like the dollar have sufficient standing to be held as official reserves to a greater or lesser degree by other national treasuries or their central banks, which conveys advantages to the country of the particular currency's origin. Private demand for the dollar in markets both at home and abroad helps sustain its global position vis-à-vis the euro, the yen, sterling, yuan, and other currencies. These dollars finance buying or selling stocks and bonds issued by American corporations, imports and exports, and direct investments in the United States or abroad. U.S. Treasury bonds are widely held by capital owners as secure assets with an assured return on investment.

While there are clear advantages, if not privileges, to hosting a reserve currency held by others, there are also substantial costs or potential pitfalls. Exchange rates (and changes in them) directly affect prices, conveying trade and investment advantages to some and disadvantages to others. Currencies that appreciate in value (revalued upward) increase purchasing power the country enjoys internationally. Imports, travel, investments, and military outlays abroad become less expensive. On the cost side of the ledger, however, exports, travel within the country by tourists from abroad, and investments there become more expensive to foreigners. Depreciating currencies (devaluations) tend to have the reverse effects.[17]

Governments also benefit when their national currency is overvalued or rising because it "goes further"—buys more at lower prices, thus reducing the budgetary cost of military and other government spending abroad. Again, the reverse also tends to be true. Devaluing or encouraging the currency to depreciate in pursuit of employment gains through export-trade or other advantages also raises the budgetary cost of government outlays. Put another way, U.S. spending abroad for the same goods and services to support military deployments increases when the dollar's exchange value declines. The privilege of oil pricing in dollars reduces this exposure somewhat when purchases of fuel for ships, aircraft, and vehicles on land are made directly in dollars rather than with local currencies.

Given the extraordinary extent of U.S. military and other obligations abroad, overvaluing the dollar conveys clear budgetary advantage to the U.S. government. It also enhances the buying power of both importers and investors looking for opportunities abroad. This comes, of course, at a very real cost to

Americans employed in agriculture, manufacturing, and other export sectors adversely affected by exchange-rate-induced, higher, and thus less competitive prices for American products in foreign markets.

THE U.S. DOLLAR AND EUROPEAN AND ASIAN CURRENCIES

For more than half a century, the German mark and French franc (now the euro), Japanese yen, and British sterling also have been key currencies for international commerce. Treasuries or their central banks also hold them as part of their reserves, but never in the quantities the U.S. has supplied dollars to global markets. Only over the last decade and a half, with the emergence of the euro— the dominant currency in Continental Europe and its major trading partners in Africa and elsewhere—have we seen a currency of sufficient size and strength that could rival the dollar's preeminence globally.

In practice, however, asymmetries in fiscal policies and the underlying economies of eurozone countries have created uncertainty, at least in the near term, of the euro's viability as rival, much less substitute, for the dollar in global commerce. Efforts have been made to strengthen the authority and resources readily available to the European Central Bank, but the ECB does not have the capabilities of the U.S. Federal Reserve, its American central banking counterpart. It is not just seventeen countries with seventeen different fiscal policies at issue, but also political limits on the ECB's access to capital that undermine its ability to ensure the maintenance of international liquidity among its members.

Working independently, but usually in close coordination with a single treasury, the U.S. Federal Reserve, by contrast, has far more authority on its own to purchase "assets" typically in the form of government bonds and other securities (both governmental and nongovernmental), thus providing capital needed by financial institutions and the markets within which they operate. "Quantitative easing" for domestic purposes (adding to the aggregate money supply by buying financial assets like Treasury or other bonds) also has important effects felt in global currency and stock markets, as does the reverse—the selling of securities in open-market operations, which reduces the quantity of money in circulation.

As with other currencies, the exchange value of the dollar and euro is a function of supply and demand, which also reflects understandings in the market about the size and strength of the domestic economic base on which the currency rests. Beyond the global need for a particular currency as a means to finance day-to-day trade and investment, the demand for it also is a function of the stability or security it provides to the owners of capital or other assets held in the country or currency area. Rules or accepted norms of the international monetary regime within which currency transactions occur matter, as do monetary policy and interest rates, influenced as they are by the capital-management actions of treasuries and central banks.

Not surprisingly, liquid capital tends to be drawn to countries with stable economies and currencies that offer a higher real return in financial markets on government and corporate bonds, bank deposits, shares of stock, and other assets. Capital also flees from countries lacking security, stability, or competitive returns, which typically are at the root of currency crises. Conditions that undermine a currency's exchange value and even its continued acceptance as payment occur when government outlays vastly exceed revenues or when private-sector owners of capital deploy their assets to other countries at levels substantially exceeding the inflow of investment capital from abroad. These are not just problems of the capital poor, but also challenges faced by capital-rich countries.

In sum, being able to spend vast sums without the same constraints others face certainly has facilitated the making and implementation abroad of U.S. decisions and actions over some seven decades since World War II. By no means is the U.S. position a function merely of good will, much less charity, by authorities in other countries. No, it is the underlying strength of the economic base that assures the viability of the dollar. Oil pricing in dollars also facilitates not only U.S. purchases for domestic consumption, but also global deployments of the armed forces. Put succinctly, national and international security depends on the viability of the dollar.

In a typical year, U.S. defense spending is almost as much as—sometimes exceeding—the total amount spent by all other countries combined![18] When U.S. government spending for defense and other purposes exceeds tax revenues, the deficit typically is made up by issuing bonds—borrowing in financial markets from both domestic and international sources. Finance ministry officials and central bankers in other countries help make this possible by holding American debt directly and by maintaining or expanding the number of dollars they already have in their official reserve accounts. Thus far, at least, it has been in their interest to do so, at least as they have understood the circumstances that vary over time.

THE CHINESE CASE

China continues to buy and hold U.S. Treasuries and other dollar-denominated assets in order to sustain its export position and capital inflows from abroad. Ironically, in this ongoing process China is effectively underwriting U.S. defense expenditures and other government outlays abroad! Ongoing Chinese trade surpluses help keep domestic production and employment there at a relatively high level. Net payments received from trade also add further to accumulation of capital from foreign investment and other sources essential to longer-term economic development. Supporting the dollar or, put the opposite way, buying U.S. Treasuries to hold as reserves to keep the renminbi (RMB or yuan) from appreciating too rapidly in value vis-à-vis the dollar serves both Chinese and American interests.

At the same time, given American balance-of-payments and employment considerations, the United States continues to press China to allow its currency to appreciate vis-à-vis the dollar to improve the U.S. export position and make further investments of U.S. capital in China somewhat less advantageous to American business interests. Although U.S. owners of capital have much to gain from an undervalued Chinese currency (put another way, an overvalued dollar that makes investments or purchases of foreign assets less expensive than they otherwise would be), this "advantage" comes at a very real cost to domestic employment in the United States.

Tensions rise from time to time on the relative advantages or disadvantages the two parties receive from a given yuan-dollar exchange rate. When U.S. officials push their Chinese counterparts to allow the yuan to appreciate, the latter counter with concerns that the dollar component of their foreign-currency holdings already vastly exceeds their need for them as reserves. The Chinese-American dispute, then, is focused on the *rate* at which the RMB appreciates, U.S. officials generally favoring larger upward adjustments sooner.

Of course, any Chinese wholesale effort to dump the dollar—selling those accumulated as reserves and no longer buying U.S. Treasuries or other dollar-denominated assets—would have potentially catastrophic economic consequences for both countries, not to mention other countries adversely affected. Given this locked-in, mutual vulnerability, shifts from the status quo have tended to be slow in coming.

The security interests of both countries are tied by these mutual vulnerabilities. Consistent with mutually agreed or accepted targets, sustaining the bilateral U.S.-China arrangement depends, then, upon both explicit and tacit understandings by officials in both countries to take steps designed to maintain or adjust existing exchange rates in global markets.

China benefits from an overvalued dollar that makes its exports less expensive not only to Americans, but also to others with accounts denominated in dollars they use to pay for their imports. Capital also moves to China as investors from abroad tend to find their overvalued dollars (euro, or other overvalued reserve currencies) go further there, particularly investments in labor-intensive production. Thus an undervalued yuan (put another way, overvalued foreign currencies relative to the yuan) helps to sustain not only Chinese domestic production and employment, but also capital formation. Running trade surpluses and attracting foreign investment produce a net capital inflow—an essential ingredient for meeting its own investment and development goals.

Although losing domestic production and employment—very real costs to those affected, particularly in labor-intensive industries—the United States and other countries with overvalued currencies relative to the yuan do benefit from lesser-priced imports from China, making them more affordable to consumers and reducing inflationary pressures in domestic markets. Capital interests are also advantaged by the enhanced purchasing power of their investment dollars spent in China, as well as by the returns they expect to realize from these investments. U.S. and other importers and retailers gain by the profits they receive from increased sales to consumers of less expensive products.

For its part, the United States benefits from external monetary support for the dollar, which, as we've noted, China continues to hold far in excess of its reserve requirements. Again, Chinese officials do so because of their national interest in sustaining their own economic growth. The Chinese position in the global economy depends on commerce with the United States and European and other countries whose officials, firms, and individuals use the dollar, euro, or other currencies to finance commercial, investment, and related transactions.

Finally, accumulated balance-of-payments and budget deficits financed by non-U.S. capital sources increase the potential financial leverage policy elites abroad can use in efforts to constrain American policy choices with which they disagree. Reminding the United States of the supportive financial role its officials play, China has cautioned the United States, for example, not to pursue policies that accommodate Tibetan nationalists or other human rights groups challenging Beijing's "domestic" policies.

Not surprisingly, the United States thus far has openly resisted such pressures. For their part, exercising leverage against the dollar to constrain U.S. policy-makers or dissuade them from taking a particular policy course can be costly to those in China or elsewhere considering the possibilities of doing so. Undercutting the dollar is not in the Chinese interest. Policy elites now in positions of authority in Beijing understand this, as do their counterparts in Washington, New York, and elsewhere.

INTERNATIONAL MONETARY REGIME CHANGE, U.S. COMMERCE, AND NATIONAL SECURITY

The U.S. trade balance moving into deficit—imports exceeding exports for the first time since the nineteenth century—precipitated President Richard Nixon's decision in 1971 to abandon the Bretton Woods regime. This change from relatively fixed exchange rates under Bretton Woods rules to "managed flexibility" enhanced the U.S. capacity to conduct an active foreign and national security policy global in scope. In the more than four decades since the end of Bretton Woods, pressure was substantially reduced on American officials concerned with the ways and means of financing continuing government spending abroad for defense and other purposes.

As principal architect of the Bretton Woods rules, the United States was still in a position to take unilateral action to change the international monetary regime when these arrangements were no longer understood as serving either its commercial or governmental interests. President Nixon's action shut the American "gold window" and allowed the dollar to float vis-à-vis other currencies for the first time since 1934, when President Franklin Roosevelt had set the dollar-gold parity at $35 per ounce. No longer required to sell gold to countries wishing to cash in surplus dollars—its obligation under Bretton Woods rules—the United States was freed from any monetary discipline France or other countries might have tried to impose in efforts to curb the American "privilege" to continue spending more than it took in, pursuing its own foreign and national security policy without the same financial need to consult or coordinate with allies, coalition partners, or anyone else.

The end of Bretton Woods thus ushered in a new era that permitted what was dubbed the "benign neglect" of balance-of-payments deficits, in principle allowing the dollar to follow the market—its value fluctuating relative to other currencies. In addition to allowing U.S. government officials to conduct American foreign and national security policy with even fewer monetary constraints, the new regime—adapted from time to time to changing circumstances by international agreement—allowed exchange rates to reflect more readily changes in market supply and demand, thus facilitating the global capital flows essential to the increasing globalization of trade, investment, and other forms of commerce. The United States was effectively freed from the more stringent balance-of-payments discipline of the Bretton Woods regime that required financing these deficits from currency reserves, gold transfers, loans, or other arrangements with the IMF, central banks, or other financial institutions.

Treasury and central bank interventions in international monetary markets have continued under the post–Bretton Woods, managed-flexibility regime that remains in effect. Conveying trade, investment, and other advantages to some at the expense of others makes efforts to keep a currency from falling (or appreciating) in value by no means politically neutral acts. Because of their standing as key currencies held as reserves, other countries using or holding the dollar, euro, or other deposits for this purpose gain or lose value when the reserve currency appreciates or depreciates. Holding a "basket" of key currencies as reserves is a way central banks can hedge their bets—as one currency depreciates, others may increase in exchange value, thus mitigating any loss.

Concerns for inflation aside, U.S. officials from time to time do seek to reduce the American trade and capital-outflow disadvantage by seeking a substantial decline in the dollar's exchange value. To avoid retaliatory measures, devaluing the dollar to encourage American exports in efforts to stimulate domestic production and employment usually requires coordination with monetary officials in other countries. To the extent that a growing U.S. economy has positive effects on their own economies (more exports to the United States and, perhaps, increased capital investment from abroad), they may be willing to do so. Allies and other countries depending on the U.S. for their security have an additional motivation for this kind of collaboration.

On the other hand, government and central banking counterparts abroad may also share concerns from time to time about an excessive supply of dollars in global markets, increasing balances in their own reserve accounts, and domestic inflationary pressures when dollars are exchanged for purchases in local currencies. Whatever domestic gain realized from reducing the dollar's exchange value comes, of course, with its own set of negative implications. As noted earlier, devaluation reduces the purchasing power of the dollar, thus raising costs not just for Americans traveling or living abroad but also for both business and government—an adverse budgetary impact particularly on the latter. Put another way, a dollar that buys less means that Defense, State, and other U.S. government agencies will have to spend more dollars to sustain their commitments abroad.

Finance ministry officials and central bankers in other countries clearly have understood their own national interests in the continued viability of the dollar as a currency that secures their own stakes in international commerce. Given their economic or financial stakes in present arrangements, undercutting the dollar is not without its economic or financial costs or risks for those who would choose to do so.

Nevertheless, increasing American dependency on others to accept the dollar, in effect their continuing willingness to afford full faith and credit to the United States, brings greater pressure on officials in Washington to pursue policies abroad consistent with security and other interests shared by other countries called upon to help finance outlays for these purposes. This is particularly so, given the more recent advent of the euro as an alternative reserve currency in a field in which the U.S. dollar previously had no rivals of comparable significance. Moreover, politically motivated actions on Capitol Hill that bring the government to the brink of defaulting on its obligations undermine the dollar's value and acceptance. The net effect of such actions is adverse to American national security. Those who persist in such conduct, often unaware of its implications, are undermining not only the dollar's standing but also U.S. national security.

SECURITY AND A GREATER PROPENSITY
TOWARD MULTILATERALISM

When the dollar stood alone as the world's leading key currency and principal reserve asset, U.S. officials enjoyed greater freedom from monetary constraint. This is no longer the case, notwithstanding short-term challenges to the euro's position. As a result, now and in the future American policy-makers—sensitive to the need to sustain the U.S. financial position vis-à-vis other countries—likely will be more prone to frame their policies multilaterally, which earlier administrations could, if they preferred, more readily avoid. After all, beyond private-sector spending, U.S. government expenditures abroad need to be financed—payments in dollars for military or other purposes readily accepted.

During the Cold War, U.S. multilateralism on security matters was institutionalized in NATO,[19] the OAS in Latin America,[20] CENTO in the Middle East,[21]

SEATO in Southeast Asia,[22] and ANZUS[23] in Australasia. Bilateral alliances with Japan, South Korea, Taiwan,[24] Canada,[25] and the Philippines cemented the foundation stones of U.S.-led regional security in East Asia. These overseas commitments (both bilateral and multilateral) required massive outlays abroad by the United States.

Essential to financing these payments was, again, a willingness by allies, coalition partners, and other countries to accept dollars for payment and hold them as reserves—seemingly without limit. Monetary challenges in the late 1950s when Germany and other countries converted some dollar surpluses into gold (and again, a decade later, when France and Switzerland did the same) were short-term exceptions to the overall level of military and monetary collaboration. These exceptions aside, cooperative security was the order of the day.

Dependency on the U.S. military contribution to security in Europe and East Asia was important leverage the United States possessed directly or indirectly to ensure this monetary support. Policy elites in major Western European powers as well as in Japan, South Korea, and other Asian countries also came to understand how support for the dollar was not just in their economic but also in their national security interests.

In the post–Cold War period, however, the security rationale for sustaining the dollar's position, though still present, is not as prominent among policy elites as before. Indeed, the Cold War years were marked by an East-West contest in Europe, the North Atlantic area, and East Asia that also touched security interests across the globe. Cooperative-security arrangements depend on active cultivation by the United States of its allies and coalition partners, coupled with an understanding by these policy elites that sustaining the dollar's global role also is in their economic and security interests.

Particularly given American economic prominence and the central role the United States played in security matters throughout this period, the propensity to collaborate monetarily with the United States rests, in large part, on customary practices and norms developed and reinforced during World War II and the decades that followed. Sustaining this support, however, requires ongoing recognition by policy-makers abroad of their own national economic stakes, as well as their own security and other interests served by continuing U.S. government outlays that finance the policies it pursues abroad. Collaborative ways and means include: (1) sharing information; (2) coordinating market interventions on exchange rates; and (3) maintaining (or increasing) dollar reserves even as they balance them with euros and other key currencies they also keep as reserves and use in financial transactions.

Cooperative measures from political and monetary authorities in other countries likely will be more forthcoming when, and if, efforts taken beforehand to develop a broad multilateral consensus have met with some success. Shared commercial and security interests—as policy elites, particularly treasury or finance ministers and central bankers in other countries, understand them—are the keys to building the kind of durable consensus necessary to sustain the external financing of American foreign and national security policy. The same is true, of course, as decision-makers in European Union countries, China, Japan, Russia, India, Brazil, or other countries in the coming decades assume an even larger policy presence in global commerce and security matters.

AFTERWORD

The dollar still enjoys primacy or, some might say, standing as primus inter pares in relation to the euro, which has joined it in center stage among the world's currencies. The dollar's privileged position has facilitated the conduct of U.S. foreign and national security policy since the end of World War II, much as, in the late nineteenth and early twentieth centuries, sterling supremacy allowed Britain to sustain a global empire. The emergence of the euro since the turn of the century—the importance of American links with EU counterparts in a cooperative two-way street to maintain international liquidity—compares to collaborative measures in the late nineteenth century as well as the sterling-dollar diplomacy of close collaboration in the 1920s between British and American monetary officials. As the currencies of other major players such as China, Russia, Brazil, and India almost certainly become more prominent than they are now, the personal and institutional bases for even greater multilateralism need to be in place if cooperative economic and national security is to be sustained. Reinforcing and expanding cooperative norms (as well as adapting national and international institutions to accommodate more players in these monetary roles) are essential steps in planning for the day when the United States no longer holds so many of the cards.

PART ONE THE EUROPEAN CENTER

STERLING, THE DOLLAR, AND SECURITY

BEFORE WORLD WAR I

1 Money, Empire, and Prewar Security

> After 1870, France did not contest British financial leadership. On the contrary, on such occasions as the Baring crisis of 1890, it supported London with a gold loan from the Bank of France to the Bank of England.
>
> —Charles P. Kindleberger

> London became "an international discount market, an international market for shipping freights, an international insurance market and . . . an international capital market."
>
> —E. H. Carr

From the outset of the new millennium, European Union planners understood that a common currency and monetary policy required comparable fiscal policies. After much negotiation, the parties had agreed on goals relating to taxing, spending, and borrowing with limits set on budget deficits and national debt as a proportion of gross domestic product. As a practical matter, however, reconciling differences in fiscal policy was more easily said than done.

Indeed, serious questions arose a decade after the birth of the euro. Expansive national fiscal policies among Mediterranean members collided head on with the more conservative tax-and-spend policies of Germany and other northern European countries. Not surprisingly, these fiscal asymmetries challenged the viability of the common currency. Which eurozone country would opt out, returning to a separate national currency—or worse, bring the whole euro project down? Could it be Greece? Spain? Portugal? Cyprus? Could it even be Italy? What could (or must) be done to keep the eurozone intact? Economic and national security were at stake not just for one country, but for the European Union as a whole. Since no one country acting alone could resolve the issue, a multilateral, cooperative security approach with the European Central Bank at the center quickly became the order of the day.

Serving the economic and national security purposes of any one member state depends on this willingness to engage in collective action. Fortunately for projects like sustaining the eurozone, this propensity to multilateralism for dealing with any number of often contentious issues has become deeply embedded in the European fabric. This multilateral norm, constructed mostly in times of peace over several centuries, also stands as a reaction to, and a bulwark against, reverting to the scourge of armed conflict that Europeans have endured time and again.

International monetary collaboration is not new in the European experience. Maintaining British, French, Dutch, Belgian, German, and (what was left of) Portuguese (mostly in Africa) and Spanish empires in the late nineteenth and early twentieth centuries depended on the same international liquidity that states require today to cover trade deficits and other net capital outflows—enough gold and foreign currencies in national reserves and access, when needed, to loans or national lines of credit. Given differences in perspectives, the course to an agreed multilateral approach is by no means an easy one. Nevertheless, it is in this cooperative approach to economic and national security that eurozone members tend eventually to find common ground. The most influential player needed for sustaining the euro, of course, is Germany, which has had the region's largest and strongest economy for more than six decades.

CONSTRUCTING AND SUSTAINING THE EURO

Bringing the euro to birth—a decade-long gestation period—came to fruition with the beginning of the twenty-first century.[1] The collaborative process that brought this about had deep historical antecedents that we begin exploring in this chapter. Not just an economic-security issue, those policy elites committed to the project saw constructing a viable euro as essential to keeping Europe competitively in the front rank globally alongside the United States and other powers. Support came from many among European capital owners and managers in both government and the private sector and, more broadly, from attentive publics across the Continent.

Dissenting voices among policy elites were particularly strong in EU member states that ultimately opted out of the euro project—the UK and Denmark. Critics observed how acceptance of a monetary exception (for the first time allowing some to opt out so that others might proceed) had transformed the European process into integration à la carte. Previously members had moved together in tandem to ever deeper forms of integration from coal and steel community (1953) at the outset to customs union (the goal set in 1958, finally achieved by 1967), and common market (the goal set in 1987, finally achieved by 1992).

European Union policy-makers opting into the eurozone discussed the linkage between monetary and fiscal policies and took steps to avoid (or at least minimize) asymmetries between the two. They sought a common, middle ground between expansionary, growth-oriented policies preferred by some and the more fiscally and monetarily conservative approach preferred by others, particularly Germany and other capital-rich countries. Guidelines on national budgetary deficits and debt limits were needed to meet the challenge of sustaining a common monetary policy while, at the same time, allowing separate fiscal (taxing, spending, and borrowing) policies among the seventeen eurozone members.

This shared understanding among policy elites of what was needed to make a eurozone work ultimately led seventeen EU countries to: (1) set aside their national currencies and adopt the euro; (2) participate in a new European Central Bank (ECB) they established in Frankfurt; (3) agree to a common monetary policy—setting money supply and interest rate targets with fiscal limits on the national budget deficit (3 percent of GDP) and debt (60 percent of GDP);[2] (4) manage the euro's value and exchange rate in relation to the dollar, sterling, yen, and other currencies; and (5) reach out to the UK, U.S., Japan, China, and other noneurozone countries to facilitate the cooperative relations essential to maintaining international liquidity not just regionally but also globally.

In spite of extraordinary efforts to keep differences in fiscal policy within narrow limits, asymmetries persisted—the Achilles' heel of the euro, common-currency project. By the end of the decade, finance ministers, bankers, and even prime ministers were in crisis mode, scrambling to avert financial default by Greece, Spain, and other countries in the European Union. It was an old European story—the capital-rich north confronting the fiscally challenged south, which we treat in greater detail below in this and in subsequent chapters.

Greater austerity was the price demanded by Germany and others in the north for the capital transfers needed to sustain the eurozone and the viability of the EU as a whole. Although the language used was technical and formally diplomatic, the underlying message had a puritanical ring—as if it were "penance" yet again for alleged profligacy in Mediterranean Europe. Budget deficits add to sovereign debt—finance ministries or central banks borrowing in financial markets the difference between expenditures and revenues, often at higher interest rates than more creditworthy countries pay.

If that were not enough, falsified and inaccurate reporting of economic data in Greece and elsewhere angered many, particularly in Germany and elsewhere in northern Europe. To them, governments that continually spend substantially more than the revenues they take in are the cause of the problem. They "deserve" the consequences of such policies so long as such actions do not undermine the whole set of monetary arrangements—putting the euro project and the EU itself in jeopardy.

By contrast, in the southern European view it was the anti-inflationary austerity of capital-rich countries in the north that was the real cause of the problem. Their tight money and fiscally austere policies resulted in reduced imports from the south and less investment there than otherwise might have been the case. Put another way, policies pursued in both camps have had negative externalities—adverse policy implications for each other.

This asymmetry among fiscal policies—relatively austere in the north and expansionary in the south—is the crux of the monetary challenge. Unlike the United States, which at the federal level has a single fiscal policy alongside its monetary policy set by central bankers on the Federal Reserve Board, each of the seventeen eurozone countries has its own fiscal policy—bound only by promises to keep within specified national deficit and debt limits.

To keep Greece within the eurozone and, more broadly, to sustain the EU's common-currency project were motivations for the initial €110 billion "bailout" loan agreed in May 2010, capital coming from the International Monetary Fund (IMF), Germany, and other eurozone participants working through ECB facilities. Worsening conditions in Greece necessitated transfer of additional capital—€130 billion being the amount finally ratified in February 2012. Severe austerity measures designed to raise government revenues, curb deficit spending, and privatize government-run enterprises were the price imposed on Greece for these loans. Complying with demands for greater austerity became the condition for actually receiving funds.

Labor strikes and domestic turmoil were the not unexpected outcome of these austerity measures. When people and businesses are adversely affected by increased taxes and reduced government spending remedies, the highly charged political climate typically leads to calls for changes in governing authorities. Notwithstanding substantial political opposition, Greek policy elites committed to keeping Greece in the eurozone prevailed in these debt-negotiation rounds.

Greece was not alone. To sustain their eurozone commitments, loans or lines of credit were extended Hungary (€20 billion, 2008), Latvia (€7.5 billion, 2008), Romania (€20.6 billion and €5.1 billion, 2009 and 2011, respectively), Ireland (€67.5 billion, 2010), Portugal (€78 billion, 2011), and Spain (€41.4 billion, 2012). Responding to the Greek and other challenges, a consensus gradually formed among politically connected European policy elites to strengthen the

ECB's capability—the resources it needed to maintain international liquidity among eurozone members.

Creation in 2010 of the European Financial Stability Facility (EFSF) and the European Financial Stability Mechanism (EFSM) was followed by calls for greater multilateral institutionalization and provision of greater capital resources for eurozone participants. The result was consolidating the EFSF and EFSM in a new €700 billion European Stability Mechanism (ESM) organizationally located in Luxembourg.

Maintaining international liquidity—access to, or reserves of, foreign currencies needed for currency exchange—within the region and globally is not just an economic challenge but also at the core of national (and international) security concerns. Financial failure in Europe, the United States, and elsewhere obviously has global ramifications, the exchange of money essential not just for economic security (sustaining trade, investment, and other forms of commerce upon which businesses and people depend for their livelihoods) but also for financing the outlays made by governments for foreign and national security purposes. Although policy-makers in the United States and other capital-rich states typically have a louder voice in collective deliberations, not even they can achieve economic and national security strictly through unilateral measures. Indeed, sustaining the international monetary regime—maintaining international liquidity—is a security objective in want of a multilateral approach.

Economic security of state- and private-sector interests, the conduct of foreign policy, and the deployment of armed forces abroad require day-to-day finance—the ready acceptance as payment in a given country's currency. Trade, investment, and other forms of commerce conducted by both state and nonstate actors drive the daily capital flows that require the exchange of currencies which, in turn, depend on each country's liquidity—its access to the currencies of other countries held in its national reserves or available by purchase or loan in financial markets or from the national holdings in other states.

Multilateralism matters. European, American, or other monetary challenges are recurring phenomena worth studying historically if, even for no other reason, than to underscore that the collective remedy to liquidity problems, though often elusive, requires an ongoing willingness to work with others. Cooperative security is not just a matter of finding ways to avoid armed conflict but also the enlightened self-interest in the minds of policy elites that results in a propensity to consult, coordinate, and construct approaches to achieving the economic and financial security that governments, business entities, other nongovernmental organizations, and individuals require to sustain their activities at home and abroad. Practical understandings that money is, after all, a social construction subject to human intervention are instrumental, whether in markets or in the national and international councils where bankers, treasury officials, and other policy elites pursue what they understand to be their interests.

FLASHBACK TO THE NINETEENTH CENTURY—
PLUS ÇA CHANGE, PLUS C'EST LA MÊME CHOSE

The more things change, the more they (seem to) remain the same. We flash back from the twenty-first century advent of the euro and the collaboration needed to sustain it to the late nineteenth and early twentieth centuries and see a similar mix of financial crises and the collective search for remedies by policy elites among capital owners and managers. Economic and national security rely on the viability of the currency a country uses to finance its spending at home and abroad. Then, as now, putting together *bailouts* (to use a twenty-first century term) was commonplace among central bankers and their private-sector counterparts.

British authorities, particularly those in the Bank of England, typically took the lead position on such international monetary matters both in Europe and globally in the late nineteenth and early twentieth centuries. This was due not only to the creditworthy standing of the UK and its pound sterling but also to the fact that British authorities saw it in the UK's economic and national security interest to play this role. After all, there was a global empire to defend—one upon which figuratively the sun never set. British political and financial policy elites understood the economic and national security interests that were at stake.

Gold and sterling, its currency equivalent, were the socially constructed cornerstones of commerce and security of the British Empire. Other countries defining their own currencies according to the same gold-exchange standard made sterling the international currency of choice—useful as unit of account, store of value, and medium of exchange for engaging in commerce, settling payments, and facilitating the conduct of their own foreign and national-security policies. Commercial or economic interest and security considerations were intertwined.

British imperial contributions by India and the dominions to sustaining sterling as the key international currency were substantial. Although some sterling deposits were maintained in London by private banks, South Africa's principal contribution was in the form of gold flows to the London market. Indeed, among other things, Britain's involvement in the Boer War (1899–1902) was directed toward gaining control over areas, inhabited by Dutch settlers, in which gold had been discovered.

Gold as backing for sterling thus became not only a means to finance imperial security but also an end in itself. Extension and consolidation of British control over all of South Africa secured a strategic position on the shipping route to India and elsewhere in the Orient. In this regard, gold production primarily from South Africa but also from Australia (and even some from India) greatly increased the world stock of monetary gold from $5.5 billion in 1904 to about $8 billion in 1914—an increase of 45 percent in just a decade![3]

This increasing supply of gold facilitated maintenance of sterling convertibility as well as the convertibility of other currencies adhering to the gold standard. A clear benefit to Britain and other countries of this increase in new liquidity was a lessening of the adjustment "discipline"—an ability "to postpone otherwise necessary contractionary adjustments" from running balance-of-payments deficits.[4]

SUPPORT FOR STERLING BEYOND THE BRITISH EMPIRE

Although the empire was largely responsible for supplying the London market with new gold and held almost 36 percent of all sterling deposits in 1913, less developed countries outside the empire also made substantial contributions. For example, Argentina was a particularly important source of capital flows to Britain. Heavy British investment in Argentine railways, utilities, and other construction projects during the last half of the nineteenth century not only stimulated purchases of British-manufactured equipment but also produced large debt-service revenues.[5] Moreover, differential interest rates were also capable of drawing significant amounts of Argentine capital to London whenever needed.

Japan was also a significant contributor to maintaining the convertibility of sterling, particularly in the years around the turn of the century and leading up to World War I. Indeed, the Bank of Japan, the government of Japan, and the Yokohama Specie Bank held 43.7 percent of all official sterling deposits in 1913—an amount greater even than the total empire contribution. This British-Japanese connection was allegedly secured by "secret agreements" following Japanese victories against China and Russia in 1895 and 1905, respectively.[6]

Aside from securing the "independence" of Korea, Japan forced China to pay her "a convertible sterling indemnity."[7] Presumably, Britain's price for allowing this extraction of resources from China was that a substantial portion of the indemnity be maintained on deposit in London. Moreover, Japan spent less than she borrowed to finance the war with Russia. The surplus from these loans was maintained in London, perhaps part of an agreement with British authorities supporting Japan in securing the war loans.

The data in Table 1.1 depict the relatively high degree of collaboration in support of the British-led international monetary regime that had been achieved by 1913, just prior to the outbreak of world war. Most countries were participating in this collaborative arrangement or formula for regime maintenance. Even though countries (or colonies) were divided into distinct currency areas on the basis of their deposits, the leaders of these currency areas were themselves committed to support of the British currency when needed.

Both official and private actors—British and non-British—were free to use sterling and the City's financial facilities to the extent of their needs and capabilities. No parties were excluded from their use. Some contributions to regime maintenance were voluntary, but others were mandatory. British-French collaboration, discussed in the previous section, is an example of the former in which the collaborative activity is entered into willingly, usually in anticipation of some mutual benefit or the mutual avoidance of some loss that would be sustained in the absence of' collaboration. By contrast, the role played by India in absorbing costs associated with maintaining the pre-1914 international monetary regime is an example of involuntary collaboration—a form of taxation imposed by Britain on a colony. This is not to claim that India derived no benefit from her forced collaboration with Britain. It is only to say that the colony did not exercise very much choice in the matter.

In the final analysis, Britain was able to maintain the convertibility of sterling largely because of her position as a lender (or capital exporter) on long term,[8] but a borrower on short term. In general, through use of the discount rate, the "larger financial centers tended to have greater command over each exchange rate than each smaller center."[9] In other words, the Bank of England was able to control the sterling-mark exchanges more effectively than the [German] Reichsbank, while the latter had greater power than peripheral Continental countries over their mark rates. Through this hierarchy, the impact of monetary tightness in London was shifted to the . . . peripheral countries that . . . incurred long-run payments surpluses. The ability of the system to tap sur-

Table 1.1: Key Currency Reserves, 1913

(as percent of total foreign-exchange reserves)

	Key currency		
Sterling group/Area	Sterling	Francs	Marks
Germany	28.2	10.1	—
Switzerland	41.9	26.7	12.8
Canada	100.0	—	—
Norway*	28.7	11.0	28.7
Australia	100.0	—	—
Ceylon	100.0	—	—
India	100.0	—	—
Japan	84.6	10.8	1.7
Franc group/Area			
Greece	24.8	43.3	0.2
Russia	7.8	72.6	17.3
Mark group/Area			
Austria-Hungary	22.8	—	48.5
Finland	15.8	5.3	25.8
Italy	11.2	14.7	36.6
Norway*	28.7	11.0	28.7
Romania	12.6	20.8	66.0
Sweden	14.3	2.1	35.5
Chile	25.3	—	74.7

Source: Table is adapted from data presented in Peter H. Lindert, *Key Currencies and Gold, 1900–1913*, Princeton Studies in International Finance no. 24 (Princeton: Princeton University Department of Economics, 1969), 10–12, 18–19.

*Norway is depicted here in both sterling and mark areas, having evenly split its reserves between the two key currencies.

plus-country funds in support of key currencies seems to have contributed to the stability of, and confidence in, the key-currency system before 1914.[10]

Both official and private deposits maintained in London and, to a lesser extent, in Paris and Berlin were supportive of sterling, the franc, and the mark.

Such support for key currencies, rendered in response to differential interest rates, convenience, and other market considerations, was central to international monetary regime maintenance in the years prior to the outbreak of war in 1914. It was not an unregulated gold standard that operated or adjusted automatically, but rather one in which treasury officials and central bankers took explicit actions to achieve and sustain the convertibility to gold of sterling and other currencies also tied to this gold-exchange standard.

In addition to Britain, France and Germany also supplied their currencies and financial facilities. Neither Paris nor Berlin was in the position, however, to replace London and thus were never serious competitors for the top position within the global monetary regime. Nevertheless, the influence of sterling was not as pervasive as is often thought. Russia held large franc deposits as a result of her special relationship with France, an alliance formed in 1892 in common opposition to the security threat posed by Germany. These deposits amounted to about U.S. $50 million after the turn of the century, but had risen to more than U.S. $300 million after 1910.[11]

Although Russian support for France was considerable—rendered in large part in return for various loans and credits—the czarist government also maintained deposits in London and Berlin. Unfortunately, from the point of view of all three monetary centers, the Russian deposits were highly volatile; frequent withdrawals did not contribute to the stability of exchange markets.[12] Nevertheless, following the French example of granting direct assistance to the Bank of England when needed, in 1890 the Russian government purchased British Treasury bonds amounting to £1.5 million in gold.[13] This, however, was not typical behavior for the czarist government.

CONTINENTAL TRADE AND THE CONSTRUCTION OF A LATIN MONETARY UNION

Prior to defeat in the Franco-Prussian War of 1870–71, Paris competed somewhat successfully with London in the finance of Continental trade. Moreover, the French collaborated with other Continental states in forming a currency area—the Latin Monetary Union. Unlike Britain, France was on a bimetallic (that is, gold and silver) standard. Hawtrey describes the French role as the center of bimetallism: "The bimetallic country is in the position of a dealer undertaking to buy and sell unlimited quantities of both metals at fixed prices. If the stock of the metals this dealer is prepared to hold is large enough in proportion to the world demand and supply, he governs the world price of both."[14]

The discovery of gold in California in 1849 and the rise in silver production had increased the world supply of both metals, upsetting to some extent the stability of exchange between the two. In addition, arbitrage associated with differences in silver coin weights (that is, variations of the amount of silver in different coins) played havoc with domestic coinage systems. For example, in the 1850s well-worn French coins were thus lighter than newly minted Belgian coins, a differential that drove the latter from circulation: "Belgium saw about 85% of the coin she had in circulation disappear beyond her borders, to be replaced by 'light' French coin."[15] In the early 1860s, French coins similarly displaced "heavy" Swiss coins. For their part, in 1862 the Italians minted a silver coin slightly lighter than the French, and it then inundated France.[16]

To deal with the situation, France held a monetary conference in Paris in

1856 attended by official representatives from Belgium, Switzerland, and Italy. The outcome was a treaty that established the Latin Monetary Union, a currency area that was to last for a fifteen-year term. Although there was considerable talk of establishing a gold standard in all the countries, certain French interests prevailed,[17] and bimetallism was retained.

The gold-silver weight ratio was defined as 1:15.5 (that is, one gram of gold was equal in value to 15.5 grams of silver), with the French five-franc silver piece defined as the basic unit. In each of the countries, the silver content of all new coins was to be a weight equal to 83.5 percent of the face value of the coins. By coordinating their policies in this fashion, the authorities in each country were committed to avoiding the coinage disruptions of the previous fifteen years. Moreover, the parties agreed to set an upper limit on the volume of silver in circulation at a rate of no more than "six francs per inhabitant of each country."[18] The latter agreement, although a modest step, set a precedent for controlling the growth of the money supply through international policy coordination.

In practice, however, the Latin Monetary Union did not display the degree of policy coordination called for in the formal agreement of 1865. The Italians were the first to defect, ending currency convertibility in May of 1866. The reason for the Italian defection was a run on its official reserves stemming from an inflationary monetary policy during the previous decade.[19] The Italians were not alone in disrupting the neat arrangement of the Latin Monetary Union. The worldwide fall in the price of silver in the early 1870s, as well as the French security need to finance the Franco-Prussian War through inflationary issue of paper and silver, were also highly disruptive of attempts at monetary policy coordination.

From London's point of view the Latin Monetary Union was less a challenge to its position than a complement that provided for some Continental monetary stability, albeit within the French sphere of influence. Earlier hopes that Prussia would join the union disappeared with the onset of the Franco-Prussian War of 1870–71. The war also precluded further attempts by France to rival Britain as a monetary center. Prussian victory effectively removed France from the competition. Not only was the war costly to the French, but they also were forced to pay the victor an indemnity that effectively drained French monetary resources.[20]

A significant outcome of the Franco-Prussian War, of course, was the rise of the German national state under Bismarck. With respect to monetary policy, adoption of a gold standard was seen as instrumental in forging the desired unification.[21] According to Hawtrey: "The French indemnity paid in the years 1871–3 supplied Germany with ample resources for carrying out a currency reform. In 1871 was adopted a new currency, the mark, which was based on gold." He adds: "Henceforward there was to be free coinage of gold and no free coinage for silver. . . . Germany thereupon started buying gold and selling silver on a huge scale."[22]

This German policy had a catastrophic effect on silver, which dropped in value relative to gold. The consequence was "that the currencies of silver-using countries began to depreciate," and in those countries on a bimetallic standard, silver tended to drive gold coin out of circulation. Ultimately "the only remedy was the suspension of the free coinage of silver," and "gold became the standard throughout the Continent except in those countries which were using depreciated paper money."[23]

With the decline of French monetary influence after the Franco-Prussian War, its franc area—the Latin Monetary Union, never strongly unified—broke down completely in subsequent years. As Kindleberger states: "After 1870, France did not contest British financial leadership. On the contrary, on such occasions as the Baring crisis of 1890, it supported London with a gold loan from the Bank of France to the Bank of England."[24]

The German challenge, however, began as the French was ending. Kindleberger notes that "with the unification of the German capital market after 1871, domestic functions focused on Berlin and finance of foreign trade on Hamburg."[25] An attempt by the private Deutsche Bank to compete with British finance did not succeed, except perhaps "in the narrow arena of the Ottoman Empire" or involving "the Italian clients of the weakened French."[26]

Although Germany rivaled Britain in trade and shipbuilding in the years leading up to 1914, it generally conceded to London the position of the world's leading financial center.[27] A number of Continental states came to be tied fairly closely to Germany, however, as is apparent by the extensive official mark deposits maintained in 1913 by Austria-Hungary, Finland, Italy, Norway, Romania, Sweden, Chile, and others.

This newly constructed mark area was still closely tied to London as indicated by the official sterling deposits maintained there. For its part, even Germany maintained about 28 percent of its total foreign exchange reserves (about 4 percent of its total reserves of gold and foreign exchange) in the form of official sterling deposits. Such deposits appear to have been maintained largely for purposes of convenience.[28] Nevertheless, it is still true that members of the

German currency area were also contributors to the cost of maintaining sterling convertibility.[29]

Finally, one other nineteenth-century currency area—the Scandinavian Monetary Union—is also worthy of mention. Formed in the mid- 1870s by Denmark, Norway, and Sweden, the purpose of the group was to enable the member states to maintain themselves on a gold standard.[30] As such, the group was supportive of the British-centered, global, gold-exchange regime. Given the standards of the day, the degree of collaboration achieved in the union was quite impressive. The three "went on the gold standard with identical monetary units."[31] In 1885, well in advance of currency swap agreements that would not be fully developed until the 1960s, the "three central banks . . . opened, for the other two, accounts on which the latter could draw . . . even if they did not have any credit balances with the drawee bank."[32]

This degree of systematic central bank collaboration was never achieved on the global regime level. Had it become routine, the central banks would have been in a better position to deal with the crisis of 1914. For our purposes in this volume, however, we note these clear examples of multilateral cooperation in support of commonly understood economic and national security interests.

INTERNATIONAL CONFERENCES

Even though international monetary collaboration was not as well developed as in the Scandinavian Monetary Union, international monetary conferences open to all regime members were held in 1867, 1878, 1881, and 1912. Although differences in viewpoint surfaced at these meetings, the participants were generally supportive of existing monetary arrangements. Nor did they challenge Britain's position at the helm of the global gold-exchange regime.

There was an initial attempt, however, to extend French influence beyond its Continental confines with the convocation in 1867 of the first World Monetary Conference in Paris.[33] Nineteen states were represented, including Britain and the United States. The conference was a high-water mark for nineteenth-century liberal ideology and for acceptance of the British preference for a gold-based international monetary regime. The American proposal was that France should coin a twenty-five franc gold piece. Then the United States would lower the gold content of the dollar to make the five-dollar gold piece exactly equivalent to the new French coin. The British could make a lesser adjustment in the pound, and universal coinage would be a fact; with the great trading nations of France, Britain, and America unified, the rest of the world would follow suit.[34]

The American Civil War over, there was domestic interest in favor of stabilizing the U.S. currency in terms of gold. With few exceptions, the conference
delegates—even the French—agreed in principle to the eventual establishment
of gold monometallism. The British, for their part, clearly were not enthusiastic
about the franc as the proposed basic international unit; however, they "sought
the adoption of gold, their own standard, everywhere."[35] Responding to pressure from the French, the British delegation specifically stated that they could
not "vote for any question tending to bind their government, nor express any
opinion to induce the belief that Great Britain would adopt the Convention of
1865."[36]

In short, the British refused to submit themselves to the French-dominated
Continental currency area, seeking only to bring it into accord with British
monetary policy. The British delegation made no commitment with respect to
bringing the pound into accord with the French twenty-five franc piece. In the
final analysis, Britain "gained by having assisted in universalizing the gold standard, yet had not compromised in the slightest her own monometallic usage or
unique coinage system!"[37]

The Latin Monetary Union for the time being remained bimetallic. In their
Paris meeting of 1874, members of the union, flooded with paper and depreciating silver, agreed to move toward establishing a gold standard.[38] The United
States, now an advocate of bimetallism, engaged in a lobbying exercise at the
International Monetary Conference in 1878 in Paris but was unsuccessful in
persuading the union to return to that position. None of the participant countries supported "the American proposal of a treaty to establish a worldwide
gold-silver ratio."[39]

The Germans did not even attend the conference, and the British, although
attending, regarded the affair as an American self-serving effort designed to
protect its silver. In a meeting held after the international conference had ad-
journed, the union membership "grudgingly approved" Italy's decision to issue
more silver coinage; however, approval was granted only under the condition
that it would be the last such issue. The union, due to expire, was renewed for
five years in 1879.[40]

The French position in the Latin Monetary Union had clearly declined, as
was apparent in union attempts to return Italy to convertibility in 1880. Although British, Dutch, Belgian, German, and Italian private banks floated a
loan to the Italian government, the French did not participate.[41] Nevertheless,

the union was able to maintain "a united anti-silver front" at the International Monetary Conference of 1881.[42]

The commitment to international collaboration in support of the global monetary regime was upheld as late as 1912 when, at an international conference held in Brussels, a resolution was adopted that urged European central banks to "hold meetings for the purpose of improving the system of international payments."[43] Formal statement of this objective notwithstanding, no concrete action toward this end was taken until almost two decades later. The seed planted, in 1930 a Bank for International Settlements (BIS) finally was established in Basel. Although the prewar collaborative arrangement that had evolved was sufficient to handle normal, day-to-day transactions in noncrisis periods, the means were inadequate to handle the forthcoming crisis of 1914.

THE CALM BEFORE THE STORM

There was thus a relatively high degree of collaboration underlying the pre-1914 international monetary regime. Britain, through the instrument of its banking network and the international acceptability of its currency, was at the center of this global regime. As discussed above, the French competed with the British to some extent prior to the Franco-Prussian War of 1870–71, but France was replaced as contender by the newly emergent German state. Although the late-nineteenth- and early-twentieth-century German naval and army buildup challenged the security of Britain and France, respectively, in monetary matters Germany remained subordinate to Britain, notwithstanding substantial gains by Berlin and its trading capital, Hamburg. Britain remained the international monetary regime leader, given both sterling's utility as an international store of value and medium of exchange and London's financial facilities that included "an international discount market, an international market for shipping freights, an international insurance market and . . . an international capital market."[44] The security provided by these socially constructed international arrangements was about to be undone by the outbreak of world war.

AFTERWORD

That monetary matters under the nineteenth-century gold standard (more precisely the sterling-gold standard) were automatic—left to the market—is the stuff of myth. In fact, central and private bankers were by no means passive. The Bank of England's use of the discount rate—raising or lowering it—had direct effect on capital flows intended to serve the bank's and the UK's global economic and national security interests. From time to time sovereign bail-out packages were essential to maintaining international liquidity in Europe. Then, as now, the preferred modality for economic and national security was use of cooperative measures involving capital transfers from both private and central bank coffers.

2 Wartime Security and Monetary Exchange in the Great War

> [The world war] cut off the means of direct remittance to London from Germany and Austria-Hungary . . . , [but] did not completely destroy every connection between the currencies of the Central Powers and those of the Allies.
>
> —William Adams Brown, Jr.

> Britain ceased to be the world's greatest creditor nation [and] heavily indebted to the USA, which ended the war as the greatest creditor nation in its turn.
>
> —E. J. Hobsbawm

Wartime finance—maintaining the exchange value and thus the purchasing power of the national currency—is often overlooked or merely taken for granted. Procurement of war materiel, fuel, and other war-related purposes requires a national currency that will be accepted as payment for these purchases. It is the work of central bankers and treasury officials in wartime—customarily out of sight and behind the scenes—that makes it possible to sustain combat operations abroad. These monetary transactions occur not only among allies and the neutral parties with which they trade but also between the currencies of adversaries. Indeed, there is wartime need to acquire and spend an enemy's currency—whether for transactions with third parties, financing intelligence operations, or other war-related purposes.

The dim outlines of the regime that came into existence with the outbreak of war were apparent well before 1914. The wartime monetary regime followed very closely already established, prewar relations among the contending Great Powers. The outbreak of war was accompanied in financial matters by hardening of prewar divisions into two principal currency blocs—monetary relations during the war described as "a wartime regime of an exchange rate pegged by foreign borrowing and restrictions."[1] There being only a minimal consensus at the global regime level, two distinct monetary blocs formed around the strategic division into Allied and Central Power camps. A larger number of neutrals and nonbelligerents dealt with one or both sides.

Although the events of August 1914 "cut off the means of direct remittance to London from Germany and Austria-Hungary . . . , it did not completely destroy every connection between the currencies of the Central Powers and those of the Allies."[2] Switzerland, for example, acting as a political neutral, served as a conduit that linked the monetary blocs of the Central and Allied powers.[3] Bloc members minimized gold exchanges among themselves, conserving available reserves for use in defending the exchange rates of their currencies and for financing purchases from neutral or nonbelligerent states. Although gold remained the legal or formal basis for currency values, the free export of gold by private interests, a right that had existed under the pre-1914 regime, was suspended in the belligerent states as governments assumed increasing control over international financial transactions. Even the United States, with its extensive gold reserves, imposed an embargo on gold exports shortly after entering the war.[4]

Although most monetary transactions during World War I took place within the separate Allied and Central Power blocs, some transactions occurred between members of the opposing blocs, typically through a neutral medium such as Switzerland or the Netherlands. Indeed, "there was even a regular trade between Germany and England through the Netherlands known to both war offices."[5] Moreover, some of the nonbelligerents, as noted above, dealt with members of both blocs. Monetary transactions not confined completely to a given bloc, some semblance of a global monetary regime remained, but the scope of financial operations outside of the blocs was understandably at a much reduced volume than had existed prior to 1914.

MAINTAINING A WARTIME MONETARY REGIME

The global monetary regime during World War I was sharply divided into opposing blocs. The level of global collaboration outside of these currency blocs was minimal compared with what had gone on before. Prewar commitment to maintaining a truly global international monetary regime was set aside. Although international exchanges continued within each bloc, there were no global monetary conferences outside of them. Mutual support efforts through managing interest rates or maintaining foreign exchange and gold deposits in support of certain currencies were confined primarily within each wartime bloc.

Events in 1914 led to a breakdown in the London financial mechanism and, with it, the prewar global regime. As the guns sounded in August 1914, the British government authorized a temporary suspension or moratorium on payment of bills, particularly those owed to foreigners by acceptance houses and other financial institutions. The bank rate was raised from 3 to 10 percent; however, rather than alleviating the panic, this action may have contributed to it.[6]

Nevertheless, considering the magnitude of the breakdown, the British government and central banking authorities acted rather quickly to restore financial activity in the London market.[7] The Bank of England made advances amounting to £200 million to various financial institutions. In addition, on August 13 the Bank of England began discounting bills accepted prior to the moratorium, support amounting to about £120 million, these actions taken under a treasury guarantee against loss to the central bank. Thus government action through the central bank was responsible for restoring the London financial market and establishing the wartime monetary bloc. Stock exchange operations also resumed in January 1915, but only after the government again intervened to guarantee "payment of advances to the Exchange."[8]

British and U.S. discount rates maintained throughout the war were set so that London's rate was always slightly higher than that maintained by New York[9]—a clear indication of Anglo-American wartime monetary collaboration during even the early years of World War I, when the otherwise "neutral" United States tried to remain politically aloof from the fray. Thus, given this interest rate differential, whatever mobile capital from the United States or others seeking higher gain tended to be drawn more to the United Kingdom than to the United States.[10] The resulting capital inflow to the United Kingdom facilitated efforts in London to maintain the wartime exchange value of sterling. From the U.S. point of view, maintaining rates lower than in the UK also had the advantage of discouraging additional capital inflow to the United States that might have had inflationary effects. Thus both sides saw benefit in the collaborative arrangement.

Until 1918 Germany was fairly successful in stabilizing the Swiss franc-mark exchange rate. Through transactions on the Swiss financial market the values of Allied and Central Power currencies remained fairly stable with respect to one another for most of the war.[11] Within the Central Power bloc, strict exchange controls were imposed by Berlin, and intervention took place in the financial markets of the Netherlands, Denmark, Sweden, Norway, Switzerland, Austria-Hungary, Bulgaria, and the United States.[12] Never having the capital-drawing power of London even before the war, Berlin was forced to rely both on exchange controls and on intervention in foreign (particularly neutral) financial markets in lieu of a differential discount rate scheme similar to the one the Bank of England was able to devise.

FOREIGN EXCHANGE DEPOSITS AND OTHER CAPITAL FLOWS

Wartime allied monetary collaboration also took the form of official deposits by foreign central banks and their treasuries in both London and its new financial rival, New York. Essential to financing the war effort, these deposits contributed directly to maintaining the exchange stability of sterling and the dollar. London and New York were now the principal centers of international finance. Indeed, "because of difficulties in remitting home, the expectation of a postwar return to 'normal' exchange rates, and special inducements offered by British banks, foreign balances accumulated in London far in excess of the need for them."[13] Also helping the British attract this capital were special rates on deposits maintained in London.[14]

In addition to the dominions and colonies, the United States, France, and other bloc members, nonbelligerents such as Norway, Sweden, Switzerland, and Argentina maintained substantial deposits in London. The United States also was a net recipient of $980 million in foreign deposits as of June 1918. Data in Table 2.1 suggest that although the U.S. held some deposits in the currencies of the European Allies, these countries maintained deposits more than six times as great in the United States.

The Central Power bloc had comparatively greater difficulty attracting the deposits of nonbelligerents such as the Netherlands, Denmark, and Sweden.[15] The consequence was that German and Austro-Hungarian trade with these countries tended to be on a cash basis that depleted the reserves of the Central Powers.

TABLE 2.1: U.S. Deposits by Region, June 1918

(U.S.$ millions)

Region	Foreign deposits in U.S.	U.S. deposits abroad
Europe: Allies	621	94
Neutrals	281	—
Central Powers	—	9
Asia	137	39
North America	134	89
South America	100	59
Africa/Oceania	3	6
Total	1,276	296
Net Balance	980	—

SOURCE: *Federal Reserve Bulletin*, December 1921, 1408–10, as cited in William Adams Brown, *The International Gold Standard Reinterpreted, 1914–1934*, 2 vols. (New York: National Bureau of Economic Research, 1940; and AMS, 1970), 152.

Table 2.2: Gold Reserves, 1913, 1918

(Gold value in national currencies*)

	1913	1918	% change
Allies			
United Kingdom	35	108.5	210
United States	1924	3081	60
France	3517	5478	56
Italy	1493	1642	10
Russia*	4313	9613	123
Central Powers			
Germany	1170	2262	93
Austria-Hungary	1241	262	−79
Others			
Netherlands	151	689	356
Spain	472	2223	371
Japan	376	1588	322
Sweden	102	286	180
Switzerland	170	415	144
Argentina	295	433	47

Source: League of Nations, *Memorandum on Currency and Central Banks: 1913–1925*, II, 34ff; and Charles Blankart, *Die Devisenpolitik waehrend des Weltkrieges* (Zurich: Arell Fussli, 1919), 21–25, as cited in William Adams Brown, Jr., *The International Gold Standard Reinterpreted, 1914–1934* (New York: National Bureau of Economic Research, 1940), 100, 104–5.

* Data on Russia are in Swiss francs at par. Due to the revolution, the reported 1918 statistic is as of October 1917.

As reflected in Table 2.2, the amount of gold held by treasuries and central banks increased in most countries during the war, in part the result of increased production and extraction from private, domestic sources. By far the greatest increases occurred in the nonbelligerent countries, particularly those acting as suppliers to the belligerents.

Throughout the war, the Bank of England purchased gold for the treasury from South Africa, Australia, and India at the official sterling rate.[16] The rate was, of course, most favorable to Britain in that it reflected none of the actual depreciation of sterling. In this manner Britain was once again able to pass off some of the costs of maintaining sterling to be borne by her empire.[17] Thus, above and beyond providing human and other resources, the empire directly contributed monetarily to British security.

Sterling was the principal currency used to purchase war-related materiel for the Allied powers. Currency bloc members including France, Russia, Japan, and Italy also shipped gold to England, which facilitated maintenance of the dollar value of sterling. The costs of maintaining sterling were also borne within Britain by private citizens who, for patriotic or other reasons, surrendered their gold and American securities in exchange for sterling,[18] and by financial institutions that deposited their gold holdings with the Bank of England."[19] For its part, Canada supported sterling "by lending securities to the British government which were suitable for pledging in New York." Even France loaned gold to England "in exchange for British credits to the French Treasury."[20] All of these monetary measures were essential to the security of Britain, its empire, and allies in their war against the European Central Powers.

Although not a belligerent in the early years of the war, the United States was a principal supplier of materiel for the Allies and thus was the recipient of much of their gold used for payment. Even so, Britain remained at the center of the Allied international monetary bloc, given her role "as middleman in the purchase of war supplies for her allies," notably France, Italy, and Russia. The British used their gold supplies to intervene in the New York and other foreign exchange markets so as to maintain the dollar value of sterling and thus prevent further depreciation of the currency in relation to its formal gold parity. Above all, London retained her position as "the market for dollars for all Europe."[21]

The monetary bloc of the Central Powers had its center in Berlin. As in the case of Britain and sterling, the costs of maintaining the gold value of the mark for foreign purchases from nonbelligerents were not borne by Germany alone. In 1915 the Reichsbank received virtually all of the Austro-Hungarian Bank's gold reserves. Considerable efforts were also made to build up the Reichsbank's gold reserves from domestic sources and from occupied territories in Belgium, Romania, and Russia. Moreover, by the Treaty of Brest-Litovsk, the new Russian government ceded an estimated 400 million marks worth of gold to the Reichsbank.[22]

Gold remained, nevertheless, a relatively scarce commodity to the European belligerents of both sides. Nonbelligerent or neutral countries faced the opposite problem of resisting the massive inflow of gold because of its potentially inflationary impact—the amount of currency in domestic markets being a function of the size of a country's gold stock. Accordingly, financing much of the war by purchasing on credit was acceptable to both belligerents and nonbelligerents. Of course, given the expected depreciation of currencies that would occur when exchange controls were removed after the war, purchasing on credit was, from the belligerent viewpoint, yet another way to pass on some of the war finance costs to the nonbelligerents.[23] In short, by extending credit so as to reduce the chance of domestic inflation, the nonbelligerents were, in effect, contributing to maintenance of currency values of the belligerent states. The nonbelligerents also benefited, of course, from the increased domestic employment stimulated by expanding exports to the belligerents through fairly liberal credit terms.

"Gold movements were controlled by the conscious, purposeful, and political direction of central banks and treasuries," processes that necessarily involved considerable collaboration.[24] Monetary officials thus played a crucial role in sustaining the war efforts of parties on both sides of the conflict. The experience of wartime monetary collaboration also set precedents and established norms for postwar collaborative efforts discussed in the next chapter.

Following the sinking by Germany of the passenger ship *Lusitania* in 1915 and continuation of German attacks on merchant ships, the United States finally came into the war in 1917. Not surprisingly in the course of the buildup for war, U.S. monetary collaboration increased. British authorities were permitted to sell Treasury bills in New York, using the dollar gains along with gold sales to support sterling. In addition to these Anglo-American dealings, French and British authorities also agreed in 1916 to collaborate in stabilizing the franc-sterling exchange rate. In 1915 the British already had extended credits to France under the condition that at least one-third of it be spent in Britain.[25]

In return for credits in London, the French government offered gold, the securities of neutral or nonbelligerent countries, and French Treasury bills. French government advances to its allies amounted by 1918 to about U.S.$ 672 million.[26] Thus, through such collaborative efforts "the sterling-dollar-franc nucleus was definitely established and it endured throughout the rest of the war."[27] Moreover, direct American support in the form of credits increased upon American entry into the war, the country thus becoming a full-fledged member of the Allied monetary bloc it had supported monetarily from the onset of hostilities.[28]

Germany and Austria also extracted loans to support their currencies from such countries as Switzerland, the Netherlands, and Romania. Indeed, Germany and other belligerents threatened to interrupt the trade of neutrals unless they granted credits and "stabilization loans."[29] Rather than allow their currencies to depreciate vis-à-vis the neutral currencies, members of both blocs extracted contributions, particularly from (but not confined to) the weaker of the nonbelligerents:

> The extraordinary spectacle was presented of the great powers of the world demanding credits from many small countries. France borrowed from Spain, Uruguay, Switzerland, Argentina, the Netherlands, Norway, Sweden, and Japan as well as from the United States and Great Britain. England borrowed from Argentina, the Nether-

lands, and Japan as well as from the United States. The United States borrowed from Spain, Argentina, and Bolivia. Russia borrowed from Italy, France, and Japan as well as from Great Britain and the United States.[30]

Moreover, preservation of stable exchange rates, as noted earlier, benefited the belligerents at the expense of the nonbelligerents by keeping the costs of imports to the belligerents less than otherwise they would have been if their currencies had been allowed to depreciate. The commonly perceived necessity among the belligerents for "enabling goods to move and maintaining a stable system of exchange rates" was the primary basis for wartime monetary collaboration within the separate blocs.[31] Security was an underlying motivation for monetary collaboration pursued by countries within both wartime blocs. Even though "collaboration" was minimized between the opposing blocs, that both pursued similar monetary objectives within their separate spheres resulted in considerable exchange rate stability on a global basis.

THE DECLINE OF BRITAIN'S MONETARY CAPABILITIES

Britain's position as international financial center was greatly weakened as a result of the war. Although British gold holdings increased by more than two times during the war, her reserves were only about a sixth those of the United States and about half of French totals. Even defeated Germany had more gold than the United Kingdom in 1918, and Japan had 50 percent more. Moreover, the British merchant fleet "was a tenth less in 1920 than in 1910, while that of the United States was more than one-half greater and that of Japan had more than doubled."[32]

The longer-term, net effect of World War I on Britain's international position was decisively adverse. In addition to the diminished "competitive position of Great Britain in international trade," the heavy costs of financing the war had drained British resources. "Her creditor position was reduced between 1914 and 1920 approximately one quarter," thus ending "the world-wide dominance of the pound."[33] Indeed, Britain and the United States exchanged financial positions, in that "Britain ceased to be the world's greatest creditor nation" and actually became "heavily indebted to the USA, which ended the war as the greatest creditor nation in its turn."[34]

The United States enjoyed a trade surplus throughout the war, which transformed the U.S. "from a net debtor on short- and long-term of $3.7 billion in 1914 to a net creditor of the same amount by the end of 1919."[35] More than a billion dollars in gold were sent to the United States by the belligerent states.

Another source of European liquidity, American securities held by private citizens in Europe, amounting to $1.41 billion, were taken over by the governments of the belligerents and used in payment for goods imported from the United States. Existing foreign loans extended by private interests to American borrowers were reduced by half a billion dollars, and new loan obligations owed to American lenders totaling around $2.4 billion were incurred.[36] The balance due in payment for American goods came from these sources and, as noted above, from extensive credits granted by the United States to her allies after U.S. entry into the war.

Although the dollar did not readily become a substitute for sterling, New York increasingly became London's rival as financial center.[37] Already the war had afforded New York the opportunity to grant extensive acceptance credits to finance trade and to receive foreign deposits that might otherwise have been concentrated in London.[38] Moreover, New York "became the chief market for the securities of both belligerent and neutral countries."[39]

In March of 1919 sterling and other Allied currencies were unpegged, and their values with respect to gold began to decline.[40] Compared to its prewar rate of $4.867, the pound reached a low of $3.42 in October 1920.[41] As has already been discussed, the war produced a substantial alteration in the relative capabilities of states in the world as a whole and, in particular, within the international monetary arena. The Central Powers were removed as opposition to the Allies, who now were clearly dominant. Among the Allied Powers, Britain had been considerably weakened and the United States had assumed an increasingly prominent position in monetary capabilities.

As the strongest state in monetary terms, the United States could have assumed monetary leadership in Europe; however, the political decision was made in the monetary as well as in most other fields to withdraw from significant involvement overseas. Given American reluctance to assume leadership, the British were more than willing to assume the role. Thus the United States effectively deferred international monetary regime leadership to Britain. The latter performed this role throughout the 1920s, albeit in coordination with the United States. Changes in the distribution of capabilities as a result of World War I thus had an effect on the construction of the initial postwar international monetary regime.

Efforts in the 1920s to maintain a fixed exchange rate regime ultimately failed following the 1929 stock market crash and the Great Depression that followed. The weakened position of Britain, France, and the other European Allies, combined with the failure of the United States to provide strong leadership, produced a floating rate regime in which the requirement for collaboration was minimal. Notwithstanding its economic and military hard-power capabilities, the United States did not want to assume monetary leadership, much less play a military role in support of European (and American) security. Agency—or more precisely, the lack of it on the part of the United States and its policymakers in the interwar years—posed no effective obstacle to the downward course of events leading to World War II.

AFTERWORD

Not only allies exchange currencies in wartime but also adversaries, who need to finance intelligence collection, espionage, purchases, and other activities in an enemy's currency. Neutrality in World War I allowed Switzerland and the Netherlands to serve as bankers to both sides engaged in trading the enemy's currency. Quite apart from adversaries, shoring up the financial means to carry on warfare for one's own country and one's allies—interests essential to national and alliance goals—is cooperative security in its wartime mode. It is a time when central bankers and treasury officials as capital managers matter in ways often overlooked in most war accounts. Money always matters when it comes to security—particularly then.

3   Restoring Sterling, Commerce, and Security after World War I

> There must be financial and currency conditions which afford sufficient security for trade.
>
> —British prime minister David Lloyd George

> [Churchill] has no instinctive judgment to prevent him from making mistakes; partly because, lacking this instinctive judgment, he was deafened by the clamorous voices of conventional finance; and, most of all, because he was gravely misled by his experts.
>
> —John Maynard Keynes

Shortly after concluding the initial agreements on reparations imposed on Germany, the parties made progress toward agreement on principles to govern a newly constructed, postwar international monetary regime. The Genoa Conference,[1] a gathering of government ministers supported by central bankers and other economic "experts" (a nascent epistemic community on monetary matters among capital managers), finally agreed on May 19, 1922, to work toward reestablishment of a gold exchange standard.[2] To a large extent the conference reflected the wishes of the British delegation led by Prime Minister David Lloyd George.[3] Behind the scenes, however, was the influential Montagu Norman, governor of the Bank of England.[4] Significantly, the Americans did not participate in the Genoa Conference. With no effective competition, the position of leadership thus passed by default to the British.

The doctrinal premises underlying the British position had been stated clearly by the Cunliffe Committee in 1918 when it advocated restoration of "the automatic functions of the gold standard."[5] Indeed, the British government had established the Cunliffe Committee in January 1918 "to consider the various problems which will arise in connection with currency and the foreign exchanges during the period of reconstruction, and report on the steps required to bring about normal conditions in due course."[6] The essence of the committee's report was that the pre-1914 regime should be restored—an "unshakeable confidence in the traditional British methods of controlling credit and supporting the exchanges ... [and] a trumpet call for a return to normal techniques."[7]

The objective was to return to normalcy by "cessation of government borrowings" and "resumption of the long tested policy of credit control through the use of Bank of England discount rate policy," even if this meant deflationary economic policies. The British conceived of gold—or, more precisely, sterling defined in terms of a given weight of gold—as being at the center of such a regime.

The doctrinal underpinnings of the Genoa Conference are clear—"a remarkable object-lesson in applied liberalism."[8] Lloyd George even told conference delegates that their "effort must include the removal of all obstacles in the way of trade." With respect to monetary matters he argued that "there must be financial and currency conditions which afford sufficient security for trade."[9]

Both Norman and Benjamin Strong of the New York Federal Reserve Bank believed in the automaticity or self-regulation of money markets that would occur under a restored gold standard. Norman argued that under a gold standard "stability in the Exchanges will be looking after itself in the old-fashioned way and artificial stabilisation will hardly be necessary."[10] For his part, Strong also opposed "management" by financial authorities. His faith was rather with free-market forces. Under a gold standard "it will be more automatic; we won't have to depend so much on judgment, and we can rely more upon the play of natural forces and their reaction to price."[11]

The resolutions on monetary matters adopted by the Genoa Conference are of particular interest,[12] because they represent a formal statement of the agreed-upon rules or norms that would be operative in the newly restored regime.[13] Each country sought to stabilize "the value of its currency" and charge central banks with conducting monetary matters "solely on lines of prudent finance" and "free from political pressure." The resolutions called for "continuous co-operation among central banks" to facilitate "coordinating their policy without hampering the freedom of the several banks."

There was an unequivocal call for restoration of gold as "the only common standard which all European countries could … adopt." Accordingly, it was agreed "that European Governments should declare … that the establishment of a gold standard is their ultimate object," and that they "should agree on the programme by way of which they intend to achieve it." The procedures by which the regime was established and maintained clearly reflected the influence of the Cunliffe Report, the Bank of England, and its governor, Montagu Norman.

No longer was a country to resort "to the creation of fiduciary money or credits" so as to "meet its annual expenditure." Instead, budgets were balanced through "adequate taxation" and "reduction of government expenditure." The latter was also to remedy "an adverse balance of external payment, by reducing internal consumption." In short, deflationary policies made it possible to "fix the gold value of the monetary unit" either at its pre-1914 parity or at a "new parity approximating to the exchange value of the monetary unit at the time." Free international exchange of currencies was to be maintained by each country's efforts to provide itself with an "adequate reserve of approved assets" to include gold and foreign exchange balances. Thus, from the beginning the new regime was a "gold exchange standard" and not a pure gold standard. Indeed, foreign balances were seen as a "means of economizing the use of gold."

The rules for day-to-day central banking under the new regime were also outlined. Currency markets were maintained, and all countries were to "buy and sell exchange of other participating countries within a prescribed fraction of parity, in exchange for its own currency on demand." The British role, moreover, was apparently as one of "certain" unspecified countries that would "establish a free market in gold and thus become gold centres."

Thus the new regime resembled pre-1914 practice.[14] Great emphasis was placed, however, on the need for central bank "collaboration" as a means of maintaining the regime. The resolutions called for some formal institutionalization of this cooperative approach through adoption of an "International Monetary Convention."

The Bank of England as the leading central bank (although not openly labeled as such) brought central bankers together, thus organizing the epistemic community of financial experts that could make recommendations to their governments for the adoption of such a convention.[15] Establishment in 1930 of the Bank for International Settlements (BIS) in Basel, Switzerland, provided an institutional setting for further development of this central-banking community.[16] The BIS, however, was established strictly as an extragovernmental body of "private" central banks with only quasi-official status.

In any event, the call for collaboration among central bankers and intervention in the financial marketplace represented something of a departure in practice from orthodox notions of self-regulation and automaticity of currency markets under a gold standard. Indeed, monetary intervention to maintain gold parities was central to the proposed regime. Central bank intervention through the buying and selling of currencies and gold made it possible for private bankers and other nongovernmental financial and commercial interests to operate without governmental restraints. Officials saw "artificial control of operations in exchange" as "futile and mischievous," and such controls would "be abolished at the earliest possible date."

With respect to capital flows, they argued that "the reconstruction of Europe depends on the restoration of conditions under which private credits, and in particular investible capital, will flow freely" across national borders. Intergovernmental loans were to be minimized and countries were to rely instead on loans and credits of private capital. Borrowing was not encouraged, but when needed, "long term loans" were "preferable to short terms." Countries borrowing capital were to follow prudent policies (balanced budgets) to avoid inflation.

Although the United States was not a participant in the Genoa proceedings, Benjamin Strong, head of the New York Federal Reserve Bank, assured Norman as early as 1919 of his interest in currency stabilization among British, French, and American central banks.[17] With respect to the Genoa deliberations, Strong favored a pure gold standard rather than the gold exchange standard regime the British had proposed.[18] Of course, only the United States had sufficient gold to operate under a pure gold standard regime, and such an arrangement would have favored the Americans over the British for monetary leadership.

Strong's principal argument against a gold exchange regime, however, was that there would be a reduction in the autonomy of center countries holding short-term deposits of peripheral countries. A gold exchange regime would force center countries to raise discount rates or offer other incentives to maintain or increase foreign exchange holdings by peripheral countries and thus stem gold outflows from the center countries. Such measures would necessarily have to be taken regardless of the domestic economic needs of the center states.[19]

From the American perspective, if a pure gold standard were adopted as the basis for the new international monetary regime, adjustments would occur more or less automatically and in response to "natural" market conditions. Such a regime would not have put peripheral countries in the advantageous position of being able to pressure the center countries by using financial leverage stemming from their holdings of sterling, dollars, or other center country currencies. Thus, there was no real conflict between American calculations of interest on the one hand and economic doctrine with respect to gold on the other. Gold standard doctrine and perceptions of American interest—maintenance of autonomy in monetary matters—were coterminous.

In the final analysis the British position won out, in large part as a result of American nonparticipation in the Genoa Conference and other gatherings considered politically to be European matters. Given the then prevalent isolationist view in the United States, monetary leadership was left to the British who, for their part, were only too happy to assume the role. Unfortunately, as Kindleberger and others have observed, Britain proved to be unable to carry out the leadership responsibilities it had assumed.[20]

MANAGING THE POSTWAR TRANSITION TO A RESTORED STERLING-GOLD REGIME

Faced with congressional opposition, President Woodrow Wilson failed in the postwar period to move the United States toward the internationalist course he understood to be in the national interest. Wilson's opponents—inspired by nationalist sentiments, isolationist in the extreme—saw the costs of involvement in European affairs as exceeding any benefits to be derived from such relations. They did not see extensive monetary or other forms of collaboration with European states as being in the national interest. The United States not having overseas military deployments outside of its own territories in the Caribbean and the Pacific, there was no national security imperative to play a leading role in international monetary matters, much less to elevate the role of the dollar commensurate with the capital-rich standing the U.S. now enjoyed.

Although U.S. government policy was not to become heavily involved in monetary or other collaborative arrangements with European states, private interests in the United States—mainly members of the banking community—sought nevertheless to make New York into the world's major financial center. An attempt was made to compete with sterling as the vehicle for financing trade by granting extensive acceptance credits denominated in dollars.[21] Private American bankers such as J. P. Morgan assumed a prominent position in international banking circles. The quasi-official New York Federal Reserve Bank under Governor Benjamin Strong was constrained from assuming too active a role in international monetary matters, however, by the White House, the Treasury, and the State Department.

Seeking to reestablish London as the world's monetary center, the British favored reestablishment of the pre-1914 gold exchange regime that had been managed largely by the Bank of England and interests in London's "City"—the financial district. Although it took some years to effect the necessary stabilization of currencies called for in the resolutions of the Genoa Conference, British leadership was apparent throughout the period.

American deference to British leadership in monetary matters was accompanied by a commitment to collaborate that manifested itself particularly in

TABLE 3.1: Central Bank Discount Rates (percentages),
1919–1925

Year	United Kingdom	United States
1919	6.00	4.38
1920	7.00	5.88
1921	5.75	5.75
1922	3.75	4.25
1923	4.00	4.25
1924	4.00	3.75
1925	4.50	3.25

SOURCE: For British data, see B. R. Mitchell, *Abstract of British Historical Statistics* (Cambridge: Cambridge University Press, 1962), 456–60. For U.S. data, see U.S. Department of Commerce, Bureau of the Census, *Historical Statistics of the United States: Colonial Times to 1970*, Bicentennial Edition, 2 vols. (Washington, D.C. : 1975) , 1001.
NOTE: Discount rates are expressed as medians between high and low for a given year.

central banking circles. As can be seen in Table 3.1, in only two of the years between 1919 and 1925 was the New York bank rate higher than that of the Bank of
England. Even in these years the bank rate in New York was only slightly higher.
This was not accidental, but rather by design. The effect was to make Britain
relatively more attractive as a recipient of foreign deposits and thus enable Britain to build up foreign exchange to augment its gold reserves. For its part, the
United States hoarded gold and minimized the foreign exchange component of
its official reserves.

As the only major currency on the gold standard, the dollar became the base
currency in terms of which the market values of sterling and other currencies
were defined. Thus monetary policies pursued in New York had direct effect on
the relative position of foreign currencies in the marketplace. Given Britain's
central position as monetary leader in Europe, Anglo-American collaboration
was essential to maintenance of the international monetary regime.

Although they were weak compared with the United States and various wartime neutrals, Britain and France were, nevertheless, dominant over the defeated Central Powers. Given this relative power position, they were able to
force Germany to make reparation payments designed to compensate for losses
sustained during the war. The effect was to pass on the costs of recovery to the
defeated. Anticipation of revenue enabled France to maintain "a comparatively
high exchange value" for the franc until 1922, "when the hopes of the receipt of
such payments vanished," at least for the time being.[22]

The United States was not a party to reparation demands on Germany, but it did insist that its allies pay their war debts. Fulfillment of this demand was, of course, contingent upon receipt by Britain and France of reparation payments. Otherwise, the American wartime allies could not have met their obligations. Thus, by pressuring Britain and France to pay their war debts, the United States clearly added urgency to demands being made on Germany. Washington chose to deny the linkage between war debts and reparation demands, although it was clear that the costs for meeting obligations to the United States were to be borne not by the Allies alone but largely by Germany.

The United States did finally agree to readjustment of debts owed by its wartime allies.[23] But "the concessions made by the United States to some debtor countries in the Debt Funding Agreements were barely sufficient to offset the increase in the burden of war debts through the appreciation" of the dollar relative to other currencies.[24] Pressure for payment of war debts continued to be a factor in British and French calculations of their reparation needs to be borne by Germany.

The floating of exchange rates from the end of World War I to the mid-1920s was never intended to be a permanent regime, but rather only a transition period to the time when gold parities could be restored. The aim was always to restore the pre-1914 gold exchange regime, sterling at its center. The parties definitely tried to achieve economic stability and the financial strength seen as needed for returning to this gold-based regime. Discussions on this subject occurred during the Peace Conference leading to the Versailles Treaty signed on June 28, 1919. A central part of the arrangement was worked out in the various reparation negotiations conducted between 1919 and 1921.

Early in 1920 a Reparation Commission convened in Paris, and on July 16 the Spa Conference, composed of ministers from Germany and the Allies, reached agreement "upon percentages for division of German reparation payments" among the recipients.[25] At meetings in London during May of 1921, Germany finally agreed to remit a total of $33 billion over a period of years, a sum that was to be divided among the Allies.

Thus Germany was to bear the heavy costs of Allied economic recovery. This enormous economic burden on Germany also played to what the victorious European Allies understood to be their short-term security interests. Heartened not just by German demilitarization, they also reassured themselves that reparations kept Germany economically down—effectively denying Berlin the economic capability (and the national currency) needed to sustain yet another military challenge to other European countries.

In his *Economic Consequences of the Peace*, John Maynard Keynes stated most eloquently how this formula was decidedly untenable. In that book Keynes argued that the burden of costs passed off onto Germany was far in excess of the economic capabilities of the German state. In his classic comment: "Little has been overlooked which might impoverish Germany now or obstruct her development in the future."[26] Time proved the Keynesian objection to be correct.

The decision to extract so much from Germany weakened its economy and undermined efforts to democratize the country's politics. The rise of Hitler and the consequent right-wing turn to national socialism ended the Weimar Republic. Short-term gains from extraction of reparations and war-debt collection proved to be contrary to U.S., British, French, and Belgian security interests in the longer-term—not to mention other European countries also victimized by German invasions during World War II.

Even in the short term, massive capital transfers from Germany to the victorious Allies were impractical. Indeed, the formula by which the Allies benefited from Germany's cost-bearing role was revised successively in the Dawes and Young plans that became effective in 1924 and 1930, respectively. The stabilization of the German mark in 1924 after its collapse in 1923 is a case in point. In order to extract resources directly, France and Belgium proceeded to occupy the Ruhr when Germany defaulted on reparation payments. Washington held steadfastly to its view that the reparations issue was not related to American demands for war debt payments.[27] Accordingly, neither the U.S. government nor the Federal Reserve became directly involved in the attempt to stabilize the mark.

Nevertheless, U.S. financial support for the effort was needed, and private U.S. banking interests filled the void created by America's official absence. American and British bankers, Charles G. Dawes and Reginald McKenna, headed two separate committees of "experts." Neither man was part either of government or his respective central bank.[28] Based on the work of these committees, the British sponsored a follow-on, month-long conference of European governments in London from July 16 to August 16, 1921.

Through its position on the Financial Committee of the League of Nations, Britain had already been the major actor effecting the stabilization of the Austrian and Hungarian currencies. Similarly, Britain took the lead in deliberations that resulted in the Dawes Plan. Not unlike the Marshall Plan of the post–World War II period, the rationale behind the Dawes loan was that a capital infusion was a "catalyst" that, in turn, "would facilitate the revival of the German economy" and thus make it possible for Berlin to meet its financial obligations.[29]

The weight of reparations imposed on Germany was a principal cause of Germany's economic collapse in 1923. Maintaining the viability of sterling and the French franc while, at the same time, restoring German financial capacity was essential to sustaining the postwar international monetary regime. Collaborating in the Dawes Loan package—a "basket" of currencies (the dollar, sterling, lire, kroner, and Swiss franc) intended to provide the liquidity needed by Germany—also set the stage for the newly restored gold-sterling exchange regime that finally came into effect in 1925.

Total subscription for the loan was $191.1 million in various currencies. The American contribution of $95.6 million represented 50 percent of the total. Although the British contribution was less than half of the American total, subscription in sterling by Britain and other countries amounted to $83.7 million, or 43.8 percent of the overall loan. Belgian, Dutch, French, Swiss, and German banks joined with British banks, making their subscriptions primarily in sterling. Indeed, as Norman had commented in a communication to Strong, sterling remained "very much the exchange of Europe."[30] The data on Dawes Loan subscriptions are contained in Table 3.2. Twenty-five-year bonds were issued on October 14 and 15, 1924, in New York, London, and other markets. The response was excellent and the issue was soon oversubscribed.[31]

Prior notions that Germany was able to bear so heavy a reparations cost—

TABLE 3.2: Dawes Loan Subscriptions

Currency of subscription	Country amount of subscription	(U.S.$ millions)
Dollars	U.S.	95.6
Sterling	Britain	46.0
	Belgium	5.8
	Holland	9.7
	France	11.5
	Switzerland	9.3
	Germany	1.4
Lire	Italy	3.7
Kronor	Sweden	5.8
Swiss Francs	Switzerland	2.3
		191.1

SOURCE: Stephen V. O. Clarke, *Central Bank Cooperation: 1924–31* (New York: Federal Reserve Bank, 1967), 70. Dawes loan contributions were expressed in gold marks, converted here, as they were then, at 4.198 gold marks to the U.S. dollar.

providing liquidity to others that it did not itself possess—were modified as it became apparent that the country was not able to meet these obligations. As noted above, for the British and French to pay their war debt to the United States required the Germans to keep paying them reparations. Rather than change the terms of reparations, much less cancel them, the wartime Allies sought a remedy in the Dawes Loan.

British and French attitudes toward postwar Germany differed substantially, but the Dawes Plan was a public demonstration of international monetary collaboration between these two countries and eight other states. When the arrangement for extraction from Germany was obviously in trouble (and with it the continued viability of the postwar international monetary regime), the major actors of the day finally came together in an effort to make Germany more economically viable, if only to facilitate payment of its reparation obligations. To say the least, it was a very narrow conception of cooperative security.

Given its own interest in receiving payments on war loans, the United States participated, but it was Britain that reassumed leadership. Montagu Norman and the Bank of England were key players in the Dawes negotiations. Another indicator of British monetary leadership was the degree currency markets resumed their prewar propensity to follow sterling's lead. On the European continent the exchange rates of Denmark, the Netherlands, Norway, Spain, Sweden, and Switzerland remained closely tied to sterling throughout the 1920–25 period.

France was the only European competitor to Britain, but French influence was largely confined to Continental ties with Belgium and Italy, members with France of the old Latin Monetary Union of pre-1914 days.[32] With the decline of the position of the franc after 1922, even this minimal monetary influence declined. In any event, French monetary influence in this period was never wielded independently of the British, the value of the franc having been closely tied to sterling until 1922.[33]

Prior to negotiations associated on the Dawes Loan, Norman had already established a close working relationship with Hjalmar Schacht, governor of the German Reichsbank. Early in January 1924 Norman agreed that the Bank of England would extend a two- or three-year credit of £5 million to the Reichsbank to augment an additional £5 million being raised in the German market. Moreover, Norman agreed that up to £10 million in German bills of exchange could be discounted in the London market.[34]

The obvious benefit to Britain of this apparent generosity was to encourage German use of sterling as its international currency. Accordingly, German deposits of sterling were maintained in London. Moreover, Schacht also won British support "in opposing a Franco-Belgian scheme to establish an independent central bank in the Rhineland."[35] Opposition to the scheme also served British purposes, of course, in undercutting the position of its French competitor. Strengthening the British economy and its monetary position were again necessary for sustaining the security of its then truly global empire.

MOVING STERLING BACK TO GOLD

Driven by these postwar concerns to restore its commercial position and provide for the security of Britain and its global empire, Chancellor of the Exchequer Winston Churchill announced the decision on April 29, 1925, to return Britain to the gold standard at the prewar parity of U.S.$4.867 to the pound. By objective standards and from the perspective of Britain as a whole, the costs of this choice turned out to be far greater than benefits received. Exports and export industries lost out in the competition with Continental rivals. Moreover, overvaluing the British currency had a deflationary impact on the domestic economy—reducing real income and increasing unemployment.

British policy-makers were generally aware of these costs before returning to gold at the prewar $4.867 rate of exchange. John Maynard Keynes met with Churchill and informed him of the economic consequences involved as he understood them.[36] Why, then, did the government choose to discriminate against British exports and to pursue a deflationary policy?

Overvaluation of sterling made outlays for security of the empire less expensive. Put another way, the pound went much further when spent for imports or other purchases abroad. Spending local currencies bought with sterling resulted in lower prices or lesser aggregate cost for these goods and services so essential for naval and other governmental spending outside of Britain.

Moreover, the owners and managers of capital deriving income from investments denominated in sterling also saw themselves as gaining from overvaluation of the pound. Although Britain as a whole might have suffered from the policy, it nevertheless served certain special interests. For their part, these capital interests tied to the City were also beneficiaries, not only from holding sterling deposits and investments that were now worth more than previously, but also because returning to the prewar parity held the promise of restoring London to its position as the center of world finance.

Such restoration was clearly seen as beneficial to the various banking houses that profited from London's position as the world's leading financial center. Moreover, the Bank of England and the Treasury saw gains from restoring foreign confidence in sterling—confidence that manifested itself in continuing and increasing sterling deposits. Economic doctrine—widely accepted understandings of the time about world monetary exchange—worked to the advantage of special interests among capital owners who asserted political pressures on the government.

Prevalent economic doctrines or established policies do affect the way "objective" conditions or facts are perceived and understood. The belief in the sanctity of gold as a monetary base and the view that restoring sterling to its prewar parity would facilitate the return of Britain to her leading position in the world were the "common knowledge" of the time. Because they were widely held beliefs, reinforced by recollection of a favorable prewar experience, there was little challenge in the political realm by working-class or other interests adversely affected by the restoration attempt. Moreover, the fact that by 1925 several other countries already had stabilized or were planning to stabilize their currencies by returning to gold gave added impetus to British political and financial leaders.[37] After all, the dominant prewar monetary power did not want to be found lagging too far behind the others in the return to gold lest its legitimacy as leader be challenged. In their minds the imperatives of empire and national security warranted extraordinary action.

The "lesson" learned or internalized from the prewar period was that sterling should be tied to gold. This view also prevailed throughout World War I. Although in practice it is true that the 1914 "crisis caused moratoria, suspensions of specie payments, and legal or de facto gold export embargoes in many countries,"[38] gold nevertheless retained its formal or legal status as the standard of monetary value. The only belligerent to maintain the formal convertibility of its currency into gold throughout the war was Britain, but even British gold exports were "obstructed, partly through the inevitable difficulties of transport in wartime and partly through official pressure."[39]

The idea that the gold standard eventually would be restored internationally was paramount in wartime monetary thinking. Although the pre-1914 freedom of international gold flows and the "interconvertibility of notes and gold" ceased during the war, efforts were made to "preserve as far as possible the traditional system of exchange rates defined by the system of mint pars existing in 1914."[40]

Official intervention in the financial marketplace was widespread, however,

and one economic historian has noted that the wartime departure "from financial orthodoxy for the sake of national defense paved the way for the school of
thought which considers it justifiable to depart from rigid orthodoxy in time of
peace in the interest of progress and prosperity of mankind."[41] Nevertheless, the
gold standard doctrine was far from dead. Currencies remained legally defined
in terms of gold during World War I, and widespread efforts were undertaken
after the war to return to gold in practice.

"LESSONS" LEARNED AND UNDERSTANDINGS OF INTEREST

Commitment to restoration of gold as the monetary center of the liberal order was reinforced by "lessons" learned and internalized in the pre-1914 period.
Internalization of such understandings—correct or otherwise—drives future
choices by policy-making elites. Even though central banks and treasury officials frequently intervened collaboratively to support each other's currencies
during the late nineteenth century and in the years leading up to the world war,
it was instead the image of an idyllic nineteenth-century governmental laissez
faire toward the market by adherence to a gold or gold exchange standard that
was the postwar mindset.

Collective understandings of this sort effectively eliminate from serious
consideration policy options that are counter to the conventional wisdom. As
a result, choices finally made may well be suboptimal, perhaps serving only the
interests of a few. Fixed exchange rates, because of their linkage to gold, were
seen as necessary to rebuilding the prewar liberal order. Notwithstanding that
the return to gold at the prewar exchange rate carried known costs, British officials were bent on that course. Given the prevailing orthodoxy at the time, it
was hard to argue otherwise.

This attempt to restore conditions that previously existed—"imitative" innovation—contrasts with the more inventive "initiative" innovation,[42] which
does not rely so heavily on learning grounded in past experience. In the years
after World War I, there were no theoretical breakthroughs or significant new
insights on monetary relations to fuel new thinking, much less new initiatives.
Nineteenth-century free trade and gold standard doctrinal beliefs were still au
courant. They carried the day.

These were the understandings that drove the Churchill decision to return
sterling to gold at the prewar parity. Donald Winch notes "that a good deal of
pride and prestige [were] attached to the pre-war parity. Most people, including the policy-makers of the day, were hypnotised by the only parity which had

any reality for them. It may not have been entirely irrational to act on such beliefs."[43] This is precisely the point. Prevalent understandings—"the decision maker's personal perceptions of reality"[44]—are what matter. Widely accepted economic doctrines and established policies influence the choices made by decision-makers. They inform the perception of reality upon which policy-makers act and also may be used by them in an attempt to legitimate their choices.

Such arguments can be used by some, of course, to manipulate others in the political process. To the extent that the policy-makers themselves are believers in the validity of a given doctrine, however, their use of such arguments may be genuine efforts to persuade others in the political process.[45] Thus references by Churchill and others to the sanctity of the gold standard may not have been, as critics allege, merely a cynical manipulation of values designed to serve the special interests of the City and, more broadly, capital owners and managers. Although these interests were indeed served, Churchill and others in the cabinet were influenced primarily by the then-prevalent gold standard doctrine.

Overvaluation facilitated government finance of foreign policy and national security policies pursued abroad. Referring to advisors from the Treasury and the Bank of England, Churchill remarked that their opinions were more important "than the clever arguments of academic theorists"—presumably a reference to Keynes.[46] For his part, not even Keynes accused Churchill of intentionally serving special interests in response to political pressures brought by them on the government. He merely attributed the decision to Churchill's being ill informed.

In a scathing attack written right after the government's policy was announced, Keynes asked why Churchill had done "such a silly thing." Keynes's reply to his own question was that Churchill "has no instinctive judgment to prevent him from making mistakes; partly because, lacking this instinctive judgment, he was deafened by the clamorous voices of conventional finance; and, most of all, because he was gravely misled by his experts."[47]

Thus Keynes did not accuse the "voices of conventional finance" or Churchill's "experts" of deliberately misleading the government. In his view "they miscalculated the degree of the maladjustment of money values which would result from restoring sterling to its pre-war gold parity," and both "misunderstood and underrated the technical difficulty of bringing about a general reduction of internal money values."[48] In a reference to Parliamentary committees and other advisors advocating a return to gold at the prewar parity, Keynes commented that "the minds" of Churchill's "advisers still dwelt in the imaginary academic world, peopled by City editors, members of Cunliffe and Currency Committees *et hoc genus omne*, where the necessary adjustments follow 'automatically' from a 'sound' policy by the Bank of England."[49] Clearly, the mindset described by Keynes was an ideological one—a belief system committed to what were thought to be the virtues of the gold standard. Indeed, Keynes viewed the gold standard as "an essential emblem and idol of those who sit in the top tier of the machine."[50]

That there was a common mindset or ideological perspective toward money within the financial elite—among the bankers of the City and the government's treasury men—is understandable.[51] But in 1925 gold standard doctrine as ideology was not just the exclusive possession of an elite among capital managers who shared a common "social environment." Indeed, belief in the alleged virtues of the gold standard was widespread. Even industrial workers who bore a disproportionate share of the costs of returning to gold apparently shared these beliefs. Opposition from working-class interests to the policy was initially very muted and only assumed strength after the consequences predicted by Keynes became apparent.

Few questioned the desirability of Britain's returning to gold. It was assumed that this was not only the most appropriate but also the only feasible course to follow. Economic doctrine, consistent as it seemed to be with national and imperial concerns, thus effectively reduced the perception of alternatives to one. Indicative of this perspective was a comment made in 1931 by a former Labour minister after sterling had finally been detached from gold: "They never told us we could do that!"[52]

The prevalent economic doctrine notwithstanding, matters were not left to "natural" forces after the British return to gold in 1925: "Britain's need to maintain a tight monetary policy in order to foster adjustment [forced] Norman . . . to ignore the gold standard tradition under which monetary policy was supposed to be linked to movements in international reserves."[53] Moreover, violation of gold standard precepts were not confined to Britain. In matters involving "pressing national problems" most central bankers "gave short shrift to orthodox preconceptions that ran counter to their views of the public interest."[54]

On the other hand, the gold standard doctrine retained considerable utility in practice when central "bankers wished to oppose policies pursued" by their counterparts in other countries. Invocation of the doctrine was selective: "Where the problems of others were concerned" the central bankers "sometimes based their judgments on the pieties of the gold standard rules of the game."[55] This manipulative function of doctrine was also employed in the domestic political arena by central bankers and other officials wishing to oppose those prone to pursue "inflationary" economic policies.

Although economic doctrine did not bind policy-makers absolutely, it nevertheless was a significant factor that influenced the perceptions of interest or rational cost-benefit calculations that resulted in Britain's return to gold in 1925 and her attempts to maintain the regime until it finally broke down in 1931. Perceived benefits at the time clearly outweighed perceived costs, even though in retrospect the actual costs to Britain in terms of unemployment and reduced export earnings of returning to gold at the overvalued rate of U.S.$4.867 to the pound seem to have been particularly burdensome. In 1925, however, restoration of London as the world's financial center and reestablishment of the national self-image as a great power, both economically and politically, were benefits perceived to be well worth any apparent costs associated with returning to gold at the prewar rate.

Inferences drawn from pre-1914 practice were consistent with (and thus supportive of) the commitment to doctrine on the alleged merits of the gold standard. This commitment and various political pressures underlay the deliberations of the Cunliffe Committee, the Genoa Conference, and other gatherings that contributed to Churchill's 1925 decision to return Britain to gold convertibility, thus restoring the pre-1914 gold exchange regime understood at the time to be so essential to both commerce and security.

In fact the measure undermined economic security, putting the United Kingdom into serious recession even before the Great Depression that began after the 1929 stock market crash. Although capital owners no doubt registered gains from investments abroad, recession at home was not to their advantage. However less expensive an overvalued pound made Royal Navy and other imperial operations abroad, the cost at home was enormous—the British working classes being particularly hard hit. For them, the Great Depression had already begun!

AFTERWORD

The interwar period illustrates clearly how money, the rules we make about its exchange, the financial institutions that process it, and the markets in which it is exchanged for other currencies are all social constructions. Ideas associated with "conventional finance," as Keynes put it, when applied uncritically in other times and circumstances, can have substantial, adverse impact. Overvaluing a currency like sterling—setting its exchange at its prewar rate, as much for symbolic reasons favored by even the learned among capital owners and managers—severely hurt not only those in the British working classes well before the Great Depression but also those among capital owners with domestic investments and stakes in what had been a very thriving export trade. Concepts and ideas that define the range of policy choice can change as newly crafted ideas displace older ones. "*They* never told us we could do that," said one Labour Party MP when the pound finally was allowed to float down to its actual market value. "*They*" were the monetary officials and other experts among the capital managers to whose advice even Labour customarily deferred! Then, as now, economic and national security depends on critical thinking about how the ideas embedded in theories are practically applied. Further tightening fiscal or monetary screws in a period of austerity (as in deliberately overvaluing the national currency) is hardly an apt prescription to remedy adverse economic circumstances at home.

PART TWO THE UNITED STATES

MOVES TO THE CENTER

DOLLAR PRIMACY AND

AMERICAN NATIONAL SECURITY

4 Money and Cooperative Security, the Interwar Years, and World War II

The inter-war misfortunes had destroyed the former faith in the efficacy of freely working market forces.

—Richard N. Gardner

It's true they [the Americans] have all the money bags, but we [the British] have all the brains.

—Lord Halifax, whispering to John Maynard Keynes

The stock market crash in 1929 and the Great Depression that followed dashed the high hopes for the security expected from a return to normalcy—the stability thought to exist in a gold exchange standard set at prewar rates. British authorities tried but could not maintain their prewar $4.867 exchange rate and, in 1931, finally let the pound float downward against the dollar and other currencies. The United States held on until 1934, when the new president, Franklin Roosevelt, let the price of gold rise from $20.67 to $35 per ounce—a devaluation of more than 40 percent!

The Smoot–Hawley Tariff Act passed in 1930 during the previous Hoover administration had imposed extraordinarily high taxes on imports intended to protect American manufactures. The combination of boosting tariffs while devaluing currencies to gain competitive trade advantage became the new norm. Countries turned inward in this narrow understanding of self-interest, thus ushering in a period of ever-higher tariffs and competitive devaluations in search of one-sided trade advantage dubbed by critics as "beggar-thy-neighbor" policies. The notion of enlightened self-interest was hard to find as authorities took measures with adverse effects on others—negative externalities that were returned in kind.

Given the size of its economy and its large gold reserve, the United States retained the capability for monetary leadership during this turbulent period in the 1930s but chose, for the most part, not to exercise this role. Charles Kindleberger saw American policy-makers as unwilling and Britain unable to provide the leadership needed for achieving a high degree of monetary collaboration.[1] The resulting global monetary regime of floating exchange rates, accompanied by "beggar-thy-neighbor" trade policies, reflected this absence of global monetary leadership.

Such zero-sum, narrow constructions of national monetary and economic interest dramatically reduced the volume of international trade and had adverse effects on security as well. The absence of leadership, coupled with changes in relative capabilities of states during the 1930s, was responsible, in part, for the emergence of competing currency blocs during the last half of the decade that became solidified with the outbreak of war in 1939.

The September 1936 Tripartite Agreement reached by Britain, the United States, and France was a significant step toward reestablishing collaboration in monetary matters among the three World War I allies. Although the degree of collaboration achieved was small compared with what would be achieved under the Bretton Woods Agreement in 1944, each of the three treasuries was at least to "be prepared to execute support orders for the other and hold the exchange for twenty-four hours, when it could ask for conversion into gold."[2]

That Germany was not part of this agreement was consistent with the growing political division into rival blocs. No longer burdened by reparations payments since a moratorium took effect in 1931 and, two years later, when Hitler came to power, German authorities took extraordinary steps to restore economic growth and reassume the country's dominant position in central Europe. Once again, the outlines of rival monetary blocs reflected the political reality of competing alliances much as they had during World War I.[3] The Axis Powers, confiscating monetary assets in the countries they invaded,[4] constituted their own currency bloc, as did the Allied Powers in their Tripartite Agreement of 1936.

As in World War I, most monetary transactions occurred within the two separate blocs. Nevertheless, some transactions among warring parties in each other's currency did continue through intermediaries between the two blocs. As happened in World War I, the opposing blocs again were linked through banks in nonbelligerent countries and, as discussed below, central bankers from warring states continued to participate in, or cooperate with, the Bank for International Settlements (BIS) in Basel. Switzerland was again a center for monetary exchange among adversaries.

The March 1941 effective date of American Lend-Lease assistance to Britain solidified Anglo-American collaboration in what had become an Allied currency bloc.[5] Although the United States was closely tied to Britain, France, and their allies, American transactions with Germany, Japan, and the other Axis Powers were not formally terminated until U.S. entry into the war in December 1941.

MAINTAINING THE TRIPARTITE AND WORLD WAR II REGIMES: 1936–45

The French government's turn to the left led to abandonment of the gold standard and a decision to join the British and Americans in the Tripartite Accord of 1936. The gold bloc that France had led was left in disarray. The commitment made by the three parties to the new regime was that each would be willing to purchase the currency of the other and hold it for at least twenty-four hours, after which it could be exchanged for gold. Even this admittedly meager foundation provided some basis for rebuilding a collaborative spirit among the United States, Britain, France, and countries associated with them. It was cooperative security on the monetary front among those who once again soon would become Western allies against Germany in its central European sphere of influence.

As shown in discount rate data contained in Table 4.1, the earlier Anglo-American collaborative pattern by which the American bank rate was kept below that in London was restored. For its part, the French interest rate was allowed to go even higher than the British to discourage further depreciation of the franc, a persistent problem after the French finally departed from the gold exchange standard in 1936. The Germans, not a party to the Tripartite Agreement, kept their discount rate constant, albeit behind a wall of strict exchange controls and other restrictions.

With the outbreak of war in 1939 exchange controls were soon put in place. Given the imposition of these restrictions on capital flows, how the discount rate was set ceased to have the same significance as a collaborative tool for maintaining the exchange regime.[6] Accordingly, the American and British central banks fixed their bank rates at 1 and 2 percent, respectively, for the duration of the war.[7]

TABLE 4.1: Central Bank Discount Rates, 1936–39

	U.S.	UK	France	Germany
1936	1.5	2.0	2.0	4.0
1937	1.0	2.0	3.0	4.0
1938	1.0	2.0	2.5	4.0
1939	1.0	2.0	2.0	4.0

SOURCE: Compiled from various January issues of the *Federal Reserve Bulletin*.

There was a slightly greater tendency to hold foreign exchange as a monetary reserve medium within the tripartite-centered regime, but the degree to which this occurred was still small compared with the 1920s. By the end of 1937, only 8.6 percent of monetary reserves were in the form of foreign exchange, compared with 5.5 percent at the end of 1933. But this was still only about a third of the 24.3 percent maintained at the end of 1928.[8]

In the years between the formal devaluation of the American dollar in 1934 and the French departure from the gold standard in 1936, the gold stock of France diminished as the American stock rose.[9] About half of the American gold inflow came from France,[10] further eroding the French effort to remain on a gold exchange standard.

This trend was reversed in 1936, however, as the French were allowed to depreciate the franc relative to both sterling and the dollar without threat of retaliation. As a result, the French were able to increase their gold supply during 1937. In May 1938 the franc was finally pegged to sterling that, in turn, was tied to the dollar. The three central banks actively coordinated by intervening in financial markets to maintain stable exchange rates. The approach of the war in 1938 and 1939, however, put increasing strain on the tripartite regime as private capital flowed from Europe to the United States, thus drawing gold to that relatively safer haven.[11]

Until mid-1938, the dollar-sterling exchange rate remained at about $5.00 to the pound. By August 1939, however, the pound had depreciated to about $4.60.[12] Even so, one estimate is that Britain lost almost $700 million in gold reserves between March and September 1939 as a result of the capital outflow.[13] After the fall of France in 1940, the sterling rate dropped as low as $3.27 until it was finally stabilized at $4.035 for the rest of the war.[14]

The extent of American monetary collaboration with Britain was extremely limited during the early days of the war. Between August 1939 and December 1940, British gold reserves were forced down from about $2 billion to just over $400 million. When the American commitment to the war became clearer, however, a new wartime regime was created. The positive effect of Lend-Lease on the British reserve position is depicted in Table 4.2.

As in World War I, Britain relied heavily on the empire for monetary support throughout World War II. Sterling deposits trebled during the war, from $5.133 billion in 1941 to $14.881 billion four years later.[15] In particular, India again absorbed the heaviest burden of this support, such that by 1945 India

TABLE 4.2: British Reserves, 1939–45

(Billions of dollars)

1939	September	2.094
1940	March	1.981
	September	0.899
1941	March	0.282
Lend-Lease begins		
1941	September	0.278
1942	March	0.658
	September	0.960
1943	March	1.194
	September	1.618
1944	March	2.034
	September	2.377
1945	March	2.433
	September	2.433

SOURCE: R. S. Sayers, *History of the Second World War: Financial Policy, 1939–45* (London: HM Stationery Office and Longmans, Green, 1956), 496.

NOTE: Dollar figures are computed at $4.03 to the pound. Data are primarily for gold reserves; however, the figures also include a small amount of foreign exchange (Canadian and American dollar) holdings.

TABLE 4.3: British External Liabilities, 1941–45

End of:	Total liabilities (billions of dollars)	% £ area
1941	5.133	52
1942	6.625	60
1943	9.482	61
1944	12.166	63
1945	14.881	67

SOURCE: R. S. Sayers, *History of the Second World War: Financial Policy, 1939–45* (London: HM Stationery Office and Longmans, Green, 1956), 497. The exchange rate for the period was £ 1.0 = $4.03.

held about 36 percent of all sterling deposits, compared with about 23 percent in 1942.[16] Table 4.3 depicts the increasing relative burden assumed by the sterling area as a whole.

In short, for its security Britain relied heavily on two sources of monetary collaboration—the United States through Lend-Lease as well as the empire and other countries willing to accept payment for wartime purchases in the form of sterling deposits maintained in London. Through these means the British were able to share some of the very heavy costs of the war effort.

The United States collaborated with Britain in the interest, of course, of its own national security in the common war effort. Aside from common national security interests, countries selling war materiel to the British certainly derived domestic economic benefits from such transactions. Accepting payment in sterling and maintaining such deposits in London was a "cost" that undoubtedly seemed worth the price, given the benefits derived.

Lend-Lease was also helpful to the U.S.S.R. in the financing of its war materiel purchases, but the monetary impact of this arrangement outside of the Soviet Union was negligible. Indeed, as during the 1920s and 1930s, the Soviets under Stalin minimized transactions within the global economy. Accordingly, the ruble was never significant as an international currency.

Belligerents on both sides also used "fiat" military currencies as a means of imposing costs on the residents of occupied territories: "Usually the occupying power attempts to force upon the occupied country the responsibility for the continued acceptance and exchange of the military currency issued during occupation, in this way saddling the occupied country with at least part of the costs of occupation represented by expenditures of military currency."[17]

The practice was followed by the Allies in North Africa and on the European continent, by the Japanese in China and other parts of Asia, and by Germany in occupied Europe.

In addition to paying the troops and compensating the owners of requisitioned property, military currencies also served as a major means of manipulating the economies of occupied territories. These currencies were declared legal tender alongside the indigenous currencies; their circulation was enforced, and no discrimination against them was tolerated. Their impact upon the economies of conquered territories was considerable. Consequently, they came to be viewed more as an aspect of occupation policy than merely as a temporary military expedient.[18]

Not surprisingly, German extraction of resources from occupied countries was extraordinary—by one estimate (1939 to September 1944) some 84 billion marks, 42 percent of this total from France alone![19] The United States and Britain also made dollar and sterling loans or open-market purchases to support various local currencies.[20] Thus, collaboration was at a high level within the Allied bloc, Germany and Japan imposing "collaborative" arrangements on countries or areas within their separate spheres. As in World War I, however, collaboration on a global basis among competing blocs understandably remained very low. What transactions did occur between opposing belligerents were conducted largely through banks in nonbelligerent or neutral states such as Switzerland, where the Bank for International Settlements also was located.

Basel was an ongoing meeting place for monetary authorities on both sides. As managers of capital, these central bankers carved out an important role for the BIS as a neutral meeting place.

CURRENCY AREAS AND THE EMERGENCE OF WARTIME CURRENCY BLOCS

Until the war, there were no major international conferences following construction of the tripartite regime except for the day-to-day collaboration among monetary officials involving "interfund operations and interchange of information."[21] Given the competing Allied-Axis hegemonies of World War II, international conferences occurred exclusively within the separate blocs. That changed, however, toward the end of the war when meetings were held in Bretton Woods, New Hampshire, in 1944 that put foundation stones in place for a new postwar international monetary regime.

Seeking "isolation of the domestic economy from international trends," the German-centered bloc operated in the late 1930s independently of the tripartite global regime.[22] The attempt was not so much to disrupt its operations as to insulate the German Reich from it. German central bankers did continue to participate with their counterparts at the BIS in Basel alongside counterparts from countries outside of the German currency area. When war broke out, "Germany secured the full benefit of favourable terms of trade through a deliberate overvaluation of the reichsmark" in countries within its sphere of influence.[23] Overvaluation of the Reichsmark clearly served German security interests, facilitating official payments abroad for military and other expenditures.

Although the French-led gold bloc disintegrated with the formation of the tripartite regime, the British-led sterling area remained intact. Not surprisingly, sterling-area countries continued to back Britain and thus the tripartite global regime of which Britain was a key member. In a similar fashion, the United Kingdom relied on support from the sterling area and the Allied bloc throughout World War II.[24] As has already been discussed, this support was manifested through acceptance of sterling in payment for war materiel and maintenance of these sterling deposits in London far above any conceivable reserve needs. Helping the UK finance wartime purchases in support of British national and imperial security interests was clear motivation for this external support.

COMMERCE BETWEEN ENEMIES:
THE BIS AND OTHER THIRD-PARTY AGENCY

Founded in 1930 as a nongovernmental but quasi-official organization incorporated under Swiss law, the BIS continued its operations as a central bankers' bank throughout the war. Although the United States in its isolationist period avoided formal membership, the Federal Reserve, particularly the New York Federal Reserve Bank, developed important links there. An executive order issued in 1940 required licensing by the Treasury of all BIS transactions in the United States. In practice, the New York Federal Reserve Bank, where the BIS maintained its American account, readily assumed this regulatory function. In practice the New York Fed adopted a more permissive stance on BIS transactions it considered "normal" or "routine." Unfortunately for the BIS, the Treasury intervened in June 1941 to revoke its license, thus making it more difficult for the BIS to operate.[25]

Thomas McKittrick, a U.S. private citizen who had acquired a European identity within the American expatriate business community, was BIS president from 1939 to 1946. National City Bank of New York had employed McKittrick early in his career, assigning him to the bank's Italian office in Genoa. Later he entered other business pursuits in New York and London but apparently did not develop any political connection to the Roosevelt administration prior to assuming the senior position at the BIS. Efforts made in 1942 on a trip to the United States to persuade government officials of the value of the BIS did not accomplish the acceptance in Washington his international colleagues at the BIS had sought.[26]

Personalities, individual understandings of interest, and informal networks matter. Treasury Secretary Morgenthau and Deputy Secretary Harry Dexter White were, to say the least, not enamored of the BIS or of engaging on monetary matters with adversaries, even if only through third-party intermediaries. On the other hand, others in the Roosevelt administration, fully aware that the German, British, and other central bankers were engaged in wartime transactions with Germany, had their own interest in not disrupting BIS operations. Although the transaction volume was small, the United States still needed access to Reichsmark sources either at the BIS or at neutral Swiss private-sector banks to finance intelligence and other European operations. Moreover, both American and British banks kept their doors open in Paris during the German occupation of the French capital.[27] Given his international position at the BIS,

McKittrick apparently deferred much to BIS economic advisor Per Jacobsson, a Swedish conservative who maintained contact for the bank with Allen Dulles, European director of the U.S. Office of Strategic Services (OSS), the wartime forerunner to the CIA.[28]

German need for the BIS and other Swiss banking connections was even greater. Foreign currency was needed to finance "imports of armaments and raw materials such as oil, iron ore, tungsten, and manganese, which were supplied by Romania, Portugal, Sweden, Spain, and Turkey."[29] Reichsbank vice president Emil Puhl represented Germany's wartime interest at the BIS, the German central bank reporting to the German government that the BIS had rendered "valuable services" to include "a great number of important gold and foreign exchange transactions."[30]

To say the least, gold transactions either at the BIS or in Swiss banks were troubling, given German acquisition of gold from Jews and other victims of genocide in the late 1930s, which continued, of course, throughout the war. Moreover, gold assets were taken from countries Germany occupied: "Out of a grand total of $860.2 million worth of gold available to the Reichsbank during 1939–45, $532.6 million was shipped abroad to settle the debts arising from the delivery of goods and services" to Germany—more than 77 percent of the gold used for these purposes shipped to Switzerland![31] Most of these transactions were with Swiss banks, although the BIS also had its share.

Even if the full extent of these wartime financial activities was not known at the time, U.S. treasury secretary Henry Morgenthau and Assistant Secretary Harry Dexter White became thorns in the side of the BIS, advocating its dissolution. After all, the new Bretton Woods institutions—the International Monetary Fund (IMF) and International Bank for Reconstruction and Development (IBRD, the World Bank)—could assume BIS functions.

On the other hand, John Maynard Keynes, the British government, other Europeans, and even some American private-sector banks argued for retaining the BIS—an institution that had demonstrated its ability to conduct financial transactions neutrally in both peace and wartime. To central bankers, of course, the BIS was not only institutionally and symbolically at the center of their epistemic community but also functionally essential, its monthly meetings, regular communications, dissemination of research findings, and conduct of monetary transactions highly valued.

Relationships among these managers of capital were close. The Bank of England's link was particularly strong, its governor Montagu Norman (1920–44) having been instrumental in the politics of constructing the BIS and a stalwart supporter since its inception of this central bankers' bank. In the 1920s it was Norman who collaborated with his American friend, Benjamin Strong, president of the New York Federal Reserve Bank. Prior to the Nazi period, Norman also established a close friendship with his German counterpart, Hjalmar Schacht (Reichsbank president, 1924–30 and 1933–39), which contributed fuel to the fire later on his alleged pro-German sympathies.[32]

CONSTRUCTING THE BRETTON WOODS REGIME— LEARNING FROM THE INTERWAR PERIOD

As World War II entered what would be its final year, monetary authorities and their academic advisers looked back on the interwar experience for insights on how to proceed in the forthcoming postwar period. In their minds one obvious thing to avoid was the turbulent period of floating exchange rates that followed the breakdown of the gold exchange regime of fixed exchange rates in 1931. They were well aware how in the 1930s the volume of trade had declined markedly and unemployment increased to unprecedented levels because of the beggar-thy-neighbor policies we have discussed—competitive currency devaluations, higher tariffs, and other barriers aimed at promoting exports at the expense of other countries. It was not until 1936 that American, British, and French collaboration finally brought a degree of stability to exchange rates. As noted above, the currency blocs persisted, becoming even stronger with the onset of war in 1939.

Various "lessons" were learned from the interwar experience by those charged with constructing a postwar international monetary regime. In this regard, Richard Gardner has stated that "it is difficult to over-estimate the influence exerted by these 'lessons' from the past on the character of American post-war planning."[33] One such "lesson" was that stability of exchange rates was preferable to a regime of floating rates that could be manipulated by individual states to the detriment of others. What was needed was "a mechanism which would ensure the stability of currencies and avoid the recurrence of competitive devaluations" and exchange controls.[34]

Moreover, instability of exchange rates was seen as having "contributed to the coming and [to] the severity of the great depression," not to mention World War II itself.[35] Indeed, thinking prior to Bretton Woods was influenced by a genuine desire that the world not be plunged again into heavy unemployment after World War II was over, lest the history of the interwar period be repeated.[36] The failure of collaborative efforts at the 1933 World Economic Conference in London should not occur again.

If anything, the collaboration achieved in the 1936 Tripartite Agreement (by which Britain, France, and the United States stabilized their exchange rates) was a benchmark or model for constructing any new, postwar international monetary regime. In short, governments should play an active role in establishing the rules that would govern postwar monetary and commercial transactions. As Gardner notes: "The inter-war misfortunes had destroyed the former faith in the efficacy of freely working market forces." Moreover, American officials responsible for designing the postwar economic order also "were not believers in *laissez faire*; they shared the belief of most New Deal planners that government had an important responsibility for the direction of economic life."[37]

This apparent departure from pure laissez-faire liberalism—advocacy of government involvement in marketplace economic matters—was not, however, a total abandonment of all classical liberal tenets. In fact, the United States became a principal champion of restoring convertibility of currencies and reducing barriers to trade.[38] In this regard, there was considerable hostility in American circles directed toward the continuation of currency blocs in the postwar period. U.S. Treasury officials "disliked and distrusted the fragmentation of the international monetary scene into currency areas—the sterling area being a particular bugbear—and the proliferation of multiple currency practices and the like."[39]

In spite of differences with the United States over the future of the sterling area, there was considerable support in British government and academic circles for liberal notions of free trade and the convertibility of currencies.[40] Although there was general acceptance of the need for expanding both trade and employment, Britain and other countries that had sustained economic devastation during the war were more inclined than the United States to view free trade and convertibility of currencies at relatively fixed exchange rates as longer-run goals to be achieved only after economic recovery.

The British sought an international monetary regime that allowed a state to correct an overvaluation of its currency as well as one that provided sufficient liquidity and credit to allow for adequate defense of existing rates against short-term pressures. The 1925–31 experience had obviously had an impact on British thinking.[41] Sterling had been overvalued, and there was ultimately a shortage of liquidity in 1931 that forced Britain to float the pound and thus abandon its costly commitment to the gold exchange regime. British authorities also were concerned lest following World War II the again-victorious allies repeat the same mistakes of the interwar period.

The link between economy and security was abundantly clear in their minds—how the imposition of reparations and the collection of war debts fiasco had undermined the Weimar Republic and contributed to the domestic turbulence in German society that resulted in the rise of Hitler's National Socialism. American representatives shared this British concern for a more enlightened approach to planning for the postwar era. The resulting U.S. policy of forgiving most Lend-Lease obligations was decidedly aimed at strengthening, rather than weakening, the various postwar financial and commercial arrangements so important for security and economic well-being in Europe and elsewhere.[42]

Informed by the British experience during the interwar period when deflation, not inflation, was the principal problem, Keynes proposed a plan for the postwar international monetary regime that put emphasis on "an expansionist, in place of a contractionist, pressure on world trade" through generous provision of liquidity and credit.[43] By contrast, the author of the American postwar plan, Harry Dexter White, and his superior, Treasury Secretary Henry Morgenthau, were not so much concerned with the danger of deflation as they were with ensuring the stabilization of exchange rates.[44]

Given these different priorities, the White Plan for the postwar international monetary regime was not so permissive as the Keynes Plan in terms of the quantity of liquidity and credit available for the finance of international economic transactions. Different lessons drawn from the interwar experience—American concern for stabilization of exchange rates and British fear of deflation—understandably resulted in rather different postwar international monetary regime plans so essential to realizing postwar security.

CONSTRUCTING THE BRETTON WOODS REGIME

The net impact of the interwar experience, then, was a dilution of classical liberal premises with respect to the role of governments in economic matters. In the United States, the New Deal policy that replaced the laissez-faire commitment of liberalism had mass popular support by workers and others who had experienced the privation of the Depression years.

Organized labor had become far more significant as a source of political pressure in the United States, Britain, and on the European continent. Demands by labor could no longer be ignored by decision-makers charged with the construction of international monetary regimes. Economic adjustment by pursuing deflationary policies, the usual prescription of gold-standard doctrine, was no longer acceptable because of the increased labor unemployment caused by such policies. Organized labor now had a political voice in both Europe and the United States.

Of course, industrial and other commercial and financial interests of capital owners also remained important as sources of political pressure. After the economically disruptive experience of the 1930s, when exchange rates were allowed to float, business interests favored an international monetary regime in which exchange rates were relatively stable. There was also support for restoring the relatively unencumbered flow of private capital across national borders, free of the exchange controls erected in the 1930s and maintained during World War II. Stable exchange rates and the free flow of capital across national borders were conditions seen as essential not only to facilitating international commerce but also enabling government expenditures in the conduct of foreign and national security policy.

The outcome at Bretton Woods sought not only to accommodate government needs to finance international expenditures for security and other purposes but also to serve *both* business and labor interests at home. Exchange rates under the new regime were to be relatively stable, but additional liquidity was also provided to preclude the necessity for any immediate resort to deflationary adjustment policies. Adherence by most states to the Bretton Woods discipline of relatively fixed exchange rates was not achieved until 1958, after allowing sufficient time for economic recovery. Although progress to the goal was incremental, the parties established a liberal regime free of exchange controls, thus achieving a stated objective at the Bretton Woods meetings.

It was a time of ferment. New ideas mattered. They were more welcome in the 1940s than before the war and during the Great Depression. The door was open now to John Maynard Keynes and other opponents of economic laissez-faire who promoted new theories that underscored the imperative of activity by government in the marketplace, both domestically and internationally.[45]

Alluding to Darwinian notions, Keynes observed what he called "a natural line of evolution" in the development of capitalism. In Keynes's view there was a need to make "improvements in the technique of modern Capitalism by the agency of collective action."[46] It was an early statement of gains to be had from cooperative security measures in international monetary matters.

Although the notion of an evolutionary trend in capitalism may be more metaphor than theory, the view nevertheless had a profound effect upon the status of established doctrines. Moreover, the effect was not confined to the domestic policy arena, but was extended to the international realm as well. Sharing a conviction that at least minimal international policy coordination was necessary in an increasingly complex world, policy-oriented scholars like Keynes made proposals for the establishment of an international monetary regime to facilitate commerce and other relations. These regime proposals typically included new organizational structures that were given varying degrees of authority to enable them to carry out assigned tasks.

Keynes saw the "need" for "an instrument of international currency having general acceptability between nations," and he argued that the quantity of this international currency should be "governed by the actual current requirements of world commerce."[47] He specifically advocated the establishment of "an *International Clearing Union* based on international bank-money, called . . . *bancor,* fixed (but not unalterably) in terms of gold and accepted as the equivalent of gold."[48]

Under such a regime, "the central banks of all member states (and also nonmembers) would keep accounts with the International Clearing Union through which they would be entitled to settle their exchange balances with one another at their par value as defined in terms of bancor."[49] Keynes also acknowledged that "measures would be necessary . . . to prevent the piling up of credit and debit balances without limit." Accordingly, the limits on a country's overdraft credit would be determined by "the running average of each country's volume of trade."[50]

In short, Keynes proposed the establishment of a world central bank with currency functions comparable to that of a domestic central bank. Its leadership and staff would have the authority to discuss with any country heavily overdrawn those measures that could be taken "to restore equilibrium of its international balances." Each state, however, was to "retain the ultimate decision in its own hands" to determine what, if any, actions were to be taken.[51] This restriction or denial of supranational authority to the proposed International Clearing Union was, moreover, consistent with Keynes's own reformist (rather than revolutionary) persuasion.

Although the proposed clearing union was clearly framed with Britain's own liquidity needs in mind, it also reflected the Keynesian commitment to the creation of organizational structures, as necessary, to perform desired economic roles. This was a clear departure from laissez-faire, but there was at the same time no commitment to radical alteration of the capitalist structure and process. On the contrary, as noted above, Keynes saw himself more as a reformist seeking to improve the functioning of capitalism than as a revolutionary committed to its overthrow.

The Keynesian proposal also reflected "lessons" learned from the interwar experience. Between 1925 and 1931, when Britain returned to gold and overvalued the pound relative to other currencies, the domestic austerity that resulted manifested itself as a direct cost to both export industries and labor—the latter paying a high unemployment cost even before onset of the Great Depression. As we have underscored above, the stability of exchange rates between 1925 and 1931 that had been purchased at so high a price gave way to floating exchange rates accompanied by restrictions on trade, competitive currency devaluations, exchange controls, and other illiberal "beggar-thy-neighbor" policies that ensued.

Changed understandings in the minds of experts matter. The Keynesian approach, then, combined lessons learned from these experiences. Exchange rates were to be stable, as in 1925–31, but sufficient liquidity also would be provided multilaterally. No single state was again to bear the burden of international regime maintenance through overvaluation of its currency as Britain had done in 1925–31. Both domestic well-being and international security depended on a more equitable, multilateral framework for international monetary exchange.

In the United States there were political pressures from isolationists who feared any American surrender of its monetary authority to an international organization and from conservative banking interests among capital managers who saw the proposed Bretton Woods regime as too expansive monetarily and not sufficiently stringent vis-à-vis debtor states.[52] In spite of these political pressures, the United States assumed leadership in constructing the new international monetary regime.

The United States persuaded Britain to join the new regime against the wishes of illiberal elements within Britain on both the right and the left.[53] The payoff to the British that enabled the government to accede to the agreement was the promise of sufficient liquidity or aid that clearly served British postwar needs.[54] Similar incentives also motivated the accession of other states to the new international monetary agreement.

The International Monetary Fund that emerged from the Bretton Woods Conference in 1944 in fact reflected more of the American White Plan than it did the British Keynes Plan. Although the White proposal was more restrictive in terms of making international credit available, it shared the Keynesian commitment to collective action when necessary to restore or to maintain the functioning of capitalism—both international monetary exchange and capital flows across national borders.

At one point in the Anglo-American discourse Lord Halifax reportedly whispered to John Maynard Keynes: "It's true they [the Americans] have all the money bags, but we [the British] have all the brains." But brainpower could only go so far and the less expansive White Plan prevailed, albeit with some modifications.

Incremental implementation of the Bretton Woods agreement would resolve Anglo-American differences in interpretation of the agreement, but in 1944 the differences still remained:

[1] The British appeared to regard the International Monetary Fund as an automatic source of credit; the Americans seemed to consider it as a conditional provider of financial aid.

[2] The British emphasized their freedom to maintain equilibrium by depreciation and exchange control, placing on creditor countries the main burden of adjustment; the Americans looked forward to the early achievement of free and stable exchanges, specifically rejecting the suggestion of any one-sided responsibility on the United States.

[3] Most disquieting of all, the British considered their adherence to multilateral principles contingent upon bold new measures of transitional aid; the Americans claimed that the Bretton Woods institutions would meet Britain's postwar needs.[55]

Notwithstanding these differences, the Bretton Woods agreement did provide the basis for the construction of the postwar regime of relatively fixed exchange rates among participating states.[56]

Coupled with its disproportionately vast capital resources, the Bretton Woods outcome left the United States monetarily as undisputed global leader. Indeed, it was the only country at the time with an effective veto in the IMF. Monetary leadership under the new regime clearly conveyed the financial means necessary not only to provide for its own security but also to take on global security tasks in coordination with governments in other countries. Liquidity provided by the U.S. Marshall Plan aid was also part of a strategy that secured an ongoing American interest in global commerce. It was a vision that accommodated the interests of both capital owners and labor—the latter by job growth from the anticipated expansion of export industries providing materiel to countries devastated by world war.

The United States finally had assumed the international monetary lead, anchoring the dollar in global commerce as the world's key currency—a decisive advantage essential to financing a postwar American foreign and national security policy requiring extraordinarily large government outlays abroad. Other countries readily accepted the American currency for payments as if it were gold—better than gold, since dollar deposits also earned interest!

As a practical matter, the problem in the immediate postwar years was not a surplus of dollars in global markets, but rather a shortage relative to demand for them. U.S. balance-of-payments deficits were welcomed abroad precisely because of their direct contribution to international liquidity. Investment of private capital expanded substantially as U.S. corporations and other investors pursued opportunities abroad, which contributed to economic growth there and returns to the capital interests at home. International trade expanded substantially with gains to export industries and labor employed in them. Job loss from imports was offset by gains in the export sector—the United States running a favorable trade balance for a quarter-century following World War II!

The U.S. government embraced this new postwar internationalism—a willingness to grant foreign assistance, make loans, and spend abroad for military and other purposes for its own national security as well as the security interests shared by allies and other countries in the newly founded United Nations organization. The international monetary advantage enjoyed by the United States proved to be a decisive factor throughout the Cold War. Deep American pockets were an essential ingredient enabling the conduct of U.S. national security policy vis-à-vis its new adversaries—the Soviet Union, China, and their respective allies.

AFTERWORD

The Great Depression years that began with "beggar-thy-neighbor" policies in the early 1930s finally gave way to cooperative security efforts in the last half of the decade within what were yet again in Europe becoming separate allied camps. Germany gradually returned to its dominant position among central European states, while Britain and France (and later the United States) were core members of what, with the outbreak of war, would become a reconstituted Western alliance.

As in World War I, wartime controls on currency exchange rates were in place within each alliance—wartime costs externalized—shared or imposed on others. With the Netherlands under occupation no longer able to play the banking role it had performed in World War I, Switzerland (to include now the Bank for International Settlements in Basel) remained the principal neutral ground for currency exchange, intelligence, and other operations requiring an enemy's currency.

"Lessons" drawn from the interwar period profoundly affected the postwar design crafted at Bretton Woods. A liberal view of cooperative security saw a return to relatively fixed exchange rates, institutionalizing in the IMF the ways and means countries easily could access the capital needed to sustain these rates. To make the new regime work would require cooperative measures by finance ministers and central bankers either within or outside of this institutional framework to provide liquidity needed to avoid exchange controls so injurious to international commerce. As in other matters in the "new" multilateralist thinking of the time, economic and national security was to be very much a cooperative affair.

5 Cold War and the Bretton Woods Years

There is no greater responsibility resting upon peoples and governments
everywhere than to make sure that enduring peace will this time—at long
last—be established and maintained. . . . The crucial test . . . for nations
today is whether or not they have suffered enough, and have learned
enough, to put aside suspicion, prejudice and short-run and narrowly
conceived interests and to unite in furtherance of their greatest common
interest.
    —Cordell Hull, Former Secretary of State upon Accepting
        the Nobel Peace Prize (December 1945)

The SDR is like a "zebra"—either "a black animal with white stripes" or a
"white animal with black stripes."
    —Otmar Emminger, Vice President, German Bundesbank, and Chairman,
        Group of Ten Deputies (on the Franco-American compromise
        resulting in the SDR being both credit and reserve)

Secretary of State Cordell Hull, Treasury Secretary Henry Morgenthau and his
deputy, Harry Dexter White, and others in the Roosevelt administration saw
the establishment of liberal trade, investment, and monetary arrangements after World War II as essential to restoring peace and maintaining postwar security. They put these issues first—setting the economic foundations for postwar
security carefully in place. Even as war was still raging in Europe and the Pacific,
delegates from forty-four wartime allies caucused in July 1944 at the Mount
Washington Hotel in Bretton Woods, New Hampshire.

As discussed in the previous chapter, the Anglo-American leadership at
Bretton Woods saw expanding postwar international trade and investment as
depending on monetary exchange at relatively fixed rates. They finally agreed
that putting the U.S. dollar convertible to gold at the core and maintaining international liquidity were essential elements of the new international monetary
regime. Only after agreement there on rules and institutional arrangements (an
International Monetary Fund to maintain international liquidity and World
Bank for investment of capital for development) was a smaller set of meetings
convened on a new United Nations organization. Putting economic or commercial matters first also reflected understandings of interest among capital
owners and managers.

Monetary and capital cornerstones put in place at the Bretton Woods talks in New Hampshire, discussions were subsequently held between August and October on transforming the earlier League of Nations and the wartime alliance into what would become the United Nations. As Allies referring to themselves in World War II as United Nations, the U.S., UK, Soviet, and Chinese delegations (the "Big Three" plus China) met in Washington, DC, at the Dumbarton Oaks mansion in Georgetown to construct an outline for this new international peace and security organization. The four plus a liberated France would reserve to themselves as Great Powers permanent seats on the new Security Council.

For their part, the French were represented at Bretton Woods a month before the liberation of Paris in August but were not players at Dumbarton Oaks. Fully integrated in the United Nations in San Francisco a year later, however, France assumed its place as one of the Euro-Atlantic "Big Four" that played leading roles in reestablishing liberal economic and multilateral security relations for the postwar years.

The Soviets were full participants at both Bretton Woods and Dumbarton Oaks, although they ultimately opted out of membership in the IMF and World Bank, which Stalin and other Soviet officials saw as overly dominated by Anglo-American and other Western capital interests. From this Moscow perspective it was enough to be a major power in the UN organization, carving out for itself a veto power in the Security Council alongside its World War II "allies"—the United States, Britain, China, and France.

Agreements finally were reached at Dumbarton Oaks on the outlines of a UN charter, which was signed in San Francisco on June 26, 1945. The preamble set the agenda already begun at Bretton Woods—"to employ international machinery for the promotion of the economic and social advancement of all peoples" and (in Article I, Section 3) "to achieve international co-operation in solving international problems of an economic, social, cultural, or humanitarian character." It was to be a cooperative approach to security.

The socioeconomic link to international security becomes clearest in Chapters IX and X, entirely given to economy, security, and the human condition "with a view [in Article 55] to the creation of conditions of stability and well-being which are necessary for peaceful and friendly relations among nations." Chapter X establishes the UN Economic and Social Council but also acknowledges generically the work conducted for these peaceful, security-oriented purposes by specialized agencies—the IMF and World Bank already having been established at Bretton Woods.

It is, after all, cooperative security efforts among treasury or finance ministry officials and central bankers in day-to-day constructive or peaceful engagement bilaterally and multilaterally that sustain the international monetary arrangements that underlie economic and national security. Serving national, capital, labor, and other interests, they manage conflicts and find the common ground in institutional and other settings that define the politics of constructing and maintaining international monetary regimes.

THE BRETTON WOODS, EARLY COLD WAR YEARS

A liberal postwar world—one ordered by the institutionalization of wartime collaboration among allies at its core—was not to be. Early East-West division between the Soviet Union and countries in its sphere of influence in Central and Eastern Europe on the one hand, and the United States and its Western allies on the other, later became institutionalized in the American-led NATO (1949) and the Soviet-led Warsaw Pact (1955). The IMF and World Bank as global institutions were open to others, but as a practical matter remained outside the Soviet sphere and thus were predominantly more "Western" in orientation. The Soviet Union, though participating in the United Nations, routinely used its veto power in the Security Council to block UN actions seen as contrary to its interests.

Absent the Soviet Union and the Eastern European states in its sphere, collaboration on monetary matters among IMF members was at a relatively high level throughout the early Bretton Woods years. By 1958, currencies from leading countries had established full convertibility into gold, dollars, sterling, or other currencies. Producer of half of world GDP and holder of 60 percent of the world's gold reserves at the end of World War II, the United States remained unquestionably the country with the strongest monetary position.[1] Not only did the United States possess the preponderance of monetary capabilities in 1945, but it also had the will to lead the effort to put the Bretton Woods rules in force globally.

During 1946 and 1947 the reserves of European states declined markedly in spite of efforts made by the UN Relief and Rehabilitation Administration (UNRRA).[2] Beginning with a $3.75 billion loan to Britain and the $1.2 billion in Export-Import Bank credits to France in 1945 and 1946, the United States embarked on the broad-based European Recovery Program (or Marshall Plan) in 1947.[3]

In addition to advancing American national security interests by strengthening European states against what officials in the Truman administration understood as a real-and-present Soviet threat, Marshall Plan aid also was aimed at reducing the shortage of dollars in the official reserves of other countries. Between 1946 and 1953, the United States transferred some $33 billion to the rest of the world (a figure that does not even include military expenditures).[4] In addition to military spending, tourism, and direct foreign investment by private interests, American grants and loans to other countries during the 1950s averaged $2.25 billion per year.

Of course, such transfers put dollars into foreign hands that, in turn, were used to purchase American goods and services. As noted earlier, the United States sustained a trade surplus until 1971, at the very end of the Bretton Woods years. Although offset somewhat by this trade surplus, heavy spending by both the U.S. government and private interests resulted in American balance-of-payments deficits that averaged $1.1 billion per year in the 1949–59 period.[5] Moreover, by 1960 U.S. gold transfers to the rest of the world amounted to almost $7 billion.[6]

Under considerable pressure from the United States, Britain made sterling convertible in 1947.[7] The experiment lasted barely a month, demonstrating that any attempt to establish full convertibility of major currencies was premature. The global monetary regime envisioned at Bretton Woods thus did not come into full effect until December 27, 1958, the date on which the major European countries, at the urging of the United States, finally established the convertibility of their currencies.[8]

In the meantime, however, Japan and European countries retained capital flow restrictions in place. The commitment to restoring convertibility of currencies was kept alive by the United States, and Bretton Woods institutions were permitted to function, although the volume of IMF lending was far below its capacity.[9]

EXCHANGE RATES IN THE BRETTON WOODS YEARS (1945–71)

Given the prevalence of exchange controls, devaluations during the late 1940s and 1950s were relatively infrequent. When they did occur, the changes in exchange rates were usually implemented only after discussions with other monetary authorities. For example, based on policy-maker understandings that exchange rates were in fundamental disequilibrium, it was the United States government that urged the 30 percent devaluations of European currencies that took place in 1949.[10] Even the French devaluation in 1958 was designed to allow French monetary authorities to maintain convertibility of the franc.[11] Thus collaboration during the period was at a high level, marked by both the extensive coordination associated with exchange rate changes and the absence of competitive depreciation of currencies that had occurred in the 1930s. Economic and national security was sustained cooperatively.

Similarly, during the 1960s, great efforts were made to avoid exchange rate changes. For example, beginning in 1964 the British went to great lengths to maintain the $2.80 to the pound rate.[12] Drawing heavily on the Group of Ten's General Arrangements to Borrow (GAB), IMF and currency swap credits with various central banks, increasing the bank rate, and raising taxes at home, the British government arranged a $3 billion credit package that effectively halted further speculation against the pound.

The currency came under attack again in 1965, however, and a program of wage-price constraints was imposed on the domestic economy. Although the French chose not to collaborate, the American, Japanese, and various European central banks began purchasing sterling in a massive support operation. An austerity budget and continued credit drawings did not prevent further monetary crises that resulted in a decision in November 1967 to devalue the pound from $2.80 to $2.40. But, consistent with the collaborative spirit of the period, even this decision was duly communicated to foreign monetary authorities prior to its public announcement.

The franc also came into difficulties in 1968 and 1969—a turbulent time domestically that resulted in President Charles de Gaulle's leaving office.[13] Drawing heavily on available credits from foreign monetary authorities and expending a large volume of its reserves, the Bank of France was able to maintain the existing exchange rate for more than a year. Finally, in August 1969, the French were forced to devalue by 11.1 percent.

For their part, the Germans and the Dutch collaborated with other monetary authorities by agreeing to revalue their currencies upward in 1961 and again in 1969. Moreover, these countries and Japan were willing to absorb billions of dollars of speculative capital inflows in the 1969–71 period—all in defense of existing exchange rates.[14]

It took some twelve years for many IMF member countries to accumulate sufficient monetary reserves and finally set an exchange rate consistent with market expectations, thus complying with Bretton Woods rules that required convertibility of currencies into dollars or gold. Once establishing convertibility, a number of measures were available (or subsequently were constructed) to facilitate maintenance of the monetary regime: (1) coordinating interest rates as a tool for managing capital flows, thus influencing exchange rates;[15] (2) holding dollars or other convertible currency deposits as official reserves, not converting them to gold; and (3) maintaining international liquidity—providing to global markets a sufficient supply of dollars, gold, and other currencies convertible into dollars or gold, all of which could be held as official reserves.

COORDINATING INTEREST RATES

As in earlier periods, central bank discount rates—a tool used by monetary authorities to manage domestic interest rates—were also a means to affect capital flows and thus manage exchange rates. Of course, the same sensitivity of international capital flows to interest rate differentials—other things equal, owners of capital tending to move liquid funds to take advantage of higher interest paying opportunities[16]—constrained monetary authorities in their use of the discount rate for purely domestic economic purposes, lest raising or lowering rates for these purposes run counter to their exchange rate objectives.

Differing views expressed from time to time aside, interest rate data, contained in Table 5.1[17] indicate a fairly high level of collaboration among the

TABLE 5.1: Central Bank Discount Rates, 1948–70

End of year	U.S.	UK	France	Germany
1948	1.50	2.00	3.00	5.00
1949	1.50	2.00	3.00	4.00
1950	1.75	2.00	2.50	6.00
1951	1.75	2.50	4.00	6.00
1952	1.75	4.00	4.00	4.50
1953	2.00	3.50	3.50	3.50
1954	1.50	3.00	3.00	3.00
1955	2.50	4.50	3.00	3.50
1956	3.00	5.50	3.00	5.00
1957	3.00	7.00	5.00	4.00
1958	2.50	4.00	4.50	3.00
1959	4.00	4.00	4.00	4.00
1960	3.00	5.00	3.50	4.00
1961	3.00	6.00	3.50	3.00
1962	3.00	4.50	3.50	3.00
1963	3.50	4.00	4.00	3.00
1964	4.00	7.00	4.00	3.00
1965	4.50	6.00	3.50	4.00
1966	4.50	7.00	3.50	5.00
1967	4.50	8.00	3.50	3.00
1968	5.50	7.00	6.00	3.00
1969	6.00	8.00	8.00	6.00
1970	5.50	7.00	7.00	6.00

SOURCE: IMF, *International Financial Statistics*, 1972 supplement, 4, 8, 24, 28 (entry on line 60 on each page).

principal monetary authorities during the Bretton Woods years. Given British monetary problems, the discount rate in New York was never allowed to exceed that in London. Except for 1959, when both countries had the same bank rate at year's end, the American rate was always lower. This was not accidental, but rather part of cooperative security on the monetary front. Similarly, the United States assisted both France and Germany during the late 1940s and the 1950s by keeping its bank rate below theirs, thus in the same spirit of cooperative security not unduly attracting capital to New York at the expense of these countries.

During the 1960s, however, the Germans and the French (now monetarily much stronger than they had been and consistent with their desire to reduce capital inflows from the United States) kept their rates lower than (or at least equal to) the American discount rate. This was true for Germany in all but two years during the 1960s. During the mid-1960s, the French were also successful in keeping their bank rate lower than the American, but this became unfeasible during the political and financial crises that faced the country in the late 1960s. Other things equal, the policy of keeping interest rates in Europe lower than in New York facilitated capital flows to the United States, thus bolstering the dollar—a mutually beneficial, cooperative measure.

FOREIGN EXCHANGE DEPOSITS

Most countries were willing to maintain reserves in the form of dollar deposits rather than convert these dollar balances to gold, thus supporting U.S. efforts to maintain the dollar's gold convertibility in accordance with Bretton Woods rules. In fact, throughout the 1958–71 period, most countries were willing to hold official dollar deposits often well in excess of their reserve needs. Data on dollar reserves maintained between 1958 and 1971 are contained in Table 5.2.

Dollars—now joined by the euro and other currencies—were (and still are) most useful for market intervention by central bankers in defense of a given currency or in coordinated efforts to move exchange rates in one direction or another. Moreover, unlike gold, dollar and other currency deposits are interest earning assets. Thus, holding dollars in lieu of gold in the Bretton Woods period was of benefit not only to the United States and the regime as a whole but also to countries receiving even modest returns on these funds.

By contrast to this kind of cooperation, beginning in 1965 France chose not to collaborate with the United States and began to demand gold in exchange for excess dollars acquired by the Bank of France, as indeed the Swiss also did from

TABLE 5.2: Collaboration with the U.S. as Regime Leader: U.S. Liabilities to Foreign
Central Banks and Governments, 1958–71

(All figures in U.S.$ billions)

Year	U.S. liabilities to central banks and governments	In Canada	In W. Europe	In Asia
1958	9.65	1.69	6.89	2.07
1959	10.12	1.86	7.67	2.64
1960	11.09	2.17	8.33	2.99
1961	11.83	2.48	9.56	2.84
1962	12.71	3.11	9.27	3.29
1963	14.42	1.79	8.51	2.74
1964	15.79	1.81	9.33	3.03
1965	15.83	1.70	8.83	3.31
1966	14.90	1.33	7.77	3.96
1967	18.19	1.31	10.32	4.43
1968	17.34	1.87	8.06	5.00
1969	16.00	1.62	7.07	4.55
1970	23.78	2.95	13.62	4.71
1971	50.65	3.98	30.13	13.82

SOURCE: IMF, *International Financial Statistics*, 1972 and selected monthly issues.
NOTE: The Asia column refers primarily to Japan.

time to time. Nevertheless, for a short period of time France was clearly the major exception, as most other countries collaborated with the United States to sustain the dollar's position as principal reserve asset and key currency in the Bretton Woods regime.

MAINTAINING INTERNATIONAL LIQUIDITY

Formation of the European Economic Community (EEC) in 1958 and the fact that it was open to foreign investment resulted in the further movement of large amounts of American capital to Europe, thus putting more dollars into international currency markets and adding to the growth of international liquidity. London banking concerns began holding dollar deposits on an increasing scale, and a "Eurodollar" market came into existence.[18] Elites among British capital managers effectively constructed the new Eurodollar market, which operated alongside the London gold market and facilitated transactions from one asset into the other. Not only was the Eurodollar market a source of capital for private investment, but it also was a source of liquidity for central bank use in making payments to other central banks.

Given the relative decline of sterling, creation of a Eurodollar market served the interest of London-based banking concerns by giving them the new business necessary for maintaining the City's competitive position vis-à-vis New York as an important center for international financial transactions. For their part, American banks operating in overseas locations such as London also benefited from participation in Eurodollar transactions. Indeed, given their overseas location, the American banks were exempted from various regulations on interest rates and other business practices imposed by the Federal Reserve Board on banks operating within the United States.

The real take-off point for the Eurodollar market, however, was the imposition by the Kennedy administration on July 18, 1963, of an interest equalization tax aimed at reducing the transfer of American capital abroad by taxing the earnings on foreign securities held by Americans at a rate that would discourage their purchase. Substantial reduction of return on investment on foreign securities had the effect of making New York less attractive as a source of capital. Accordingly, the Eurodollar market, centered in London, received a considerable boost, substituting itself for New York as the primary source of needed capital.

As was true in the years leading up to 1958, the largest single contribution to regime maintenance was made by the United States in the form of balance-of-payments deficits that contributed to growth of the Eurodollar market and supplied additional liquidity to foreign central banks in the form of gold and gold-convertible dollar deposits. Data depicting the growth of international liquidity between 1958 and 1971 are contained in Table 5.3.

Loss of its gold reserves was a cost borne by the United States in exchange for the benefit of having a liberal monetary regime that allowed the dollar and other currencies to be mutually convertible for government expenditures abroad for foreign policy or national security purposes, as well as the conduct of commercial, investment, and other financial transactions across national borders. In particular, the arrangement gave the United States the undisputed benefit of access to European and other foreign economies for trade and investment by American private interests.

Moreover, general acceptance of the dollar made possible the continuing heavy expenditures by the U.S. government in support of its military and other foreign policy objectives. Sustaining American alliances, meeting UN and other obligations, and pursuing a broad range of foreign policy objectives depended on the wide acceptance of the dollar globally. The dollar enjoyed the legitimacy that conveyed hard-power capabilities to U.S. leaders.

Although the flow of new liquidity stemming from American balance-of-

TABLE 5.3: The Growth in Aggregate Regime Liquidity, 1958–71
(U.S.$ billions)

Year	Total reserves	Year	Total reserves
1958	57.6	1965	70.5
1959	57.4	1966	72.6
1960	60.3	1967	74.3
1961	62.4	1968	77.4
1962	63.0	1969	78.3
1963	66.4	1970	92.6
1964	68.7	1971	123.2

SOURCE: International Monetary Fund, *International Financial Statistics*: December 1973, 19 (1966–71); December 1969, 13 (1959–65); and December 1967, 16 (1958).

payments deficits was beneficial to overall international monetary regime maintenance, the flow clearly had its costs to the recipients of the dollar inflow. New liquidity from abroad stimulated the growth of the domestic money supply (particularly in Germany), with consequent inflationary impact. Various EEC countries, especially France, came to resent the influx of dollars used by some American interests among capital owners to gain control over domestic industries. To many in France this was a very real cost.

The American response to European complaints in the late 1950s and early 1960s took the form of "Buy American" campaigns to reduce imports of foreign-made goods, leading to open discussion in the Eisenhower administration about withdrawing family members of military personnel living overseas as a means to reduce the gold outflow stemming from these expenditures. Other attempts to reduce U.S. government spending abroad included imposing the interest equalization tax of 1963 and instituting a "voluntary" program of restraint on direct investment abroad, announced by President Lyndon Johnson on February 4, 1965. The aim of these tactics, of course, was only to curb, not entirely eliminate, balance-of-payments deficits. Quite apart from private-sector capital interests in continued access to global markets for trade and investment purposes, the continuing U.S. government ability to sustain its overseas operations and military deployments defined its national-security stake in maintaining Bretton Woods arrangements.

For their part, the Germans levied "a 25% withholding tax on remittance of interest to foreign holders of fixed-interest securities . . . effective July 1, 1965," and the French announced in January 1965 that henceforth, currency reserves (particularly dollars) would be minimized in favor of holding gold.[19] As discussed in greater detail in the next chapter, the aim of the French policy was to put pressure on the United States to restrain both governmental and private expenditures abroad, in effect subjecting the regime leader to the same monetary discipline imposed on other regime actors. France thus raised the first serious challenge to American leadership of the global monetary regime.

INSTITUTIONALIZING COLLABORATION

During the 1960s the machinery of international conferences designed to cope with various monetary crises had become institutionalized in such organizations as the Group of Ten,[20] the London Gold Pool,[21] Working Party Three (WP3) of the Organization for Economic Cooperation and Development (OECD),[22] the Bank for International Settlements (BIS), the International Monetary Fund (IMF), and the Monetary Committee of the EEC. Meetings took place both formally and informally within these overlapping, institutionalized structures.[23]

As forums for collaboration, these institutions permitted "the formation of friendships of an enduring nature among influential policy makers from several countries."[24] Although the individual participants in deliberations within these organizations often differed in their perspectives on different issues, it is also true that they typically shared certain values, not the least of which was a commitment to international monetary regime maintenance.

A liberal orientation in favor of free capital movements across national borders was an ideal sponsored by American officials, but also generally accepted by their European counterparts. In addition to efforts at the BIS since 1930, for its part the IMF also served as an agent of socialization in favor of the liberal values contained in its own charter: (1) to promote international monetary cooperation; (2) to facilitate the expansion and balanced growth of international trade; (3) to work toward the elimination of foreign exchange restrictions; (4) to promote exchange stability; and (5) to avoid competitive exchange depreciation.[25] Not only did IMF staff members become oriented toward the liberal values embodied in these monetary objectives, but the agency also actively trained individuals for service in less developed countries as central bankers, thus undoubtedly infusing them with attitudes that reflected "the general Western obsession with monetary equilibrium and balance."[26]

There is a danger, of course, in overstating the significance of these transnational or transgovernmental ties among policy elites, their networks in international organizations and conferences, and the epistemic communities they form. Although they share certain value orientations and predispositions in common, particularly among central bankers, they also have been divided by different national cost-benefit or interest calculations, as well as by different theoretical persuasions or ideological commitments.[27]

Nevertheless, viewed as a whole, the 1960s are replete with examples of collaborative activity through both formal and informal international conferences—managing day-to-day financial transactions, meeting monthly at the Bank for International Settlements in Basel or annually at the International Monetary Fund in Washington, and gathering periodically in other, less formal settings. More than other politically connected elites, it is the high degree of pragmatism among central bankers tasked with maintaining international monetary exchange that moderates the theoretical or ideological differences that typically divide policy-makers.

An operational venue that also brought the players into contact was the gold market in London that began operations in March of 1954 and where, until March 1968, the free-market price of gold was kept by coordinated interventions at about $35 an ounce—monetary officials having formed a Gold Pool in October 1961 to facilitate these interventions.[28] The U.S. Treasury previously had collaborated from time to time with British monetary officials at the Bank of England in market interventions designed to stabilize the price of gold.[29] Indeed, a stable price for gold within very narrow limits of fluctuation was essential to maintenance of the Bretton Woods regime.

Collaboration between the United States and the United Kingdom expanded substantially after formation of the Gold Pool. By joint efforts to avoid any rise in the price of gold, the Belgian, French, German, Italian, Dutch, Swiss, British, and American monetary officials were, in effect, precluding any devaluation of the dollar that would undermine the Bretton Woods regime. France, consistent with its less collaborative, more independent stance in the late 1960s, defected from the Gold Pool in June 1967.[30] This was also when the French president decided to withdraw from the American-led military command structure within NATO, thus ending any sign of French military subordination to the United States.

By agreement, the Gold Pool was finally terminated in March of 1968—a two-tier gold market established in its place. The new arrangement held that although the $35 per ounce gold parity price for transactions among central banks would be maintained, open market prices for the metal would be free to fluctuate without central bank intervention. After all, the Gold Pool had been of their own making, so they were free to alter the rules, constructing in its place their own "second-tier" market for official gold exchanges.

Still remaining, however, was the Group of Ten—the world's most industrially developed, noncommunist countries, which was formed soon after the Gold Pool was originally set up in October 1961. Seeking common means for coping with monetary crises that threatened existing exchange rates, the Group of Ten dealt first with problems arising from weakness in sterling. In an attempt to develop a mechanism for dealing collectively with such crises in the future, the Ten agreed to establish the General Arrangements to Borrow (GAB) in January 1962. A credit facility available to Group of Ten members amounting to $6 billion, the participation of GAB subscribers is summarized in Table 5.4.[31]

Prior to the development of the GAB, American influence had been responsible for an agreement on March 12, 1961 at the Bank for International Settlements that pledged participating central banks to cooperate by "holding each others' currencies to a greater extent . . . instead of converting them immediately into gold or into dollars," and by "short-term lending of needed currencies."[32]Support for sterling under this so-called Basel Agreement amounted to almost a billion dollars between March and July 1961.[33]

In February 1962, U.S. officials experimented with various short-term financial expedients undertaken in cooperation with foreign central banks.[34] The swap arrangements were essentially lines of credit between the American and other central banks that could be drawn on in mutual defense of existing ex-

TABLE 5.4: Regime Collaboration: General Arrangements to Borrow (GAB)

(January 5, 1962)

Country	Contribution (U.S.$ millions)	Contribution as % of total
United States	2000	33.3
United Kingdom	1000	16.7
Germany	1000	16.7
France	550	9.2
Italy	550	9.2
Japan	250	4.2
Canada	200	3.3
Netherlands	200	3.3
Belgium	150	2.5
Sweden	100	1.7
	6000	100.1

SOURCE: Lawrence A. Veit and Rona S. Woodruff, *Handbook of International Finance, 1958–1966* (New York: National Industrial Conference Board, 1967), 16; and J. Keith Horsefield, ed., *The International Monetary Fund, 1945–1965*, vol. I (Washington, DC: International Monetary Fund, 1969), 512.

TABLE 5.5: Regime Collaboration: Swap Arrangements, 1962–64

Central Bank	Credit line (U.S.$ millions)	Credit line as percent of total
United Kingdom	500	24.4
Canada	250	12.2
Germany	250	12.2
Italy	250	12.2
Japan	150	7.3
Switzerland	150	7.3
Bank for International Settlements (BIS)	150	7.3
France	100	4.9
Netherlands	100	4.9
Austria	50	2.4
Belgium	50	2.4
Sweden	50	2.4
Total	2050	99.9

SOURCE: J. Keith Horsefield, *The International Monetary Fund, 1945–1965*, vol. I (Washington, DC: International Monetary Fund, 1969), 484. The figures contained in the table amount to lines of credit extended

change rates.[35] In the first eighteen months of the swap arrangements, total American drawings amounted to $978 million with credits repaid "generally within six months" of each drawing.[36] The totals of these lines of credit (reciprocal credit facilities) for the two-year period starting in February 1962 are contained in Table 5.5.

The British were frequent recipients during the 1960s of such short-term assistance for sterling, either through the GAB, other IMF drawings, or currency swaps.[37] Drawings on the IMF and GAB took place in 1964, 1965, 1967, and 1969.[38] But, as shown in Table 5.6, Britain was certainly not the only object of collaborative activity among regime participants. Indeed, 57 percent of the IMF member countries used Fund credit on at least one occasion during the 1958–71 period.[39]

Less developed countries were heavy users of IMF credit facilities and thus were also principal beneficiaries of regime collaboration. In 1959 and the early 1960s the less developed countries lobbied within the UN Commission on International Commodity Trade, the Organization of American States, and in the IMF itself for support to compensate for balance-of-payments deficits produced by price declines in commodity exports.[40]

The outcome of this lobbying effort was the establishment by the IMF in February 1963 of compensatory financing for countries "encountering payments difficulties produced by temporary export shortfalls."[41] The compensa-

TABLE 5.6: Regime Collaboration, 1958–71: Use of IMF Credit Facilities

Year	Column A: Countries using IMF credit	Column B: Countries with standby credits	Column C: Total use of IMF credits (A+B)
1958	19	10	29
1959	15	11	26
1960	17	11	28
1961	23	18	41
1962	22	17	39
1963	22	13	35
1964	25	14	39
1965	26	15	41
1966	31	19	50
1967	31	20	51
1968	34	21	55
1969	36	23	59
1970	32	15	47
1971	31	12	43

SOURCE: IMF, *International Financial Statistics*, 1972 supplement. Countries tallied under Column A are those with an entry on country pages under line 2e (use of Fund credit); countries tallied under Column B are those with an entry on the country pages under line 2a (stand-by credits).

tory financing arrangement was not only an attempt by the United States and other major actors within the IMF to satisfy the demands of less developed countries, but also to keep them within the global regime.

Collaboration thus was not confined just to the industrial countries but was supposed to benefit less developed countries as well. Certainly if the less developed countries were to adhere to the regime rule of maintaining exchange rate stability, IMF credit would have to be on sufficiently liberal terms. Although the bulk of the payoffs from regime collaboration remained with capital interests in industrial countries, it was also in their interest to contribute to exchange rate stability in less developed countries through such mechanisms as compensatory finance.

To say the least, the early years of compensatory financing were understandably a disappointment to less developed countries. Allowable drawings were not normally to exceed 25 percent of quota, and countries drawing such credits were subject to IMF scrutiny and policy guidance aimed at eliminating the tendency toward balance-of-payments deficits.[42] Lobbying by less developed countries at the UN Conference on Trade and Development (UNCTAD) in 1964 and within the IMF, particularly at annual meetings, resulted in a decision in September 1966 to liberalize the rules for drawings under the compensatory financing facility. In addition, the limit on drawings was raised to 50 percent of quota.[43] The effect of the liberalization on the number of countries drawing

TABLE 5.7: Regime Collaboration: Compensatory Drawings Outstanding, 1963–71

(Number of countries)

1963	1964	1965	1966	1967	1968	1969	1970	1971
2	2	3	5	12	13	15	12	9

SOURCE: IMF, *International Financial Statistics*, 1972 supplement.

TABLE 5.8: Regime Collaboration: Value of Compensatory Drawings, 1965–71

(SDR millions)

Country/Region	1965	1966	1967	1968	1969	1970	1971
Iceland			3.8	3.8			
New Zealand			29.2				
Latin America		6.6	21.2	17.7	12.5		39.5
Middle East			9.5	23.0			4.5
Asia			117.0	24.1			6.5
Africa	11.3	17.3				2.5	19.0
Totals	11.3	23.9	180.7	68.6	12.5	2.5	69.5

SOURCE: IMF, *International Financial Statistics*, February 1977 and various other issues.

compensatory finance is apparent in Table 5.7, the value of these drawings for the 1965–71 period shown in Table 5.8.

Throughout the negotiations there was considerable debate over whether the Bretton Woods regime needed additional liquidity in the form of new reserve units or whether provision of additional credits or drawing rights would be sufficient. The original French proposal made in 1963 was for creation of a collective reserve unit (CRU) that would be closely tied to gold. Participant states would deposit their currencies in exchange for CRUs in accordance with a prearranged formula. CRUs could then be exchanged for needed foreign currencies.[44]

Recognizing its privileged position afforded by the use of the dollar as key currency, the American view was initially hostile toward the idea of creating any substitutes for gold-convertible dollars as reserves useful in transactions among central banks. The dollar's position advantaged both the U.S. government and private sector capital interests. Instead of creating a new reserve unit that might challenge the dollar's role, the United States favored merely an expansion of regime liquidity through increasing IMF quotas. Not wishing to surrender its privileged position as creator of the reserve unit most commonly used in intercentral bank transactions (the dollar), the United States continued to oppose the French CRU proposal.[45]

The French altered their position on CRUs in February 1965. Influenced by advisors such as Jacques Rueff,[46] President de Gaulle announced at a press conference his decision to seek reestablishment of a gold standard regime as had existed in the pre-1914 period. Clearly directed toward eliminating the privileged American position in monetary matters (and thus in foreign policy and national security), the French proposal for a return to gold would have imposed the same balance-of-payments discipline upon all countries.

No longer would the United States have been able to finance its balance-of-payments deficits merely through the expenditure of dollars. Instead, dollars so spent would have been exchanged promptly for gold and thus would have been a drain upon relatively scarce assets held by the U.S. Treasury. Financing the U.S. presence abroad, particularly deployments of U.S. armed forces in NATO and elsewhere, would have become decidedly more difficult. Again, this same independent strain in Gaullist foreign policy was present in the decision the following year to withdraw France from the integrated American-led NATO command structure, thus ending any sense of French military subordination to the United States.

The French finance minister (later president) Valery Giscard d'Estaing, though not entirely at odds with the new French policy line, was somewhat more pragmatic in his orientation. His earlier advocacy of CRUs was based on the view that the new reserve unit "would be both distributed and then used in strict accordance with an unspecified ratio to gold."[47] By contrast to Rueff, however, Giscard was not favorably disposed toward reestablishing a gold standard that, in one observer's view, would have been "incompatible with national commitments to maximum domestic growth."[48] The January 1966 appointment of Michel Debré as finance minister was a move, however, that solidified French government policy behind advocacy of a return to gold as the basis for a new international monetary regime.

For its part, the United States also modified its views. Having replaced C. Douglas Dillon as treasury secretary early in 1965, Henry Fowler announced in a July 11 speech that there now would be American support for creation of a new reserve asset. Significantly, the new asset would not replace but would merely supplement the dollar or other national currencies used as reserves. The United States thus would not lose its privileged position as had been implied in the original CRU proposal. At the same time, creation of new liquidity would not be dependent solely on gold mining output and American balance-of-payments deficits.[49]

Although both of their positions had changed, the French and the Americans still remained in different camps. The consistent thread underlying the French proposals was a determination to offer a counterweight to American monetary (and thus political-military and, more broadly, economic) dominance stemming from use of the dollar as key currency for the global regime. Not only was the American monetary position to be reduced, but also there would be a new monetary constraint on American spending abroad—a significant limitation on the execution of American foreign policy and on the ability of U.S. corporations and other private interests to invest abroad.

By contrast, the common thread underlying American monetary proposals was a determination to maintain U.S. monetary preeminence and the monetary privileges that permitted considerable freedom to American private investors and importers as well as to U.S. government agencies committed to extensive military and other spending abroad. Of the other members of the Group of Ten, the task of mediator fell to the Germans. The German view was clearly regime supportive: "The Germans, unlike the French, wished to build on the gold-exchange standard, not dismantle it. They wanted to control the international role of the dollar, not destroy it."[50] Similarly, the other members of the Group of Ten also were regime supportive, favoring an increase in liquidity either through new credit arrangements or creation of a new reserve unit.

Although France had no support either from her EEC partners or from other Group of Ten members on the proposal for a return to gold, the seemingly uncompromising French negotiating position afforded the country considerable leverage. Germany and the other EEC countries wished to bring French policy into accord with their own views and thus were willing to compromise.

Discussions within the EEC or within the Group of Ten failed to move France from her reliance on gold and her opposition to the creation of any new asset. At first, most of the European states lined up behind U.S. advocacy of a new reserve unit. But then in an April 1967 compromise agreement reached in Munich, Germany and her EEC partners agreed to focus on drawing rights or credits instead.[51] In return for this major concession, France also agreed to stand behind efforts of the Group of Ten in the group's planning for an expansion of liquidity within the global regime.[52]

Having moved France from her absolutely pro-gold stance, the way finally was clear for working out the technical details of what was to become a new drawing right mechanism. Negotiations were prolonged.[53] The United States still insisted on the need for creating new reserve units, a view no longer held by the EEC as a result of the compromise with France. Finally it was agreed to establish Special Drawing Rights (SDRs) in such a way that they would have characteristics of both a reserve unit and a drawing right or credit.

Provision was made for reconstitution or repayment of drawings so as to limit a participant's average daily use of allocated SDRs over a five-year period to no more than 70 percent.[54] Moreover, it was decided to charge interest to those countries using their SDRs and award interest to those countries willing to accept them in exchange for national currency. Although reconstitution and the payment and charging of interest are characteristic of a credit instrument, SDRs were also referred to in journalistic accounts as "paper gold."

Indeed, SDR allocations are, in effect, lines of credit sufficiently reliable to be counted as part of the participant states' monetary reserves. In a metaphorical reference, Otmar Emminger of Germany, then chairman of the Group of Ten deputies charged with conducting these negotiations, described the SDR as a zebra. Their dual nature as both credit and reserve unit is such that one can describe them as "a black animal with white stripes" or as a "white animal with black stripes!"[55]

A significant gain in power for the EEC was the change in IMF decision rules. It was agreed that "for decisions on the basic period for, timing of, amount and rate of allocation of special drawing rights, an 85 percent majority of the voting power of participants shall be required."[56] IMF decisions had required an 80 percent majority, thus giving the United States, with 22 percent of the vote, an effective veto. By raising the requirement to an 85 percent majority, the six EEC members, collectively holding 16 percent of the IMF voting power, also acquired an effective veto.[57]

The proposed amendments to the IMF Articles of Agreement creating the new SDR asset were submitted to the IMF board of governors in April 1968 and were approved the following month. The new amendments became effective on July 28, 1969, when at least three-fifths of IMF participating countries with 80 percent of total voting power accepted them.[58] After some debate, the board of governors approved a plan in October 1969 for the first three-year SDR period for a total allocation of about SDR 9.5 billion. The first allocation took place on January 1, 1970, with additional increments made on January 1 of both 1971 and 1972.[59]

AFTERWORD

Establishment of the SDR mechanism was an attempt to institutionalize and make more automatic the kind of collaboration necessary for regime maintenance. As subsequent events would demonstrate, however, the SDR agreement and the general increase in IMF quotas in 1966 proved insufficient as a means for maintaining the Bretton Woods regime. The German interest in keeping the United States firmly committed to NATO and its forward-defense position along the European central front was a powerful motive for working out Franco-American differences. At the end of the day, the U.S. had survived the French challenge and still held most of the cards.

6 Sustaining Dollar Primacy—
From Bretton Woods to Managed Flexibility

The Smithsonian Agreement is "the most significant monetary achievement in the history of the world."
—President Richard M. Nixon

I am working for the adoption of a more flexible system, one which reflects the diversity of the real world, and allows nations greater freedom of choice in specific exchange rate arrangements, provided they act in accordance with an agreed code of international behavior.
—Treasury Secretary William Simon

For most of the years since World War II, the continuing American balance of payments deficit had been a primary source of new international liquidity and thus the means by which the Bretton Woods regime was maintained. U.S. investors found many opportunities for their capital abroad. Military and other government outlays abroad added to the mounting global supply of dollars in currency markets. Throughout the period the United States also enjoyed an export surplus in its balance of trade, a fact of no small importance both to American industry and to organized labor.

But capital inflows from the trade balance were no match for the massive outflows from investment and government spending in Europe, East Asia, and elsewhere. NATO and other allied commitments, day-to-day military operations, wars and sustained troop deployments in Korea and Vietnam, and timely responses in other relatively minor contingencies consumed enormous amounts of U.S. capital. The massive U.S. economy—the capital, technologies, and skills from which the armed forces draw—and the ready acceptance of the dollar made the United States the only country capable of conducting prompt and sustained combat operations worldwide. The dollar's position as the world's leading currency privileged the United States economically and politically, but it also had benefit to others wanting the U.S. to contribute to their defense.

Acceptance of the dollar in foreign countries also facilitated investment and transfer of technology by American corporations and other interests. American private citizens enjoyed freedom to travel abroad, unconstrained by exchange controls that would have limited their purchases or investments. Finally, in financing its expenditures abroad for foreign policy and national security purposes, the U.S. government derived a distinct advantage from the dollar's position both as the key currency used in international commerce and as the world's principal reserve currency. In the minds of American policy-makers, this benefit clearly outweighed the cost of a gradual loss of monetary reserves from sustained balance of payments deficits.

CHALLENGES TO AMERICAN PRIMACY

Challenges to American primacy began to emerge in the 1960s, particularly toward the end of the decade. On top of commitments in Europe, Japan, South Korea, and elsewhere, spending for the Vietnam War added substantially to U.S. balance of payments deficits. American officials increasingly complained about the burdens of leadership, including the U.S. responsibility to maintain the gold-convertibility of the dollar at $35 per ounce under Bretton Woods rules then in force.

Economic growth and levels of development in other countries and the exchange values of their currencies had resulted in an overvalued dollar.[1] This overvaluation increased the purchasing power of the dollar and, as a result, the budgetary cost of U.S. government overseas expenditures was less than it otherwise would have been for the same level of goods and services purchased. Imports were less expensive for Americans and their investment dollars went further abroad, but these advantages came at high domestic cost. Less expensive imports from foreign firms gave them a competitive advantage over American producers. Moreover, U.S. export market shares also declined as American-produced goods and services became more expensive than those of their foreign competitors—losses to both capital and labor interests.

Given its position as the *numeraire*—or unit of account—of the global regime, there was considerable reluctance, however, to devalue the dollar (as in raising the price of gold above $35 an ounce, the price that had been maintained since President Franklin Roosevelt set it in 1934). Nevertheless, deterioration in the American trade balance resulted in increasing domestic pressures from organized labor, industries, and retailers hurt by foreign competition. Industry and labor had both benefited from free trade when American-made products could compete successfully in foreign markets, but overvaluation of the dollar made maintaining export market share difficult, if not impossible, to sustain. Indeed, the reversal by the AFL-CIO of its pro–free trade position and its new advocacy of protectionist legislation were indicative of growing domestic pressure to change policy course.

Foreign governments also became increasingly reluctant to continue accepting dollars in excess of their central-banking reserve needs, particularly since heavy dollar inflows also had a potentially inflationary impact on their domestic economies. As a result of such thinking, in the first half of 1971 Canada and Germany allowed their currencies to float upward in an attempt to resist the massive inflow of American dollars to their central banks. There was also considerable talk within the European Economic Community, notably by the French and Belgians, of erecting various exchange controls to include a two-tiered regime in which dollar values for normal trading purposes would be maintained in accordance with Bretton Woods rules, but allowing a floating rate to determine dollar values for other purposes.[2]

These foreign and domestic political pressures forced a reassessment of the American calculus upon which maintenance of the Bretton Woods regime so heavily depended. Unlike the dollar shortages of the late 1940s and early 1950s, the dollar was now in surplus as a result of Vietnam War and other security outlays, as well as imports and investments abroad that had increased the aggregate supply of the currency well in excess of aggregate demand for it in global markets.

It was the declining U.S. trade position, however, that probably affected American perceptions of relative costs and benefits more than any other single factor.[3] Having run the first trade deficit since the nineteenth century, both the balance of trade and the balance of payments were now in deficit—the consequence being ever-increasing net capital outflows from the United States. In a surprise announcement on August 15, 1971, President Richard Nixon effectively put an end to the Bretton Woods regime unilaterally by halting further official sales of gold, allowing the dollar to float downward in global currency markets, and imposing a 10 percent surcharge on all imports. Although the earlier Canadian and German decisions to float their currencies were indicative of a gradual breakdown in the regime rules, their abandonment by the regime leader, the United States, marked their final demise.

In the months that followed, negotiators sought a collaborative arrangement to restore the Bretton Woods regime, albeit with certain modifications. In particular, a consensus emerged to the effect that exchange rates under the new regime must somehow be more flexible while, at the same time, providing the stability seen as necessary for conducting trade and other financial transactions on a global basis.

The regime that emerged from negotiations finally concluded at the Smithsonian Institution in Washington, DC, was hailed by President Nixon as "the most significant monetary achievement in the history of the world." Notwithstanding this hyperbole, the Smithsonian regime was relatively short-lived. Exchange rates were realigned and the margin of fluctuation of currencies around their parities was increased from 1 to 2.25 percent. These measures did not halt heavy speculation against the dollar, however, and in March 1973 the Smithsonian rules also were abandoned.

The return to floating exchange rates was not considered to be a permanent solution to the problems that had plagued the Bretton Woods regime and its attempted restoration under the Smithsonian accords. Nevertheless, the flexibility of the new regime was agreed in November 1975 at a summit meeting at Rambouillet in France, details worked out and formalized in the Jamaica accords of January 1976. Under the new regime, governments—acting through their respective central banks—were to manage the fluctuations of exchange rates through collaborative action.

Cooperative security had taken a new turn. Trade, investment, other forms of commerce, and government outlays for security and other purposes would continue, the value of currencies managed in relation to market forces as opposed to fixed parities. Market interventions by treasuries and central banks—buying and selling each other's currencies in coordinated efforts—were to provide some stability. Economic and national security were strong motive factors bringing authorities among capital managers to a consensus in favor of managed flexibility—a counter to the market-driven turbulence they saw as adverse to commerce of all kinds.

CONFLICTING PERSPECTIVES

If the learning outcome drawn from the American experience of the 1960s and early 1970s was that exchange rates needed greater flexibility, this was countered by recollections of the 1930s, when fluctuating exchange rates resulted in competitive depreciation of currencies and disruption of the international economy. During the 1950s and 1960s economists had made various proposals for reforming, adapting, or substantially changing the rules and methods by which international monetary relations are conducted. Closest to the Keynesian view were various schemes for increasing international liquidity devised by

Robert Triffin, Maxwell Stamp, and others,[4] as well as those who advocated developing institutional means for the collective management of exchange rates.[5] But none of these schemes were really equipped to deal with chronic balance of payments deficits run by major players for ongoing expenditures in both commercial and security transactions.

Still fresh in most of their minds, however, the interwar experience some four decades earlier encouraged monetary authorities seeking reform to seek remedies through collective action, avoiding any return to the disruptive unilateralism of the Depression era. Before them were a variety of measures available to policy-makers seeking to increase reserves or otherwise reduce a liquidity shortage—arrayed here in a spectrum from the most to the least consistent with liberal principles: (1) establishing new (and expanding existing) lines of credit; (2) devaluing or encouraging others to revalue their currencies upward in a coordinated effort to bring exchange rates in line with market expectations; (3) instituting wage and price controls or encouraging others to follow a more inflationary path through more expansive fiscal and monetary policies; (4) imposing tariffs or other barriers designed to curb imports or encouraging others to reduce their barriers to trade—in the minds of most capital owners or managers a dreadful return to "beggar-thy-neighbor" policies of the 1930s; or (5) establishing exchange controls as in wartime—the least desirable option because of its immediate, adverse impact on international commerce and global capital flows.

Milton Friedman's monetary school and others adhering to a similar viewpoint reacted against what they saw as a quarter-century of Keynesian and neo-Keynesian institution building in international monetary matters better left to the market. Friedman, an outspoken proponent at the time of laissez-faire international monetary policy, advocated freely floating exchange rates. Under such a regime, adjustment is theoretically "automatic" and there is no need for monetary reserves because governments allow market forces to determine exchange rates. At the equilibrium price resulting from market transactions there is in theory neither a shortage nor a surplus of the currency.[6] Following this understanding, then, central-banking authorities need (or ought) not intervene in the marketplace. If they do intervene, an exchange rate other than "natural" equilibrium will result, and a surplus or shortage of the currency will be the outcome.

To say the least, not all agreed with this idealized construction, much less its application as the basis for a new international monetary regime. For Friedman's plan to have worked, state and international monetary authorities would have to be as deeply committed to his laissez-faire ideological position. As a practical matter, former U.S. Treasury Undersecretary Robert Roosa commented in a debate with Friedman: "No country able to control its own exchange rate will in practice allow it to float."[7] Put another way, political realities challenge the application of laissez-faire economic theories.

Accordingly, adoption of flexible exchange rates during more than four decades following the breakdown of the Bretton Woods regime (and the Smithsonian attempt to save it) has meant *managed* floats in which central banking authorities have intervened regularly in global currency markets. Dubbed critically by ideological purists as "dirty" floating (as compared with the pure variant of freely floating rates advocated earlier by Friedman and others), such managed flexibility rests on building multilateral consensus among treasury officials and central bankers from different countries on the interconnectedness of their commercial and security interests. It is cooperative security that depends upon collaborative measures.

Massive capital flows on a global scale make most unilateral actions ineffective. There is no assurance of success, of course, even when multilateral consensus among monetary authorities supports extending lines of credit, international borrowings, making currency swap arrangements, and coordinating buy-and-sell operations to stop a fall in value of a particular currency or, alternatively, selling it to avoid an unwanted appreciation. Apart from short-term interventions of this sort, coordinated efforts to drive a major currency like the dollar down or euro up typically require not just concurrence by central bankers but also the political authority of treasury officials on the interest-based wisdom of such a course.

Nevertheless, a flexible exchange rate regime, even if it is a managed one, does provide more opportunity for independent or autonomous behavior for government officials to make expenditures abroad for foreign policy and national security purposes than a regime of relatively fixed rates as under the Bretton Woods rules. When outlays exceed net revenues from trade and other capital inflows, the "price" typically felt is downward pressure on the currency's exchange value. These pressures are more easily managed under a flexible-rate regime than one in which there is a commitment to defend fixed exchange rates.

Regardless of regime type, monetary authorities are more prone to find collective remedies when there is broad agreement on the value added by a particular country's economic role or foreign policy expenditures that also serve commercial or security interests in other countries. Certainly this was the case when, during the first quarter-century of the Cold War, the United States maintained the official gold parity of the dollar as part of its Bretton Woods obligations, increasingly opened its own markets as it sought greater liberalization of trade and investment across national borders, and made massive defense expenditures abroad that served the security interests not only of the United States but also NATO and other allies.

Notwithstanding differences on some issues, this broad, multilateral consensus on security goals was sustained over the next two decades of the Cold War and after. Coupled with commitment to sustaining the dollar's role as a key currency essential to global commerce, the security consensus facilitated efforts by monetary authorities to take collective action when needed to maintain the post–Bretton Woods, flexible exchange rate regime.

Managed flexibility thus has reduced, but by no means eliminated, the need for international cooperation in the coordination of exchange rates. Although a disappointment to laissez-faire purists, those favoring accommodation of market forces see managed flexibility as still more desirable than relatively fixed rates. It was, in fact, this perspective that, to a large extent, guided policy choices of U.S. decision-makers in the construction of the post–Bretton Woods regime.

But this American preference for flexible exchange rates was not universally held. No longer in a position to dominate the process, much less dictate the terms of a new international monetary regime (as had been the American experience at Bretton Woods), other major players challenged U.S. officials with differing views. French advocacy of a gold-based international monetary regime, for example, stemmed from an aversion to fiat money by political conservatives then in power, particularly given the adverse French historical experience with debasement of the national currency. As noted in the previous chapter and below, the French position also reflected its wish to trim somewhat the decided advantage the United States realized from the dollar's roles as key currency, unit of account, and principal reserve asset.

As observed in earlier chapters, gold exchange standards in the nineteenth and early twentieth centuries never achieved in practice the automaticity of adjustment advocates claimed. That reality never conformed to this claim was of little concern, however, to those ideologically committed to the use of gold as the international monetary standard of value. Moreover, domestic political pressures were brought to bear by numerous private gold holders in France and elsewhere who saw themselves as losing from demonetization of the metal.

French government officials also calculated that returning to a gold standard could be a means to bring international monetary discipline to the American propensity toward unilateralism in expenditures abroad for foreign policy and national security purposes. Massive U.S. outlays to support its efforts in Indochina—the former French sphere of influence—were a particular thorn in the French side, given the U.S. decision in the early 1950s not to support France in the failed attempt to secure its colonies. Requiring the United States to pay its obligations in gold would constrain the U.S. by making balance of payments considerations not so easily set aside—or, as some Americans described it, treated with "benign neglect." This French advocacy of a return to gold thus was also a political challenge to American leadership, not just in international monetary but also in both commercial and security matters.

Thinking well embedded among Germans, underscored by the experience with debasement of the mark in the 1920s and 1930s, made them more sympathetic to French concerns about any debasement of currencies, particularly when the inflationary cause is government spending. Even though they understood their own security dependency on the United States and other NATO allies, this did not keep German officials from complaining about excess liquidity produced by American expenditures overseas in dollars. The Germans did not intend at the time to challenge American leadership either of the alliance or of the monetary regime, as the French were wont to do. These complaints were merely part of an ongoing German effort to resist the "export" of inflation to Germany by the United States or any other country spending substantially more abroad than it took in.

The German preference, then, was not for a return to gold. Rather, it was for conservative fiscal and monetary policies that keep domestic spending under control and thus reduce the likelihood of inflation. From the German perspective, countries experiencing chronic balance of payments deficits should have been willing to pursue at least mildly deflationary (tighter fiscal and monetary) policies calculated to bring about the needed adjustment.

Consistent with understandings of their own interests, it is not surprising that the Germans felt the burden of adjustment should be borne primarily by deficit countries. Indeed, since the end of its postwar recovery period, Germany had been a "chronic" surplus country. Given political pressures from its export industries, the German government was understandably reluctant to revalue its exchange rate upward or take other measures that would cut its trade advantage.

By contrast, the United States and Britain—countries in deficit during the 1960s and early 1970s and whose short-term liabilities regularly exceeded short-term assets—held that chronic surplus countries should share the burden of adjustment. In practice this resulted in American urging of surplus countries such as Germany and Japan to revalue their currencies upward to ease pressure on the dollar and sterling.

Both American and British monetary policy elites, responsive to domestic political pressures from labor and certain export industries hurt by overvaluation of the dollar and sterling, sought an international monetary regime in which both countries could remain competitive commercially by allowing exchange rates to vary. Given commitments to continued liberalization of the international trade and investment environment favored by most capital owners and managers, this clearly was preferable to policy elites in both countries lest they be forced by domestic pressures to adopt protectionist measures.

The American liberal preference was to preserve in any new international monetary regime a world of increasingly open commerce as well as one that maximized its autonomy or independence in the execution of its foreign and national security policies. This was clearly consistent with an overarching U.S. preference for minimal government regulation of the private sector in commercial matters, a view that contrasted sharply with the French commitment to governmental planning and intervention deemed necessary by policy-makers dealing with economic matters.

THE FRANCO-AMERICAN DEBATE

These contrasting perspectives were visible most clearly in the Franco-American debate over fixed versus floating exchange rates. Fixed exchange rates have the potential payoff to businesspersons and bureaucratic planners of reducing uncertainties associated with commercial transactions. On the other hand, maintaining fixed rates requires greater government involvement in monetary matters. Although greater government involvement in maintaining a gold-based, fixed exchange rate regime was of relatively little consequence to the French, it certainly was counter to the American preference at the time for a market-based monetary regime that minimized government intervention, much less regulation.

Treasury Secretary William Simon represented the official U.S. view in the discourse leading to establishment of the new international monetary regime. In a statement to the 129 member nations attending the 1976 IMF/IBRD annual meeting in Washington, Simon set forth the American position:

> A country with an unsustainable deficit should resort to internal stabilization, accompanied by exchange rate change *in response to market forces* [emphasis added]; a country with a tendency toward surplus shouldn't simply accumulate reserves but should allow its exchange rate to move in order to accommodate these fundamental adjustments of others.[8]

To Simon, the concept of managed flexibility was more consistent with his preference for a market-based regime than fixed exchange rates, whether linked to gold or not. In his view, however, marketplace interventions by the United States and other monetary officials normally should be restricted to countering "irrational" changes in currency values of a short-term nature, but not preclude adjustments dictated by "underlying economic circumstances."[9]

The introduction of even this limited degree of management, necessitating as it does the day-to-day consultation of monetary officials, represented something of a compromise from Simon's earlier position. Before becoming treasury secretary himself, Simon had been deputy treasury secretary to George Shultz. In March of 1973, when the short-lived Smithsonian regime was clearly breaking down, Simon advocated floating rates in much the same way Friedman did. Simon told Shultz: "The markets are rational, not emotional. You may get some swinging around from day to day, and maybe more than that at the beginning. But they'll settle down and reflect the fundamental forces, which is what you want."[10]

Of course, the markets never did settle down on their own. Only government intervention—"dirty" floating—produced the desired stability in exchange rates. Opposition to a "pure" float of the dollar grew within the American business community as experience with floating exchange rates clearly demonstrated their relative instability. Reflecting these views, an editorial published in the *Wall Street Journal* in mid-1975 accused the Treasury of having "a position oblivious to experience."[11] The editors admitted that "initially" they had been "reasonably receptive to the advent of floating exchange rates," but noted that "since their actual advent the world economy somehow [did] not look healthier."

They added that "in theory, the advantage floating rates were supposed to offer was the opportunity for each nation to run its own monetary policy independently of international conditions," but that "in practice this advantage" had proven "highly illusory." Monetary interdependence, whether involving exchange rates or interest rates and capital flows, was taken as a fact that dictated greater policy coordination. Referring to the need for "collective management," the editors asserted that the United States "and the other developed nations are locked into a complicated system none of us can manage independently."

In his reply to the *Wall Street Journal*'s call for a return to fixed exchange rates and collective management of international monetary relations, Simon asserted:

> I am working for the adoption of a more flexible system, one which reflects the diversity of the real world, and allows nations greater freedom of choice in specific exchange rate arrangements, provided they act in accordance with an agreed code of international behavior. Additionally, I am working for a system in which the role of gold is reduced, in order to lessen the destabilizing effects of that commodity on the monetary system.[12]

Moreover, he added that returning "to a rigid, gold-based international monetary" regime would certainly "prove disruptive of international trade and investment and damaging to the U.S. and foreign economies."

Joining this internal debate among capital managers, two academic economists—Milton Friedman and Gottfried Haberler—argued with the *Journal* and other advocates of fixed exchange rates. Mirroring the debate between France and the United States, Friedman and Haberler took issue with the *Journal* on several theoretical points.[13] The motivation for this critique was particularly clear in Friedman's comment that "fallacies" in the *Journal*'s argument "are capable of doing great harm to the economic freedom of which *The Wall Street Journal* is ordinarily one of the few effective defenders."

In Friedman's view, the extent of governmental intervention in the marketplace necessitated by fixed exchange rates is an abridgement of economic freedom and, therefore, ought to be avoided. Although his first preference was for a "freely floating exchange rate" regime, he argued that even a "managed float" is "vastly superior to the Bretton Woods" regime. Managed floating

> has enabled the world to weather in good shape political and economic disturbances that undoubtedly would have produced major crises under the earlier system. It has enabled the world to suffer widespread recessions without "beggar-my-neighbor" policies. It has not, of course, eliminated interdependence among countries. Such interdependence is both unavoidable and desirable. The greatest virtue of floating exchange rates is precisely that they provide effective shock absorbers that reduce the pressures toward autarchy arising out of disturbances of the past few years.

Thus, the debate between France and the United States on fixed versus float-ing exchange rate regimes had its parallel within the American financial and academic communities. Given uncertainties associated with the alternative monetary regimes under consideration, prior theoretical understandings and experiences from which "lessons" were drawn were particularly important as factors influencing policy choice.

Even though Treasury Secretary Simon was the official spokesman on the subject for the U.S. government,[14] his views were not shared unanimously by American officials. For example, chairman of the Federal Reserve Board Arthur Burns was clearly not as hostile to official intervention or regulation of finan-cial markets as was Simon. After all, central bankers are usually not laissez-faire actors hostile to the idea of intervening in markets to secure their goals. Nev-ertheless, official differences rarely surfaced in the public media as the United States negotiated with one official voice (Simon's).

Ultimately, Simon compromised in the dispute with the French. The spirit of Rambouillet, discussed below, led to the Jamaica agreement and the routini-zation or formal institutionalization of the managed flexibility regime that had evolved incrementally since March of 1973.[15]

INSTITUTIONALIZING MANAGED FLEXIBILITY AT RAMBOUILLET AND JAMAICA

In mid-November 1975 the heads of state of France, Germany, Italy, Japan, the United Kingdom, and the United States met just outside Paris at Rambouil-let. In a joint statement at the end of the summit meeting the six made the following declaration:

> With regard to monetary problems, we affirm our intention to work for greater sta-bility. This involves efforts to restore greater stability in underlying economic and fi-nancial conditions in the world economy. At the same time our monetary authorities will act to counter disorderly market conditions, or erratic fluctuations, in exchange rates.[16]

The six chiefs of state thus committed themselves formally to management of the global monetary regime.

The mechanics of this coordination were outlined in a separate agreement between the two main protagonists—the United States and France. The two had been at loggerheads: the United States had taken a position in favor of a free or floating currency market,[17] while France advocated a fixed exchange rate regime with all the government intervention or management such a regime implied. The ideological underpinnings of the conflicting views were apparent to observers, many of whom referred to it as a "theological dispute."[18]

The outcome was a compromise. Exchange rates were to remain flexible, but monetary authorities would intervene when needed to avoid excessive instability in currency markets. Day-to-day contact among deputy finance ministers of the Group of Ten was to be maintained in order to coordinate central bank interventions in currency markets. Finance ministers were also to confer periodically.[19] Decision-making authority was thus retained by treasury officials. Nevertheless, as coordinated market interventions became routine, central bankers would, as a practical matter, have a greater day-to-day voice in such concerns.

Having achieved this basic agreement at Rambouillet, the stage was set for a meeting of the Interim Committee of Fund Governors in Jamaica in early January 1976.[20] The various agreements of preceding months were formalized. Floating exchange rates were legitimized subject to ratification of an amendment to the IMF Articles of Agreement. The parties reaffirmed earlier decisions to abolish official gold prices, reduce the IMF gold stock by one-third, increase quotas and revise voting rules,[21] and set up a special trust fund. The trust fund was to receive proceeds from the gold sales and distribute these to the poorest of less developed countries for balance of payments assistance.[22]

The most important outcome of the Jamaica meeting, however, was a formal statement in the proposed amendment to the Articles of Agreement underscoring the principle of managed flexibility as core to the international monetary regime that had come into existence in March 1973. Significantly, the principle of managed flexibility, involving as it does the coordination of exchange rate policies, was specifically aimed at avoiding the competitive devaluations of currencies prevalent during the 1930s.

The new regime thus provided national, trade, and capital investment interests greater economic security from the turbulence of markets while, at the same time, giving greater flexibility in the finance of outlays for foreign policy and national security purposes. Put another way, flexible exchange rates could accommodate balance of payments deficits more readily than the relatively fixed exchange rates of the Bretton Woods years. The new monetary regime clearly served American purposes as U.S. authorities understood them.

REGIME MAINTENANCE—THE EARLY EXPERIENCE
MANAGING FLEXIBLE EXCHANGE RATES

Even though the United States was not able, strictly speaking, to dictate the terms of the new regime, there is no doubt that American preferences were most influential in determining the final outcome. The United States resisted reimposition of a fixed exchange rate regime and consented only to formalizing the coordination among monetary officials that already had evolved in practice.

As during the Bretton Woods years, the United States kept its discount rate in the 1970s below that of the Bank of England to encourage capital inflows to Britain and thus support the relatively weak pound. Other Group of Ten advanced-industrial countries for the most part also allowed Britain to maintain the highest interest rates so as to strengthen the international position of sterling.

As can be seen in Table 6.1, German authorities kept their discount rate consistently below that in both the United Kingdom and the United States. Aside from rendering support to the British and American currencies, the policy was also of benefit from the German perspective because it discouraged heavy and inflationary inflows of dollars and sterling to Germany. By contrast, other countries with relatively weaker currencies pursued interest rate policies calculated to encourage dollar inflows or, at least, not discourage them. Although these interest rate policies were formulated to serve domestic economic objectives, the rates of principal countries also were coordinated to support relatively weaker currencies, thus contributing to global maintenance of the managed-flexibility regime.

Advocates of flexible exchange rates had pointed to the theoretical advantage minimizing, if not eliminating, the need for reserves in a regime in which adjustment was automatic—left to market forces. As a practical matter, however, monetary officials intervene in financial markets on a regular basis and thus influence the exchange rates they manage. Decidedly not leaving matters entirely to the market, they still need continuing access to both reserves and credit. They intervene more effectively, of course, when they do so multilaterally in coordinated efforts.

There is, therefore, no automatic adjustment that one, in principle, would find in an idealized regime of freely floating exchange rates. Effective management of exchange rates requires consensus on the use of reserves and lines of credit in currency purchases and sales in service of commercial and security interests. It is a multilateral, but essentially *political,* process.

TABLE 6.1: Managing Exchange Rates by Coordinating Central Bank Discount Rates, 1972–76

(All rates expressed as percents)

Country	1972	1973	1974	1975	1976
United Kingdom	9.00	13.00	11.50	11.25	14.25
United States	4.50	7.50	7.75	6.00	5.25
West Germany	4.50	7.00	6.00	3.50	3.50
Austria	5.50	5.50	6.50	6.00	4.00
Belgium	5.00	7.75	8.75	6.00	9.00
Canada	4.75	7.25	8.75	9.00	8.50
Denmark	7.00	9.00	10.00	7.50	10.00
France	7.50	11.00	13.00	8.00	10.50
Italy	4.00	6.50	8.00	6.00	15.00
Japan	4.25	9.00	9.00	6.50	6.50
Netherlands	4.00	8.00	7.00	4.50	6.00
Norway	4.50	4.50	5.50	5.00	6.00
Sweden	5.00	5.00	7.00	6.00	8.00
Switzerland	3.75	4.50	5.50	3.00	2.00

SOURCE: IMF, *International Financial Statistics*, March 1977.

NOTE: Interpretation of differential discount rates has to be tempered by recognition that capital flows are also sensitive to differential inflation rates. Thus a country with a relatively high rate of inflation may not attract foreign capital in spite of a relatively high discount rate. The loss of purchasing power due to inflation may not be compensated sufficiently by the relatively higher interest rates to make purchases of securities profitable to foreign investors. This caveat is particularly relevant in the years since World War II, when inflation rates have varied considerably from country to country.

In 1976 and 1977 members of the Group of Ten, the EEC, and the IMF also provided several billion dollars in loans and credits to Britain and Italy to support their faltering currencies. The IMF sold gold on a number of occasions, a portion of the proceeds going to a special fund for less developed countries. The IMF was less successful in raising capital for its oil facility, which was created in 1974 to assist countries in deficit because of drastically increased expenditures for imported oil; failing to gather sufficient contributions (only $4.5 billion had been raised by January 1976), the IMF announced plans to dismantle the facility in April 1976.

Thus the degree of commitment to multilateral collaboration was certainly not unlimited. Instead of seeking multilateral solutions, bilateral arrangements were made that involved trade agreements with various OPEC countries as well as decisions by the latter to reinvest capital earnings from the sale of petroleum (petrodollars) in the United States and other industrial countries. Although the industrial countries were able to cope with balance of payments difficulties through such devices, less developed, low income countries were not so fortunate. Accordingly, their indebtedness to international and private lending institutions grew significantly.

TABLE 6.2: Early Post–Bretton Woods Collaboration: Use of Compensatory Drawings and the IMF Oil Facility, 1972–76

(Figures in SDR millions)

Country/Region	Compensatory drawings					Oil facility		
	1972	1973	1974	1975	1976	1974	1975	1976
Australia					332.5			
Finland							71.3	115.1
Greece					58.0	36.2	119.0	
Iceland					11.5	15.5	10.1	13.6
Italy						675.0	780.2	
New Zealand				50.5	101.0	85.7	106.1	46.9
Portugal					58.5			114.8
Romania					95.0			
South Africa					160.0			
Spain							496.2	75.9
Turkey				37.8	37.8			169.8
United Kingdom								1000.0
Yugoslavia						139.0	16.2	185.5
Latin America	151.5		18.3	110.0	537.4	156.1	306.1	156.1
Middle East	12.5	49.9			174.5	15.7	152.1	61.1
Asia	88.2	63.6	82.9	3.8	436.6	462.7	577.3	187.2
Africa	47.2		6.0	37.0	305.3	130.0	238.9	95.7

SOURCE: IMF, *International Financial Statistics*, February 1977.

TABLE 6.3: Regime Collaboration: SDR Users and Recipients, 1970–76

(Holdings as Percent of Original SDR Allocations Made by the IMF to Participating Countries)

	1970	1971	1972	1973	1974	1975	1976
Industrial countries	106	108	106	107	110	112	113
Other developed	77	70	82	84	64	59	44
Less developed	56	57	62	65	66	60	57

SOURCE: *International Financial Statistics*, various issues.

NOTES: SDR users are those that surrendered SDRs in their IMF accounts in exchange for needed foreign currency and thus are shown as having some percentage *less* than 100 percent, their original allocations. SDR recipients are those that have accepted SDRs in exchange for their currency needed by other countries; they are shown as having some percentage *greater* than 100 percent, their original allocations.

The figures in the chart for less developed countries in 1975 and 1976 include OPEC figures of 80 percent and 88 percent, respectively. Of 9.315 billion SDRs created, 66.3 percent had accrued to the industrial countries as of December 31, 1976. By contrast, the figure for other developed countries was 8.5 percent, and for less developed countries, 25.2 percent. See IMF, *International Financial Statistics*, February 1977. The total volume of SDR transactions had exceeded SDR 9 billion by late 1976—an average of about $1.3 billion per year over the first seven years of the facility's existence.

IMF quotas for all countries were increased in 1976 from a total of SDR 29.2 billion to SDR 39 billion. Drawings from this general account and from SDR, compensatory finance, and oil facilities reached record high levels during the period. In particular, low income country dependency on IMF lending facilities is apparent in Table 6.2. The tenfold increase in compensatory drawings between 1975 and 1976 was due mainly to easing of the rules of eligibility for

TABLE 6.4: Regimewide Liquidity/Reserves, 1971–1976

(Assets are as a percent of total liquidity in a given year)

Reserve asset	1971	1972	1973	1974	1975	1976
Gold	29.1	24.3	23.4	19.7	18.3	16.1
SDRs	4.8	5.9	5.8	4.9	4.5	3.9
Reserve position in the Fund	5.2	4.3	4.1	4.9	6.5	8.1
Foreign exchange	60.9	65.5	66.8	70.4	70.7	71.8
Total	100.0	100.0	100.1	99.9	100.0	99.9
Tot (SDR billions)	123.2	146.5	152.2	180.2	194.3	219.4

SOURCE: IMF, *International Financial Statistics*, March 1977, 21–25.

NOTE: Eurocurrency borrowings have also been quite heavy, with more than $26 billion drawn in 1976 alone. Of this, more than half ($14 billion) was borrowed by less developed countries.

TABLE 6.5: Collaboration with the United States: American Liabilities

(U.S.$ billions, 1972–76)

	U.S. liabilities to central banks and governments	In Canada	In W. Europe	In Asia
1972	61.5	4.28	34.20	17.57
1973	66.80	3.85	45.72	10.88
1974	76.66	3.66	44.18	18.61
1975	80.65	3.13	45.68	22.51
1976	87.65	2.41	44.02	33.86

SOURCE: IMF, *International Financial Statistics*, various issues.

seven years of the facility's existence.

such drawings. As shown in Table 6.3, these less developed countries were also the heaviest users on a proportional basis of the IMF's then still new SDR facility.

Finally, monetary authorities demonstrated their willingness to continue accepting dollars and other foreign exchange, often well in excess of reserve needs. As depicted in Table 6.4, there was an increasing regimewide tendency to hold dollars and other currency deposits, the proportion of total regime liquidity represented by gold declining by 45 percent. Specifically, the continuing and increasing tendency at the time to hold U.S. dollars as reserves is shown in Table 6.5.

The data underscore the preeminent position the United States still held within the global monetary regime. Moreover, as listed in Table 6.6, some two out of five countries still pegged their currencies to the dollar. Strong evidence for the still preeminent position of the United States within the global monetary regime is the extent to which other countries continued to define their currencies in terms of the U.S. dollar. Table 6.6 contains a listing dated mid-

TABLE 6.6: International Monetary Leadership

COUNTRIES MAINTAINING EXCHANGE RATE LINKED TO:

A. *The U.S. Dollar: 55 countries*
Argentina, Bahamas, Bahrain, Barbados, Bolivia, Botswana, Brazil, Burundi, Chile,
Rep. of China, Colombia, Costa Rica, Dominican Rep., Ecuador, Egypt, El Salvador, Ethiopia,
Ghana, Grenada, Guatemala, Guyana, Haiti, Honduras, Indonesia, Iraq, Israel, Jamaica, Korea,
Laos (PDR), Lesotho, Liberia, Libya, Mexico, Nepal, Nicaragua, Oman, Pakistan, Panama,
Paraguay, Peru, Romania, Rwanda, Somalia, S. Africa, Sudan, Syria, Thailand, Trinidad and
Tobago, United Arab Emirates, Uruguay, Venezuela, Yemen Arab Rep., PDR Yemen, Zaire,
Zambia

B. *The French Franc: 13 countries*
Benin, Cameroon, Central African Rep., Chad, Congo (PDR), Gabon, Ivory Coast,
Madagascar, Mali, Niger, Senegal, Togo, Upper Volta

C. *The Pound Sterling: 4 countries*
Bangladesh, the Gambia, Ireland, Sierra Leone

D. *The EEC Snake: 7 countries*
Belgium, Denmark, FR Germany, Luxembourg, Netherlands, Norway, Sweden

E. *Special Drawing Rights (SDRs): 11 countries*
Burma, Guinea, Iran, Jordan, Kenya, Malawi, Mauritius, Qatar, Saudi Arabia, Tanzania,
Uganda

SOURCE: IMF, *Annual Report*, 1976, 70–73.
NOTE: In addition to the countries shown in the table, 38 IMF members either allowed their currencies to
float independently or defined their currencies in accordance with other arrangements.

1976 of the various ways in which IMF member countries chose to define their currencies.

The data in the table portray the extent to which France was able to retain its close monetary connection to former African colonies. By contrast, the British sphere of monetary influence had declined markedly. In this regard, defections from the sterling area during the 1960s and 1970s were consistent with Britain's decision in 1964, except for Hong Kong, to withdraw within seven years from positions east of Suez. Withdrawal of official sterling balances from London contributed further to currency problems that beset the United Kingdom in this final phase of its retreat from empire.[23]

AFTERWORD

The fixed exchange rates of the Bretton Woods regime (and the challenges it posed to American policy-makers) were gone in favor of a more flexible exchange rate regime. Instead of treasuries and central banks intervening to maintain relatively fixed rates (fluctuating within 1 percent of official parity), rates were now to follow market supply and demand, radical swings checked by monetary authorities coordinating their interventions. As a practical matter, this enhanced the policy freedom for American and other policy-makers previously constrained by the pressures of relatively fixed exchange rates under the Bretton Woods rules. Increased government purchases abroad, particularly for wars and lesser contingencies, now could be financed more readily simply by allowing the value of the currency to move downward a notch or two. So long as the creditworthiness of the country and the acceptance of the dollar were not in jeopardy, the new regime facilitated financing massive American foreign policy and national security outlays abroad.

7 The Dollar, the Euro, and Cooperative Security

The financing plague is wreaking greater and greater havoc throughout the world. As in medieval times, it is scourging country after country. It is transmitted by rats and its consequences are unemployment and poverty, industrial bankruptcy and speculative enrichment. The remedy of the witch doctors is to deprive the patient of food. . . . Those who protest must be purged, and those who survive bear witness to their virtue before the doctors of obsolete and prepotent dogma and of blind hegemoniacal egoism.

> —Mexican president José López Portillo (a critique of "neoliberal" IMF "adjustment" remedies imposed on less developed, low income countries)

Collaboration with other countries in international undertakings . . . is needed not so much as a protection for others . . . as it is for ourselves. . . . Not the self-trumpeting leader in great moral causes but the modest, willing worker together with others in the vineyard of international collaboration: that is the image that America should wish to project to others, but primarily to itself, as the twenty-first century, so replete with uncertainties and dangers, begins to impose itself upon us.[1]

> —George F. Kennan, American Diplomat and Foreign Policy Scholar

Seeking multilateral remedies on most matters—monetary challenges among them—is by no means new to European policy elites. The late-nineteenth- and twentieth-century record presented in the previous pages makes this clear. Indeed, the multilateralism of cooperative security has become well established as a European norm for dealing with complex issues in which understandings of interests often vary substantially among policy-makers within and across the countries in the European Union (EU). Indeed, the norm has been socially constructed over several centuries devastated by war, but also marked by periods of peace in which the players typically engaged multilaterally.

Now embedded in the policy-making culture as the legitimate way to conduct international affairs, multilateral collaboration was core to realizing immediate post–World War II economic-security goals in Europe for reconstruction and economic development. Beyond membership in the United Nations organization (1945) was participation in such regionally focused entities as the

Organization for European Economic Cooperation (OEEC),[2] a multilateral institution formed largely to administer aid from the United States under the Marshall Plan that later became the Paris-based, globally focused Organization for Economic Cooperation and Development (OECD).

In the security domain, institutionalized multilateralism was established in the 1948 Brussels Pact that forged all-European defense links in the Western European Union (WEU), its functions transferred to the European Union in an incremental process in the first decade of the twenty-first century. In 1949 two institutions were established: the forty-seven-member Council of Europe that promotes democracy and civil society, and the twenty-eight-member North Atlantic Treaty Organization (NATO), which routinizes European multilateralism in security matters with the United States and Canada.

Prior to the 1993 decision to adopt the title EU, three European Communities (EC) were instrumental in the integration process—formation in 1953 of the European Coal and Steel Community (ECSC) and, in 1958, the European Economic Community (EEC) and European Atomic Energy Community (EURATOM). Finally, the all-inclusive fifty-seven-member Organization of Security and Cooperation in Europe (OSCE) that includes the United States and Canada emerged in 1995 from the earlier Conference on Security and Cooperation in Europe (CSCE). Indeed, the institutionalized multilateralism found in international organizations and alliances is very much a part of the European fabric.

Multilateralism, however difficult it may be to reach decisions, remains the prevailing European norm. In the section below, we explore the roots of postwar European multilateralism on the monetary front. It is a backdrop for the emergence of the euro at the beginning of the twenty-first century that depends fundamentally on sustaining this propensity to multilateralism. It is the stuff of cooperative security in Europe essential not only to economic but also to political and security purposes pursued in both global and regional institutions—the UN, NATO, WEU (now part of the EU), OSCE, and, for that matter, the EU as a whole.

RESTORING CONVERTIBILITY OF EUROPEAN CURRENCIES

The aim of the European Payments Union (EPU), formed at American urging in 1950, was to handle routine international monetary transactions multilaterally among its members. Well beyond commercial interests, support for European economic recovery was clearly part of the U.S. security calculus in its

Cold War competition with the Soviet Union. An economically strong Western Europe meant stronger allies to help carry the defense burden against the USSR and countries in its East European sphere of influence.

The Bank for International Settlements (BIS) in Basel acted as agent for the EPU. Rather than settle accounts bilaterally, in these arrangements each European country had either a net claim or net debt vis-à-vis the EPU as a whole. Although European currencies remained nonconvertible into gold or dollars, the EPU arrangement permitted members to conduct payments transactions with relative ease. Significantly, there was a reduction in balance of payments pressures that might have led EPU members to erect even higher tariffs or impose new exchange controls or other barriers to trade.

The European monetary area organized around the EPU was supportive of the liberal economic objectives the United States and its European partners were advocating for the design of global monetary and trade regimes. To the United States, the EPU was merely a temporary substitute for currency convertibility that would obtain when the Bretton Woods rules became fully effective for principal EPU members in 1958. The successful economic recovery in Europe as well as U.S. overseas spending had increased the supply of monetary reserves held by EPU members, finally enabling them, as Bretton Woods rules required, to make their currencies convertible. With some prodding by the United States, the European states signed the European Monetary Agreement (EMA) in 1955 and thus created a new fund to replace the EPU in 1958.

Drawings from the EMA's funds lacked the automaticity of credit approval of the EPU. Moreover, the EMA was never intended to serve as a clearinghouse. Administered by the OECD, successor to the OEEC, its operations were very limited. Nevertheless, both the EPU and the EMA served functions consistent with the overall Anglo-American design for the Bretton Woods regime and the security arrangements in NATO that depended on it for ready access to capital.

At the same time that the transition from the EPU to EMA was taking place, the United States supported Continental European negotiations then underway to move beyond merely the 1953 ECSC to formation of a European Economic Community. The United States did insist as price for this support that European markets remain open to American trade and investment. In a broader sense, however, American support was also a central part of the same security-based, Cold War effort to strengthen its allies economically.

The Treaty of Rome that established the EEC and the European Atomic Energy Community (EURATOM) in 1958 gave the EEC relatively weak monetary powers, although Article 6 does state that EEC members are to "coordinate monetary policies in close cooperation with Community organs." With respect to exchange rate policy, Article 107 asserts that each member country should act "in the common interest," but gives the power to the Commission, based on Monetary Committee recommendations, to authorize countermeasures in response to any damaging exchange rate changes undertaken by other parties.[3]

The two institutions designated to conduct international monetary policy within the EEC, then, were the Monetary Committee and the Committee of Governors of the Central Banks.[4] Each EEC member state sent two representatives to the Monetary Committee—typically one central banker and one finance ministry official. The Monetary Committee performed only an advisory role, whereas the Committee of Governors of the Central Banks was in a position to begin the spadework for later coordination of national monetary policies and taking joint actions. In laying these cooperative foundations, the governors met regularly with a member of the EEC Commission in attendance for the purpose of reviewing monetary issues of concern to the central bankers.

The primary emphasis within the EEC in its earlier years, then, was more on reducing barriers to trade among member countries than it was on constructing an international monetary area with substantial policy-making authority. The European monetary area that did exist in these years was, in any case, consistent with the American global design, just as the EPU had been in the 1950s. There was no apparent need at the time to pursue monetary integration, since policy elites in EEC countries could rely on the stability of the dollar's gold parity ($35 per ounce of gold) as the cornerstone of the Bretton Woods regime. Regional organization in monetary matters thus was quite minimal—primarily consultative rather than involving any designation of binding authority to EEC institutions. In the first half of the 1960s there were adjustments in exchange rates, but no great monetary crises necessitating community action.

For the most part, currency values were relatively stable—thus minimizing the adverse effect on prices of goods and services produced by exchange rate fluctuations. Indeed, the Bretton Woods regime seemed to be working fairly smoothly, particularly among the six EEC members.[5] This allowed them to work toward the goal of becoming a customs union. Each EEC member acted with considerable autonomy in the formulation and execution of its monetary policy. Consultation with EEC organs was kept to a minimum.

TABLE 7.1: The U.S., Bretton Woods, and the Cold War: U.S. Balance of Trade on Current Account and Direct Defense Expenditures Abroad, 1960–71

(All data in U.S.$ millions; minus signs indicate increases in overall balance of payments deficit)

	Balance of trade: exports–imports	Overseas defense expenditures
1960	2824	–3087
1961	3822	–2998
1962	3387	–3105
1963	4414	–2961
1964	6823	–2880
1965	5431	–2952
1966	3031	–3764
1967	2583	–4378
1968	611	–4535
1969	399	–4856
1970	2331	–4855
1971	–1433	–4819

SOURCE: U.S. Department of Commerce, Bureau of Economic Analysis.

In the latter half of the decade, however, monetary difficulties emerged that gave impetus to a strengthening of monetary collaboration within the EEC. Dependence by member countries on the U.S. dollar as the principal medium of international exchange and major reserve currency was debated seriously for the first time. The U.S. balance of trade was still in surplus, but, as shown in Table 7.1, it declined in the last half of the 1960s at the same time that the military contribution to the overall U.S. balance-of-payments deficit was increasing substantially.

Although U.S. deficits contributed to international liquidity, the dollar was already well in surplus in currency markets. European officials saw further, massive additions of dollars as not only fueling inflation in Germany and elsewhere but also putting more pressure on them for monetary support—the United States already finding it difficult to sustain gold convertibility at its fixed exchange rate of $35 per ounce.

The first, albeit mild, EEC challenge to American leadership of the global regime occurred within the context of negotiations leading to establishment of SDRs. As noted earlier in Chapter Six, EEC members insisted on a change in the IMF voting rules that gave them a veto, much as the United States had had since the IMF began operations in 1946. Significantly, the new veto power for the EEC broke the power monopoly in the IMF previously held by the United States.

The late 1960s were also a period of renewed interest in European monetary integration. Not merely an attempt to advance the EEC as a competitor to the United States, monetary integration was seen as a means to resolve problems within the EEC itself. The currency crises of 1969 that culminated in an 11.1 percent devaluation of the franc in August and a 9.3 percent upward revaluation of the mark in September and October upset the Common Agricultural Policy (CAP)—an agricultural pricing scheme that had been the result of very difficult negotiations among France, Germany, and other EEC members. Changing exchange rates had direct effect on import and export markets, altering the carefully negotiated price points.

In February and March of 1971, the EEC Council of Ministers, following consideration of various proposals,[6] finally adopted a ten-year plan for achieving European economic and monetary union by 1980. Monetary unification was to include "the total and irreversible convertibility of currencies, the elimination of margins of fluctuation in rates of exchange, the irrevocable fixing of parity ratios and the total liberation of movements of capital."[7]

During the first of three stages (1971–73), there was to be extensive monetary policy coordination,[8] with a further narrowing of currency exchange margins from the 1 percent fluctuation either side of parity permitted under the Bretton Woods rules. A monetary cooperation fund was also to be created in the first or second stage as part of the eventual consolidation of European central banking in the final stage.

Exchange rate margins of fluctuation were reduced in June 1971 from 0.75 percent to 0.60 percent—all exchange rates still tied to the dollar, still fixed in gold at $35 per ounce. Credits amounting to $2 billion for two to five years also were set up.[9] These actions taken within the EEC to further the development of the emerging European monetary area were certainly consistent with Bretton Woods rules. Indeed, the aims to be served were identical: unrestricted currency exchange at stable rates, thus promoting trade and investment across national boundaries.

SNAKES IN TUNNELS

The formation of a European monetary area with this degree of unification and potential strength was interpreted by some as a direct challenge to the preeminent American position within the global monetary regime. The collapse of the Bretton Woods regime in August 1971 and the initiation of floating exchange rates was indeed a setback for European plans to effect greater stability of exchange rates within the EEC. Constructing an EEC "snake"—a joint float against the dollar—was a decidedly European remedy and an early multilateral challenge to U.S. dollar supremacy.

The Smithsonian agreements in December 1971—a failed attempt to restore the Bretton Woods regime—set new, wider limits for fluctuations. Each currency within the new regime was allowed to float within 2.25 percent above or below its parity with the dollar. The old Bretton Woods regime had allowed only a 1 percent margin above or below parity, thus creating a maximum 2 percent band around the dollar.

By contrast, the new 2.25 percent margin resulted in a maximum 4.5 percent total range—later referred to as a "tunnel" that contained fluctuations above and below the dollar. Such a wide band was particularly problematic to EEC members committed to narrowing the extent of exchange rate fluctuations. To make matters worse, a 4.5 percent band vis-à-vis the dollar meant that the difference in fluctuation between any two EEC currencies could be as much as 9 percent![10]

Dollars continued to flood currency markets in the late 1960s and beginning of the 1970s. As shown in Table 7.2, the U.S. trade balance did go into the black briefly after the August 1971 American decision to end the dollar's $35 per ounce gold convertibility, which allowed the dollar to float downward. Nevertheless, defense spending abroad continued to increase.

The turbulence that currency fluctuations of this magnitude created for import and export prices threatened to upset trade and investment patterns and arrangements that had been constructed since the EEC was formed in 1958, some thirteen years prior. Prices for manufactures, resources, and services traded across borders quickly became highly variable—price, counter to economic

TABLE 7.2: The Post-Bretton Woods Transition:
U.S. Balance of Trade on Current Account and
Direct Defense Expenditures Abroad (1972–74)

(All data in US$ Millions; minus signs indicate increases in overall balance-of-payments deficit)

	Balance of trade: Exports–Imports	Overseas defense expenditures
1972	–5795	–4784
1973	7140	–4629
1974	1962	–5032

SOURCE: U.S. Department of Commerce, Bureau of Economic Analysis.

theory, more a function of exchange rate variations than the quality or fair market value of a particular good or service traded.

Going beyond tariff-free trade in its path toward greater economic integration, in 1967 the EEC became a customs union—with agreement by all members to impose the same tariff on imports from non-EEC members. Given domestic pressures from the agricultural sector in each member country, particularly France, painstaking diplomatic efforts were expended to bring agricultural products within the larger agreements. Sensitive, of course, to the effect of exchange rate changes on prices, these agricultural commodity price agreements, already upset by currency adjustments within the EEC, now were in complete disarray.

Given these drastically altered circumstances, community members quickly decided in April 1972 to reduce exchange rate fluctuations within the EEC to no more than any currency individually would be allowed to vary with respect to the dollar. As a first step toward reducing these fluctuations, any EEC currency adhering to the agreement was not allowed to deviate more than 2.25 percent above or below its central rate,[11] with respect to other participating currencies within the community.

The resulting narrower limits in differential fluctuations against the dollar for EEC currencies soon became known metaphorically as a "snake" within the larger 4.5 percent "tunnel." Under the arrangement, participating central banks intervened in currency markets to manage what had become a joint float against the dollar. With the passing of the Smithsonian rules in March 1973, the EEC snake was allowed to float freely—that is, without any such "tunnel" constraint. At the same time, of course, exchange rates of EEC members were stable in relation to each other, thus avoiding adverse impact on prices. The degree of collaboration achieved for economic security purposes foreshadowed the kind of efforts EU members undertook some two decades later in their construction of the euro.

Monetary difficulties at the time, however, soon forced Britain, France, Ireland, Italy, and Sweden to defect from the snake. Nevertheless, there was a strong commitment, particularly on the part of German monetary authorities, to maintain the currency area even if key members had to absent themselves from its discipline from time to time. After all, the snake already had brought greater price stability among EEC members than if each had floated its national currency independently against the dollar.

European integration advocates also feared that complete failure of the currency snake not only could destroy any lingering hopes of achieving greater European monetary and economic integration but also would amount to failure in Europe's economic competition with the United States. To the extent that European leaders wished to avoid or, at least, reduce monetary dominance by the United States, they saw their best hope for success in maintaining a currency area that at least would allow Europe to hold its own—if not a challenge to, then at least a check on, American foreign policy and national security choices.

At the same time, of course, EC members remained dependent on the United States in NATO and other security arrangements. Understood from this perspective, coordinating their exchange rates within the snake was also a means to sustain the dollar-based regime upon which international liquidity depended. For its part, the U.S. could continue to make defense outlays abroad, deficits absorbed in the managed flexibility of the post–Bretton Woods monetary regime.

COOPERATIVE SECURITY IN MONETARY CRISES

Notwithstanding significant differences with the United States from time to time over monetary policy, EEC members decidedly supported efforts to maintain the flexible exchange rate regime during the Cold War and afterward. Among other things, this meant joining with the United States, Japan, and other capital-rich members of the IMF and World Bank to extend credits and restructure or, in some cases, forgive loans owed by less developed, low income countries hit by extraordinarily high, short-term interest rates in global financial markets during the late 1970s and early 1980s—themselves the result of tighter monetary policies driven up by the U.S. Federal Reserve to curb double-digit inflation in the U.S. domestic economy.

Recession in the United States and other countries in the North reduced imports from Third World countries in the South that, combined with high interest rates and falling commodity prices, brought matters to a head in Mexico in 1982. Lest Mexico be forced to default on its loans, perhaps starting a chain reaction to be emulated by other low income countries in similar financial straits, the U.S. Federal Reserve (then under Board Chairman Paul Volcker's leadership) took action within the Bank for International Settlements, initially setting up a $700 million swap with the Bank of Mexico and following up with a $1.85 billion credit arranged multilaterally—50 percent U.S. and the rest from the Fed's central banking counterparts in Japan and Europe.

Whether to Mexico or other less developed countries in need, IMF loans were not without strings attached. A quid pro quo for any loan or credit, the

IMF typically imposed a regimen requiring tighter fiscal and monetary policies—usually some combination of government spending cuts and increased
taxes on the fiscal side and, on the monetary side, higher interest rates and
reductions in the supply of money in circulation.

The highly controversial "neoliberal" economic rationale for such austerity
measures was a need for structural adjustment in economies gone awry—those
suffering from inflation, spending beyond their means, and other maladies.
The domestic political impact of cutting spending, increasing taxes, raising interest rates, and the like was clearly adverse to those in power. The resulting
animosity directed toward the IMF and those understood to be holding these
strings—monetary officials, managers of capital in the United States and other
First World countries—is not surprising.

One of the more articulate examples in this critical genre was the statement
made on September 1, 1982, by outgoing Mexican president José López Portillo—a broad-brush indictment of capital interests:

> The financing plague is wreaking greater and greater havoc throughout the world. As
> in medieval times, it is scourging country after country. It is transmitted by rats and
> its consequences are unemployment and poverty, industrial bankruptcy and specu-
> lative enrichment. The remedy of the witch doctors is to deprive the patient of food
> and subject him to compulsory rest. Those who protest must be purged, and those
> who survive bear witness to their virtue before the doctors of obsolete and prepotent
> dogma and of blind hegemoniacal egoism.[12]

López Portillo had threatened to rebuff the IMF and other foreign lenders, na-
tionalize the banks, and impose exchange controls, but finally relented in favor
of a more moderate position vis-à-vis the IMF favored by his successor in the
Mexican presidency, Miguel De La Madrid.[13]

Although this stemmed the short-term crisis in Mexico, efforts then turned
to building international consensus for an increase in IMF quotas, thus enhanc-
ing the fund's lending facilities in particular for use by low income countries
facing the same debt-servicing problems.[14] As a practical matter, more short-
term lending was not sufficient. It would take a global decline in interest rates
as well as depreciation of the dollar (and thus Third World currencies tied to it)
for the debt crisis finally to subside.

Indeed, an appreciating dollar in the 1980s made American exports less and
less competitive. Table 7.3 depicts the dramatic increases in both trade deficit
and military expenditures abroad. Responding in September 1985 to domestic
pressures to do something about exchange rate induced loss of American trade

TABLE 7.3: The Managed-Flexibility Regime during the
Cold War Years: U.S. Balance of Trade on Current Account
and Direct Defense Expenditures Abroad, 1975–89
(All data in U.S.$ millions; minus signs indicate increases in overall balance
of payments deficit)

	Balance of trade: exports–imports	Overseas defense expenditures
1975	18116	−4795
1976	4295	−4895
1977	−14335	−5823
1978	−15143	−7352
1979	−285	−8294
1980	2317	−10851
1981	5030	−11564
1982	−5536	−12460
1983	−38691	−13087
1984	−94344	−12516
1985	−118155	−13108
1986	−147177	−13730
1987	−160655	−14950
1988	−121153	−15604
1989	−99486	−15313

SOURCE: U.S. Department of Commerce, Bureau of Economic Analysis.

competitiveness, U.S. treasury secretary James Baker organized a meeting in
New York at the Plaza Hotel. He sought concerted action by finance ministers and central bankers from the G-5 countries (the United States, Japan, Germany, France, and the United Kingdom) to coordinate buying and selling in
global currency markets. The aim of these operations was to increase the value
of other major currencies and thus depreciate the dollar, moving it gradually
downward from its high plateau.

The Plaza agreement was followed a year and a half later in Paris by the Louvre accords of February 1987, the G-5 (United States, Japan, Germany, France,
United Kingdom) and Canada agreeing subsequently to keep the dollar within
an agreed target range. Buying and selling operations resumed vis-à-vis the
dollar—still the world's principal key currency and reserve asset. Cooperative
security in monetary matters had become the order of the day. Managed flexibility had thus become routinized in a common interest shared by major players to provide greater stability to the international monetary regime in which,
as always, all had both commercial and security stakes.

The decade of the 1990s had its own set of monetary challenges—the Mexican peso in 1995 and the Asian financial crisis in 1997 noteworthy examples. In

TABLE 7.4: The Pre-Euro, Post–Cold War Managed-
Flexibility Regime: U.S. Balance of Trade on Current
Account and Direct Defense Expenditures Abroad

(All data in U.S.$ millions; minus signs indicate increases in overall balance
of payments deficit)

	Balance of trade: exports–imports	Overseas defense expenditures
1990	–78968	–17531
1991	2897	–16409
1992	–51613	–13835
1993	–84805	–12087
1994	–121612	–10217
1995	–113567	–10043
1996	–124764	–11061
1997	–140726	–11707
1998	–215062	–12185

SOURCE: U.S. Department of Commerce, Bureau of Economic Analysis.

both of these and other cases, multilateral loans—needed capital transfers to
maintain liquidity—were the initial monetary remedy. The IMF, BIS, and G-7
members (the United States, Japan, Germany, France, United Kingdom, Italy,
and Canada) were major players in building consensus essential not only to
managing the crisis before them but also to maintaining the managed-flexibility monetary regime as a whole. Less publicized day-to-day interventions of one
sort or another were commonplace. Indeed, the climate was ripe for creating
a World Trade Organization in Geneva, which opened its doors in 1995, thus
finally completing the institutional part of the post–World War II design. As
shown in Table 7.4, the U.S. balance of payments remained ever more deeply in
the red with imports (to include the cost of increased petroleum consumption)
rising faster than exports, albeit defense expenditures abroad declined by more
than 40 percent from the high point at the end of the Cold War. Units rede-
ployed to the United States with reductions of more than 60 percent in personnel assigned to European locations substantially lessened monetary pressure on
the dollar from defense expenditures abroad.

THE SOVIET AND EAST EUROPEAN CURRENCY AREA

During the Cold War years, Europe's other side—the currency grouping
composed of the U.S.S.R. and other Eastern European countries—remained
formally outside of the global monetary regime. Although they obviously had
to conduct market transactions to finance their commercial and other gov-

ernmental outlays abroad, they were reluctant to accept the preeminent position the United States held within the global regime. Organized by the Soviet Union, the Council of Mutual Economic Assistance (abbreviated at the time as COMECON, CEMA, or CMEA) thus was not directly supportive of the global monetary regime, but there is no evidence that the Soviet-dominated currency zone was disruptive of it either. It was live and let live.

Recognizing that participation in the Bretton Woods regime as a practical matter meant taking a subordinate position to the United States and, to a lesser extent, the United Kingdom, the Soviet Union also chose not to join either the International Monetary Fund or World Bank. Nevertheless, the need for access to hard currencies to finance trade and other transactions with the West led the U.S.S.R. and other East European countries to cooperate, albeit tacitly, with other players in the dollar-based global monetary regime. In the Cold War—as in the two world wars that had preceded it—adversaries found ways to cooperate when the authorities saw doing so as advantageous.

Soviet dollar deposits placed in London banks to avoid possible confiscation by the United States may have given initial stimulus to growth of the Eurodollar market. To conduct its business in Western countries, Moscow worked through the Narodny Bank, an official Soviet institution situated in London, and its Parisian counterpart, the Banque Commerciale pour l'Europe du Nord.[16] The rapid growth of East-West trade in later years also led to a significant increase in letters of credit and other financial transactions handled by private banks in Switzerland and Liechtenstein.[17]

Bilateral clearing was the primary method used for payments among currency area members.[18] The Soviet State Bank (Gosbank) began handling some multilateral clearings in 1957, but the volume of such transactions was then relatively small.[19] An attempt to increase multilateralism was made in late 1963 with the creation of the International Bank for Economic Cooperation (IBEC). The purpose of the Soviet-dominated bank was to extend credit to COMECON members suffering balance-of-payments deficits with other members.[20] The bank was not very successful, however, and much of COMECON finance remained on a bilateral basis.[21]

The Soviet Union and East European countries thus participated in gold and foreign exchange transactions without disrupting the global monetary regime. For its part, and contrary to Soviet wishes, Romania joined the IMF, thus attempting to solidify its links with the West. Another significant tie between East Europe and the West was membership in the Bank for International

Settlements in Basel. Indeed, "all the East European countries (except Albania) [were] members."[22] Nevertheless, the Soviet ruble remained nonconvertible and, as a result, COMECON remained formally outside of the global monetary regime. Again, given their need for access to Western capital for their own trade and security-oriented purposes, COMECON members did not pose significant challenge to the global monetary regime throughout the Cold War. Security challenges to the West took nonmonetary forms. The East depended upon access to global currency markets and thus was not inclined to disturb (much less disrupt) them.

FROM WEST EUROPEAN MONETARY SYSTEM TO THE EURO

Worried in the mid-1980s about European competitiveness in forthcoming decades vis-à-vis the United States and Japan, the European Commission in Brussels worked to develop consensus among the members to move beyond both the free trade and common external tariff of the customs union.[23] Achieving greater monetary integration with closer coordination of currencies in the European Monetary System, the aim was to establish by January 1992 a common market within the EEC, thus enabling the free flow of natural resources—(land), labor, and capital—across national borders, much as occurs across state borders within the United States.

The "Europe 1992" common-market goal set in 1987 was reached methodically through acceptance by EEC members over some five years of more than 150 new regulations—detailed blueprints for liberalizing the movement of the three factors of production. Meeting at a summit in Maastricht in the Netherlands in December 1991, the heads of government ratified a consensus to push economic integration to the next stage by the end of the decade—a full economic and monetary union (EMU) with a common currency later dubbed the "euro" and a common central bank, its location later determined to be Frankfurt—the central European capital and home of the German Bundesbank.

There was also a name change. The EU absorbed the EC, which had been the official designation of the EEC, EURATOM, and ECSC. Coordinating fiscal and monetary policies—setting and meeting particular macroeconomic criteria essential to economic and monetary union (EMU)—became the difficult agenda throughout the 1990s. Efforts were also undertaken to develop a Common Foreign and Security Policy (CFSP) for the European Union, but this goal proved, not surprisingly, to be more elusive—even more difficult to achieve than the economic and monetary objectives. The EU did reaffirm preferential trade, monetary, and security commitments to former colonies—the ACP (Africa, Caribbean, and Pacific) countries.

In this regard, developing a single EU currency also would facilitate external payments for security and other foreign policy commitments by members acting individually for their own purposes or collectively as in UN, NATO, OSCE, WEU, or EU-backed contingencies. Much as worldwide acceptance of the dollar facilitates the conduct of U.S. foreign and national security policy, EU members sought the same advantage from using a common European currency, the euro, readily accepted in payment for government purchases and other outlays abroad.

To reach the deep level of integration in the EMU did require compromising a well-established EC principle—moving all members to each new integration level in tandem. Instead, provision was made to allow members to opt *out* or, particularly for new EU members in Eastern Europe, an ability to opt *in* incrementally as they met fiscal and monetary requirements in stages. Widening the membership of the EU to include these countries with less productive economies had made deeper integration more difficult to achieve. Critics referred to it as integration à la carte, but it was still integration—and at a very deep level!

Little progress was made on a common foreign and security policy for the EU, but institutional arrangements were put in place by folding into the EU the long-standing, all-European alternative to NATO—the WEU, originally established in 1948 by the Brussels Pact. Most important for both commercial and security interests, however, was creation of the European Central Bank (ECB) with the euro as its currency to manage.[24] The dollar now faced a currency with the potential to be its competitive rival, its cooperative partner, or perhaps more optimistically, a hybrid between the two—a competitive partner in a global marketplace linked by shared security and commercial interests.

THE EMERGENCE OF THE EURO—
MANAGING FOREIGN POLICY AND SECURITY INTERESTS

Data on U.S. trade deficits and defense outlays abroad after the creation of the euro are contained in Table 7.5. Both the trade deficit and overseas defense expenditures more than doubled, the latter fueled by Gulf and Central Asian deployments following the 9/11 al-Qaeda attack upon the World Trade Center and Pentagon in 2001. The broad international consensus supporting the U.S. global security role still remains robust, though perhaps not as durable as in the

TABLE 7.5: U.S. Deficits in a Dollar-Euro, Managed-
Flexibility Regime: U.S. Balance of Trade on Current
Account and Direct Defense Expenditures Abroad, 1999–
2008

(All data in U.S.$ millions; minus signs indicate increases in overall balance
of payments deficit)

	Balance of trade: exports – imports	Overseas defense expenditures
1999	−301630	−13335
2000	−417426	−13473
2001	−398270	−14835
2002	−459151	−19101
2003	−521519	−25296
2004	−631130	−28299
2005	−748683	−30075
2006	−803547	−31032
2007	−726573	−32820
2008	−706068	−36452

SOURCE: U.S. Department of Commerce, Bureau of Economic Analysis.

Cold War, when the real-and-present national security stakes to American allies
in Europe and northeast Asia were difficult even for critics to overlook.

Initiated multilaterally within the NATO alliance under Article 5 of the
North Atlantic Charter, the war in Afghanistan began in 2002. It was a col-
lective response to an attack on one of its members—in this case the United
States attacked by al-Qaeda operating from its base in Afghanistan. By contrast,
the military intervention in Iraq in 2003 divided the NATO allies, the United
Kingdom also splitting from other EU members to join forces with the United
States. So much for a common European foreign and security policy within
the EU!

Nevertheless, shared commercial and security interests proved to be deeply
rooted enough to allow the parties to weather the divisive storm over invading
Iraq and the occupation that followed. As before, finance ministers and central
bankers have continued to work with their American counterparts to maintain
the managed-flexibility regime. Notwithstanding their policy differences with
the U.S./UK–led intervention in Iraq, they facilitated its finance by sustaining
monetary transactions.

The cost of military interventions was on top of massive U.S. trade deficits
that continued through the decade. Whatever their positions on the course of
U.S. policy, European and other countries (to include China and Japan) effectively supported U.S. efforts by accepting, as always, the dollars used abroad

by both the private sector in daily commerce and the U.S. government and its allies engaged in both the Afghanistan and Iraq wars. The same was true, of course, for the UK and its outlays in sterling, and outlays in euros by NATO allies. Indeed, monetary authorities in these countries saw it in their own commercial and security interests to do so.

One modality of cooperation was to allow the dollar to float further downward in the wake of increasing trade deficits and massive defense spending abroad. The dollar-euro exchange rate, captured in beginning-of-the-year annual "snapshots" in Table 7.6, shows the transition from a strong, perhaps overvalued, dollar before 9/11 losing value to the euro over the course of the decade in the lead-up to the global recession that began in 2008. In practical terms, an appreciating euro meant the dollar price of each euro purchased in currency markets was substantially higher. Although there were variations during the decade, data in Table 7.6 show the euro appreciating by some 40 percent! Put the opposite way, since one euro bought one dollar in 2000, by 2010 it took only about €0.70 to buy the same dollar! Europe's own financial problems—maintaining commitment to the eurozone—was reflected in a drop in the euro's position vis-à-vis the dollar after 2010.

Another ramification of the dollar's relative decline vis-à-vis the euro during the first decade of the new century was an increasing propensity to substitute euros for dollars as reserves—or at least strike a better balance between the two in national-reserve portfolios. In Table 7.7 we can see the declining ratio of dollars to euros held as monetary reserves—from almost four times as many dollars to euros in 1999, declining to just over twice as many a decade later! Reflective of their cooperative stance with the United States on monetary

TABLE 7.6: Dollar-Euro Exchange Rate, 1999–2013

(at beginning of January each year)

	$/€		$/€
1999	1.1789	2007	1.3270
2000	1.0090	2008	1.4688
2001	0.9423	2009	1.3866
2002	0.9038	2010	1.4389
2003	1.0446	2011	1.3182
2004	1.2592	2012	1.2893
2005	1.3507	2013	1.3155
2006	1.1826	2014	1.3740

SOURCE: European Central Bank. Compare http://www.oanda.com/currency/historical-rates.

TABLE 7.7: Ratio of Dollars to Euro as Official Reserves, 1999–2013

Year	Worldwide	Advanced economies	Developing economies
1999	3.97	4.03	3.82
2000	3.89	3.96	3.72
2001	3.73	3.88	3.41
2002	2.82	2.99	2.47
2003	2.62	3.02	1.99
2004	2.66	3.04	2.06
2005	2.78	3.37	2.09
2006	2.61	3.18	2.03
2007	2.44	2.82	2.22
2008	2.42	2.99	1.97
2009	2.29	2.76	1.88
2010	2.26	2.57	1.97
2011	2.30	2.56	2.07
2012	2.48	2.84	2.14
2013	2.63	2.58	2.57

SOURCE: International Monetary Fund, Currency Composition of Foreign Exchange (COFER) Data: http://www.imf.org/external/np/sta/cofer/eng/cofer.pdf.

NOTE: Even before the euro went into general circulation in January 2002, it was already in use as a unit of account by central banks. More than €800 billion—approaching a trillion euros—are now in circulation.

(as on security) matters, high-income countries kept dollars in their reserves to a greater extent than was true in the low-income countries where euros assumed a larger place in their reserve portfolios than before. Nevertheless, the data also make clear that the euro has not displaced the dollar, but instead has taken a seat, admittedly a rather large seat, alongside it and other reserve assets.

Sustaining the consensus to support the managed-flexibility regime and the dollar's role in it remains an ongoing, multilateral process. By contrast, a more unilateralist approach by the United States in its conduct of foreign and national security policy—as occurred in the first decade of the twenty-first century—tends to undermine the kind of support needed to sustain the dollar's position globally. Multilateral efforts not just to inform but also to consult and develop consensus for concerted action are a requirement for both monetary arrangements and, more broadly, in the foreign policy and national security domains to which they are linked.

The threat posed to global economic security by the collapse of banks and falling stock exchanges beginning in 2008 was met by a multilateral response of pumping liquidity into banking systems worldwide. As the pages in this book make clear, central bankers are no strangers to collaborative multilateralism or to cooperative security on monetary and economic matters that also have significant implications for foreign policy and national security.

Central bankers and their finance ministers were quick to respond to the crisis—much as they had in 1988 when the bottom also seemed to drop out of stock markets and many financial institutions. Widely accepted norms provide a basis for such concerted action, coupled as they are with understandings of national and capital interests. Not only national economies, but also the global markets in which they operate depend upon national and international liquidity. Given these circumstances, it is not surprising that treasury and central banking authorities rescued banks and other financial institutions first. However culpable these sectors were in producing the crisis, providing capital to the banks was the remedy dictated by understandings of economic theory that also served both national and capital interests.

Securing the economic base also buttressed the dollar and sustained U.S. capabilities to operate globally in its conduct of foreign policy and pursuit of national and international security objectives. Beyond the persistence of patterns of acceptance for performance of these roles by the United States, NATO and EU members, and other coalition partners are new-found challenges to international security, whether stemming from national and ethnic strife in the 1990s or terrorist and insurgent threats in the early years of the 21st century. If we take the long view well beyond these important near-term concerns, however, it is not hard to conclude that there is good reason for U.S. administrations to continue to engage multilaterally on these economic and monetary, diplomatic, and security matters—always a patient, but decisive search for common ground and agreed courses of action.

AFTERWORD

The US (its dollar) and the EU (its euro), however competitive, can at the same time cooperate constructively. The same is true for other major players like Japan, China and other rising powers with which the U.S. will deal in coming decades. In the nearer term, the United States does remain in a position to continue to cultivate and further institutionalize the collaborative norms in monetary and other matters it has advanced since the end of World War II. Doing so is a conservative, future-protecting policy—a hedge against the day when the country no longer enjoys the same relative position it has enjoyed—when it no longer may be able to play the same preeminent, often decisive monetary regime-maintenance role it has played since assuming global monetary leadership at Bretton Woods in 1944.

Multilateralism and cooperative security as norms can, over time, become embedded as structures that pattern behavior of major (and lesser) actors globally. Achieving this end requires both vision and persistence in the social construction of normative and institutional frameworks that serve national and international security. The U.S. capability to defend itself and continue to pursue opportunities abroad depends on the work done well beforehand to institutionalize even further multilateral norms favoring pragmatic, peaceful approaches to the oftentimes vexing monetary and security challenges that face policy-makers.

Conclusion:
Money and Cooperative Security

The year is 2035. Under UN Security Council auspices, the United States has helped organize a multilateral coalition to restore peace and secure human rights in central Africa. The U.S. dollar is still a key currency, unit of account, and store of value, but is now among several major currencies readily exchanged one for another to finance private-sector trade and investment as well as government foreign policy and national security outlays for contingencies like these. The links between security and economy, particularly the international monetary component, are clear to everyone.

Major players are the dollar, the euro, and sterling (kept stable in value by coordinated market interventions by the European Central Bank), the Chinese yuan, Japanese yen, and three new regional currencies: the Indian rupee, the Brazilian-Argentine-Chilean andino, and pan-Arab pound. From among these is a new global currency confined for the time to use only by central banks, its value defined as a basket of these national or regional currencies—some rising in value offset by others that decline in market transactions. In addition to traditional meetings in Basel and elsewhere, central bank interventions to manage exchange rates are routinely coordinated in virtual meetings conducted in cyber space.

Finance ministers and their staffs conduct similar meetings, sometimes joining with their central bank counterparts. Indeed, the new currency dubbed the "global" has been so stable in value that it has begun to replace national currencies as principal reserve assets. Plans are to move in stages to bringing the "global" into common use, perhaps over time replacing separate national currencies. Support has grown for establishing a worldwide central bank or, at least, an expanded IMF with a new central banking function. Diverse ideas are under discussion, *perhaps leading to a new "Bretton Woods"-style meeting. The Persian director of the IMF indicates that Iran—a key player in both monetary and security collaborations—has offered Tehran as venue for the conference.*

How realistic is this scenario? Is it any more likely than the more dismal scenario in the preface to this volume? Put another way, will cooperative security become the global norm, whether dealing multilaterally to manage currency matters or in efforts to resolve conflicts endangering international peace and security? Given the more pessimistic tone of the preface scenario, is this one unduly optimistic? Perhaps the future reality lies somewhere between these pessimistic and optimistic scenarios sketched out here in the preface and conclusion to this volume.

Some may think the concluding scenario to be a fanciful, futurist dream— idealism unleashed. But this critique ignores the actual experience detailed in these chapters in which central and private bankers, finance ministers, and their staffs—the principal agents for action among capital managers on the monetary component of hard power—did not sit by passively, simply leaving monetary matters to the market. No, even in the nineteenth and early twentieth centuries they intervened when they saw the need to do so, putting together bailout packages and collaborating to implement other constructive measures.

This reference to owners or managers of capital (OMC) is shorthand that identifies a category of players, many of them constituting policy elites not just in monetary and economic matters but also across a wide range of other issues. Americans and others with liberal or pluralist sentiments have tended to avoid making references of this kind, since doing so evokes images of a rigidly defined capital-owning class reified as if these units had a life of their own apart from the individuals constituting them. No, our focus instead is on people who are among the policy elites.

Notwithstanding the author's own democratic preferences, elites matter more on monetary matters than other individuals and groups within the mass public who do not enjoy the same access to those holding political or economic reigns of power and authority. Moreover, the monetary matters that dominate these pages are the stuff of experts—for central bankers and those closely linked to them—an epistemic community that discusses technical issues in a specialized central banking and financial language that typically limits participation even by less informed capital elites, not to mention mass publics. The latter matter in terms of the influence they have in markets and other public fora, but those who matter more in day-to-day management of economy and security are those capital managers who hold financial positions of authority in the private or public sector.

As we look toward the future, some things do seem clearer than others. In the short run, we need to focus on the near-term and continued viability of the dollar as key currency and reserve asset. The United States no doubt will remain a great power with enormous economic and military capabilities, but it likely will not always have the extraordinary relative advantage in relation to other countries it has had in the decades following World War II (and even in the quarter-century since the end of the Cold War).

Those of us with concerns about an uncertain future can find security resting not just on raw economic and military capabilities that constitute hard power but also in the ongoing construction and reinforcement of multilateral norms by which policy elites conduct their international relations. These norms legitimate national objectives through collaborative processes—if not to eliminate, then to manage conflicts more effectively.

It is the stuff of cooperative security that, as reflected in the pages of this volume, is by no means a new phenomenon. Whether within alliances or in multilateral institutions and less formal coalitions, dealing with money and security collectively has a long track record going back to the nineteenth century and before. Among capital managers are the bankers, finance ministers, and their staffs that have played decisive roles in monetary-regime maintenance, thus sustaining the international liquidity essential to both government and commercial transactions.

Just as Britain once depended on the global acceptance of sterling to finance the security of its empire and commonwealth, the dollar's global standing as key currency, unit of account, and store of value has allowed U.S. authorities to conduct American foreign and national security policy abroad with relatively few constraints on the outlays they need to make. It is an extraordinary privilege, but one that also carries the obligation to take steps from time to time to maintain the global monetary regime. Indeed, this international monetary role of the U.S. dollar is an essential (even if often overlooked and understated) component of hard power upon which American national security has relied.

THE MONETARY BASES OF U.S. ECONOMIC
AND NATIONAL SECURITY

National security in general, military capabilities in particular, depend upon (and are directly affected by) the economic base that sustains them. By economic base we refer to productive capacity that in itself is a function of human capabilities in relation to combinations of capital and resources. The dollar's standing among other currencies reflects understandings in markets about these underlying economic capabilities. Monetary and fiscal policy, especially national-debt politics, that puts the creditworthiness of the United States at risk also jeopardizes national security by undermining over time the currency's acceptance for payment of obligations, domestic or public.

Put another way, the U.S. global position is primarily a function of understandings about its economic capabilities and the relative value that the dollar enjoys in relation to other currencies—an indicator of the country's economic standing. After all, the real *value* of the dollar or any other currency is not only its exchange rate vis-à-vis other currencies but also its acceptance as a medium of exchange, store of value, and unit of account. The underlying economy and collective understandings of its relative capabilities matter most.

The dollar still enjoys primacy or, some might say standing as primus inter pares in relation to the euro, which has joined it in center stage among the world's currencies. The dollar's privileged position has facilitated the conduct of American foreign and national security policy since the end of World War II—much, as noted above, as late-nineteenth- and early-twentieth-century sterling primacy allowed Britain to sustain a global empire. Given the global position of the dollar as key currency, unit of account, and store of value for both payments and national reserves, American policy-makers deploy U.S. armed forces at will. When U.S. policy-makers want to conduct military operations or finance other projects abroad, they spend these readily accepted dollars.

The emergence of the euro since the turn of the century has not proven to be the challenge some had anticipated. In fact, generally cooperative twentieth-century American links with major EU counterparts (Germany, the United Kingdom, France, and others) have been sustained in a monetary field in which the dollar, euro, and sterling are among the key currencies. For the most part in this European-Atlantic area, it is a cooperative, two- or three-way street in a common effort to maintain international liquidity. In some ways, the dollar-euro and sterling connections are similar to the sterling-dollar diplomacy of close collaboration in the 1920s between British and American monetary officials. Then, as now, cooperative security in the monetary realm depended on pragmatic approaches to challenges pursued by treasury and central banking officials.

As the currencies of such other major players as China, Russia, Brazil, and India almost certainly become more prominent than they are now, the personal and institutional bases for even greater multilateralism need to be in place to sustain economic and national security on these cooperative bases. Reinforcing and expanding cooperative norms—adapting national and international institutions to accommodate more players in these monetary roles—are essential steps in planning for the day when the United States no longer holds so many of the cards.

HISTORICAL REFLECTIONS

There are instrumental lessons we can draw from the historical account. Proactive measures among treasuries and central banks and in markets are key to sustaining the international monetary regime. That monetary matters under the nineteenth-century gold standard (more precisely the sterling-gold standard) were automatic—left entirely to the market—is the stuff of myth. In fact, central and private bankers were by no means passive. The Bank of England's use of the discount rate—raising or lowering it—had direct effect on capital flows intended to serve the bank's and the UK's global economic and national security interests. From time to time sovereign bail-out packages were essential to maintaining international liquidity in Europe. Then, as now, the preferred modality for economic and national security was use of cooperative measures involving capital transfers from both private and central bank coffers.

We also reflect historically how important cooperative security was even in wartime—at least within alliances. On the other hand, not only allies needed to exchange currencies, but also adversaries who sought finance for intelligence collection, espionage, purchases, and other activities in an enemy's currency. Neutrality in World War I allowed Switzerland and the Netherlands to serve as bankers to both sides engaged in trading the enemy's currency. Quite apart from adversaries, shoring up the financial means to carry on warfare for one's own country and one's allies—interests essential to national and alliance goals—is cooperative security in its wartime mode. It is a time when central bankers and treasury officials matter in ways often overlooked in most war accounts. Money always matters when it comes to security, particularly then, and it is the owners and managers of this capital and what they choose to do that are decisive.

The interwar period illustrates clearly how money, the rules we make about its exchange, the financial institutions that process it, and the markets in which it is exchanged for other currencies are all social constructions. Ideas associated with "conventional finance," as Keynes put it, when applied uncritically in other times and circumstances, can have significant adverse impact. Overvaluing a currency like sterling—setting it at its prewar rate, as much for symbolic reasons favored by even the learned among capital owners or managers—not only severely hurt those in the British working classes well before the Great Depression but also disadvantaged those capital interests with stakes in what had been a very thriving export trade.

Concepts and ideas that define the range of policy choice can change as newly crafted ideas displace older ones. "*They* never told us we could do that," said one Labour Party MP when the pound finally was allowed to float down to its actual market value. "*They*" were the monetary officials and other experts—the capital managers to whose advice even Labour customarily deferred! Then, as now, economic and national security has depended on critical thinking about how the ideas embedded in theories are practically applied. Further tightening fiscal or monetary screws in a period of austerity (as in overvaluing the national currency) is hardly an apt prescription to remedy adverse economic circumstances, either at home or elsewhere abroad.

The Great Depression years that began with "beggar-thy-neighbor" policies in the early 1930s finally gave way to cooperative security efforts in the last half of the decade within what were yet again in Europe becoming separate allied camps. Germany gradually returned to its dominant position among central European, Axis states, while Britain and France (and later the United States) were core members of what, with the outbreak of war, would become a reconstituted Western alliance. As in World War I, wartime controls on currency exchange rates were in place within each alliance—wartime costs thus externalized—shared or imposed on others to some degree. With the Netherlands under occupation in World War II, Switzerland (to include the Bank for International Settlements in Basel) remained the principal neutral ground for currency exchange, intelligence, and other operations requiring the enemy's currency.

"Lessons" drawn from the interwar period profoundly affected the postwar design crafted at Bretton Woods, New Hampshire. A liberal view of cooperative security saw a return to relatively fixed exchange rates, institutionalizing in the International Monetary Fund (IMF) the ways and means countries easily could access the capital needed to sustain these rates. To make the new regime work would require cooperative measures by finance ministers and central bankers either within or outside this institutional framework. As in other matters in the "new" multilateralist thinking of the time, economic and national security was to be very much a cooperative affair.

Establishment of the Special Drawing Rights (SDR) mechanism in the late 1960s was an attempt to institutionalize and make more automatic the kind of collaboration necessary for regime maintenance. As subsequent events would demonstrate, however, the general increase in IMF quotas in 1966 and the subsequent SDR agreement proved insufficient as means for maintaining the Bretton Woods regime. The German interest in keeping the United States firmly committed to NATO and its Cold War, forward-defense position along the European central front was a powerful motive in German efforts to help resolve Franco-American differences. At the end of the day, the U.S. had survived a French challenge and still held most of the cards.

The fixed exchange rates of the Bretton Woods regime (and the challenges they posed to American policy-makers) yielded in the 1970s to a more flexible exchange-rate regime. Instead of treasuries and central banks intervening to maintain relatively fixed rates (fluctuating within 1 percent of official parity), rates were now free to follow market supply and demand, radical swings checked by monetary authorities coordinating their interventions. As a practical matter, this enhanced the policy freedom for American and other policy-makers previously constrained by the pressures of relatively fixed exchange rates under Bretton Woods rules. Increased governmental purchases abroad, particularly for wars and lesser contingencies, could be financed more readily now simply by allowing the value of the currency at such times to move downward a notch or two. So long as the creditworthiness of the country and the acceptance of the dollar were not in jeopardy, the new regime facilitated financing massive American foreign policy and national security outlays abroad.

American and European central banking and treasury officials dealing with the dollar, euro, and sterling, though competitive, at the same time have cooperated constructively. The same is true for the Japanese yen and, notwithstanding differences on monetary valuation, the Chinese yuan or renminbi (RMB). In a larger sense, helping institutionalize norms favoring collaborative conduct while the United States has been in a position to assist in doing so is also a conservative, future-protecting move.

When the United States no longer enjoys the primacy it has had in international monetary matters, it may no longer be able to play the same preeminent, often decisive monetary regime–maintenance role it has played since World War II. The net effect on the U.S. capability to defend itself and continue to pursue opportunities abroad will depend on the work done well beforehand to institutionalize even further multilateral norms favoring pragmatic, peaceful approaches to the oftentimes vexing monetary and security challenges that face policy-makers.

CONCLUDING REFLECTIONS

The value of the dollar and its acceptance as reserve currency is a national security issue. This should be (but is not always) obvious. It is troubling that so many in policy circles tend to take the dollar's international standing for granted. In particular, members of Congress who threaten government shutdown or default on financial obligations weaken the country's credit worthiness and put the dollar's privileged standing at risk. Whatever the legitimacy of their policy or ideological motivations, little do they know (or typically realize) that they also are undermining national security.

Indeed, as is clear in the narrative above, the U.S. funds its foreign and national security policy merely by spending dollars abroad in much the same way the United Kingdom once sustained its late-nineteenth- and early-twentieth-century empire with outlays in sterling, then the world's principal reserve currency. Since the end of World War II the U.S. government has spent its dollars for foreign and national security policy purposes seemingly without the limits other countries face. This capability depends fundamentally upon the dollar's standing—how the underlying economy and governmental creditworthiness are understood in financial markets, and whether governments will continue to accept them often substantially in excess of their need for dollars as currency reserves. Much as money itself is a social construction, so is its role as a reserve currency.

Aside from American foreign policy or military purposes, national security in its broader understanding also includes economic security. Economic productivity, capital investment for growth and returns on these investments, trade and other forms of commerce domestically and globally all depend on the continued acceptance of the U.S. dollar as a global "legal tender" or medium of exchange.

The remedy in crises lies in the cooperative security relations developed multilaterally among central bankers and treasury officials in less stormy times.

Periodic person-to-person meetings in Basel or elsewhere, ongoing telecommunications connections, and routinized interactions among them are key to maintaining the international monetary regime as a whole and the viability of their respective currencies. Cooperative security relations are key to maintaining the viability of the U.S. dollar, the euro, and the currencies of other countries upon which the global economy depends.

Cooperation among monetary officials remains, then, an essential (if often unrecognized) component of national security. Indeed, the increased globalization of commerce in the present period amplifies enormously the magnitude of negative externalities experienced in monetary crises with adverse effects on national economies and global commerce not easily contained.

So understood, national security in the monetary realm is obviously not a Department of Defense or State Department function. It is instead the responsibility of Treasury officials and central bankers, but it is every bit a national security function upon which government departments and agencies depend in executing U.S. foreign and national security policy. We need not create domestic challenges in Washington that in any way threaten the dollar's standing.

We conclude this narrative then, with a summary list of major themes articulated in this volume:

First, the monetary value of the U.S. dollar is an essential (if often overlooked or understated) component of hard power upon which American national security depends.

Second, fiscal (spending, taxing and borrowing) and national-debt politics that put the creditworthiness of the United States at risk also jeopardize national security and the worldwide conduct of American foreign policy.

Third, national security, in general, and military capabilities, in particular, depend upon and are directly affected by the economic base that sustains them.

Fourth, as with the British and other nineteenth- and twentieth-century empires, the U.S. global position is primarily a function of its economic capabilities and the relative value of the dollar in relation to other currencies—an indicator of its economic standing.

Fifth, the real *value* of a currency is not only its exchange rate vis-à-vis other currencies but also its acceptance as a medium of exchange, store of value, or unit of account. The economy and understandings of its relative capabilities matter most in determining this real value of the dollar or, for that matter, any currency.

Sixth, all of these economic determinations of value and relative value are based on understandings held not just by policy elites but also by the mass publics that constitute the markets in which the dollar operates.

Finally, maintaining economic and national security depends on cooperative measures in relation to the international monetary component of hard power. In this regard, norms and the institutions in which they are embedded, matter. As the late Ernst Haas often stated, ideas grounded in interests (of the relevant players) remain the motive forces that drive politics.

Reference Matter

Notes

INTRODUCTION

1. See the quotation by Galbraith at the beginning of the Preface, taken from John Kenneth Galbraith, *Money* (New York: Houghton Mifflin, 1975), 18–19.

2. See Rodney Bruce Hall, *Central Banking as Global Governance* (Cambridge: Cambridge University Press, 2008). Compare detailed histories of central banking in Gianni Toniolo and Piet Clement, *Central Bank Cooperation at the Bank for International Settlements, 1930–73* (Cambridge: Cambridge University Press, 2005); and Claudio Borio, Gianni Toniolo and Piet Clement, eds., *Past and Future of Central Bank Cooperation* (Cambridge: Cambridge University Press, 2008).

3. John Herz identified the security dilemma in "Idealist Internationalism and the Security Dilemma," *World Politics* 2, no. 2 (January 1950): 157–80. Compare his *Political Realism and Political Idealism* (Chicago: University of Chicago Press, 1951). As Dan Caldwell reminds me, Thucydides also observed how the Athenian military buildup caused fear in Sparta, which was a cause of the Peloponnesian War. Thus measures taken to advance security may actually undermine it, since such actions may lead adversaries, in turn, to take steps to defend themselves—a spiral of mutually threatening behaviors.

4. See Klaus Knorr's comment cited at the beginning of the Preface, taken from his *Power and Wealth* (New York: Basic Books, 1973), 40. On global capital flows, see Barry Eichengreen, *Globalizing Capital* (Princeton: Princeton University Press, 1996).

5. This important nexus between economy and security was examined earlier in Charles P. Kindleberger, *Power and Money* (New York: Basic Books, 1970); and Knorr, *Power and Wealth*. Compare Knorr and Frank N. Trager, eds., *Economic Issues and National Security* (Lawrence: Regents Press of Kansas, 1977). The monetary component was explored in Robert O. Keohane and Joseph S. Nye, eds., *Power and Interdependence*, 3rd ed. (New York: Longman, 1977, 2001), part II, 4–6; and in Robert Gilpin, *The Political*

Economy of International Relations (Princeton: Princeton University Press, 1987), esp. ch. 4.

6. See Robert O. Keohane, *Power and Governance in a Partially Globalized World* (London: Routledge, 2002), esp. part III on globalism, liberalism, and governance. See also Jonathan Kirshner, *Currency and Coercion* (Princeton: Princeton University Press, 1995, 1997).

7. For a brief overview of these developments, see Madeleine O. Hosli, *The Euro* (Boulder, CO: Lynne Rienner, 2005).

8. RMB is an abbreviation used for renminbi—the people's currency—which is denominated in units called yuan.

9. For development of this theme, see Michael Mastanduno, "Economics and Security in Statecraft and Scholarship," *International Organization* 52 (1998): 825–54. Compare Peter Dombrowski, ed., *Guns and Butter* (Boulder, CO: Lynne Rienner, 2005).

10. See Joseph S. Nye, Jr., *The Paradox of American Power* (Oxford and New York: Oxford University Press, 2002), 8–12. By contrast, Kenneth Waltz does not divide power into separate kinds, treating these capabilities instead as an integrity—a single unit. See his *Theory of International Politics* (Boston: Addison Wesley, 1979), 129–31 *et passim*.

11. For an early statement of the concept, see Ashton B. Carter, William J. Perry, and John D. Steinbruner, *A New Concept of Cooperative Security*, Brookings Occasional Papers (Washington, DC: Brookings Institution, 1992).

12. Members of an epistemic community typically have shared (1) "normative and principled beliefs, which provide a value-based rationale for social action"; (2) "causal beliefs" relevant to the "possible policy actions" they explore and the "desired outcomes" they seek; (3) "notions of validity" or "intersubjective, internally defined criteria for weighing and validating knowledge"; and (4) "policy enterprise" or "set of problems to which their professional competence is directed." See Peter M. Haas, ed., *Knowledge, Power, and International Policy Coordination* (Columbia: University of South Carolina Press, 1992), 3.

13. They do keep contact with each other through telecommunications links, particularly when economic crises or other challenges emerge, meeting periodically in the International Monetary Fund, World Bank, Organization for Economic Cooperation and Development, and other institutional settings as well. Although there is some overlap between treasury officials and central bankers, there is enough difference between them to warrant considering them separate communities—the latter more of an epistemic community.

14. Ethan Kapstein sees central bankers as acting only "like" an epistemic community. See his "Between Power and Purpose," in *Knowledge, Power, and International Policy Coordination*, ed. Haas, 265–87. There is substantial evidence now, however, to warrant calling central bankers an epistemic community. See Hall, *Central Banking as Global Governance*; Toniolo and Clement, *Central Bank Cooperation at the Bank for Interna-*

tional Settlements, 1930–73; and Borio, Toniolo, and Clement, eds., *Past and Future of Central Bank Cooperation.*

15. See Barry Eichengreen's take on this Gaullist complaint in his *Exorbitant Privilege* (New York: Oxford University Press, 2011).

16. With European, Japanese, and other economies in shambles after World War II, capital continued to flow from foreign markets into the United States, fueled by its strong export position—positive trade balances sustained throughout the period. The capital flow reversed over time as a result of increased U.S. military expenditures, Marshall Plan assistance and other foreign aid, American private investment abroad, and dollar-denominated loans from domestic and multilateral institutions. Essential to its role as a key currency to finance international trade and investment that could be held along with gold as official reserves, the supply of dollars finally met market demand for them, thus ending the dollar shortage. With a sufficient supply of dollars to serve as key currency for international transactions, its role as an official reserve currency became increasingly prominent.

17. All expected economic outcomes or tendencies expressed are with the usual ceteris paribus (other things equal—remaining the same) caveat.

18. In a typical year U.S. defense spending is about 45 percent of the world's total ($696,268 billion for the United States, $1,547,801 billion the global total in 2008, funds used to finance global commitments). See, for example, the London-based International Institute for Strategic Studies (IISS), *The Military Balance, 2010* (London: Routledge, 2009), 462, 468.

19. The North Atlantic Treaty Organization, formed in 1949 with Canada, Iceland, and Western European and Mediterranean countries further east—namely, Greece and Turkey. Post–Cold War NATO expanded from 16 to 28 members.

20. The Organization of American States, formed in 1948, but with foundation stones in 1890 in what was called the Pan American Union.

21. The UK-led Baghdad Pact (1955) included Iraq, Turkey, Iran, and Pakistan, becoming the Central Treaty Organization (CENTO) in 1959 after Iraq withdrew from the alliance. Since British authorities saw this region as lying within their historical sphere of interest, the United States never was a formal member of either the Baghdad Pact or CENTO. Nevertheless, the U.S. was a principal supporter of both organizations. The alliance dissolved after the Iranian revolution in 1979.

22. The U.S.-led Southeast Asia Treaty Organization (SEATO) or Manila Pact, formed in 1954, resisted the spread of communist regimes in the region. In addition to the United States and the Philippines (independent, but then still a U.S. client state), other members included Thailand, France (Vietnam, Cambodia, and Laos—its historical spheres of influence), the UK (Hong Kong, Malaya, and Burma within the British sphere), Pakistan (including East Pakistan, now Bangladesh—both originally part of British India), and Australia and New Zealand (members of the British

Commonwealth). After the communist victory in Vietnam (1975), SEATO dissolved in 1977.

23. An Australia-New Zealand-U.S. alliance, agreed in 1951, the treaty became effective in 1952.

24. The Taiwan Defense Command (TDC) formed in 1955, ending in 1979 with completion of the normalization process in U.S. diplomatic relations with the People's Republic of China.

25. NORAD, the North American Air—now Aerospace—Defense Command, formed in 1957.

CHAPTER 1

1. One of the best sources on the construction of the European Monetary Union (EMU) is Harold James, *Making the European Monetary Union* (Boston: Harvard University Press/Belknap, 2012). See also Madeline O. Hosli, *The Euro* (Boulder, CO: Lynne Rienner, 2005). For a critical perspective, see Jürgen Habermas, *The Crisis of the European Union* (Cambridge, UK: Polity Press, 2012).

2. Per the Stability and Growth Pact (1997), annual budget deficits (government revenue minus outlays) were not to exceed 3 percent and overall debt not to exceed 60 percent of GDP. In practice, keeping within these ceilings has proven difficult even among the more capital rich, large economies of EU members: in 2011 German debt was 81.2 percent of GDP (its 1.0 percent of GDP budget deficit well within bounds), France 85.8 percent (5.2 percent budget deficit), and (outside the eurozone) the United Kingdom at 85.7 percent (8.3 percent budget deficit). These numbers, already more than a third above the 60 percent of GDP debt ceiling, seem relatively small compared with Greece at 165.3 percent (9.1 percent budget deficit), Italy 120.1 percent (3.9 percent budget deficit), Portugal 107.8 percent (4.2 percent budget deficit), and Ireland 108.2 percent (13.1 percent budget deficit). Spain's difficulties were due less to aggregate debt (68.5 percent of GDP with 8.5 percent budget deficit) than to real estate speculation and other domestic factors. Source: European Commission, May 2012.

3. The raw data on gold are provided by G. F. Warren and F. A. Pearson, *Gold and Prices* (New York, 1935), as cited by Marcello deCecco, *Money and Empire* (Oxford: Basil Blackwell, 1974), 247. The world stock of monetary gold by selected years follows (all figures in $ millions): 1860: 2108; 1870: 2708; 1880: 3121; 1890: 3493; 1900: 4816; and 1910: 7028.

4. Peter H. Lindert, *Key Currencies and Gold, 1900–1913*, Princeton Studies in International Finance no. 24 (Princeton: Princeton University Department of Economics, 1969), 73–74.

5. By 1913, British capital represented 6 percent of total foreign investment in Argentina. Moreover, this was about 10 percent of total British foreign investment. Repatriation of earnings to foreigners climbed from an annual average of 57 million gold

pesos (£11.4 million) at the turn of the century to an annual average of 156 million pesos (£31.2 million) in the 1911–14 period. If one assumes that 60 percent of these debt service payments were made to British accounts and not reinvested, then the British may have received as much as £18 million or £19 million each year from the Argentine source alone. The data from which this inference is drawn are in A. G. Ford, *The Gold Standard, 1880–1914* (Oxford: Clarendon Press, 1962), 88–89. The exchange rate of five gold pesos = £1.0 is used in the above calculations and is found in ibid., 67. See also Ford's discussion of British-Argentine relations on pages 66–67, 84–89, 148, 155–58, 168–69, 182, 189–93.

6. Lindert, *Key Currencies and Gold*, 32. Compare Junnosuke Inouye, *Problems of the Japanese Exchange* (London: Macmillan, 1931), 74; and Ushisaburo Kobayashi, *War and Armaments Loans of Japan* (New York: Oxford University Press, 1922), 186.

7. Lindert, *Key Currencies and Gold*, 31. Russia, France, and Germany jointly opposed Japan's extensive territorial claims following the defeat of China. Their emissaries to Japan were not well received, a fact that opened the door to British interests. The latter agreed to some territorial demands and sterling indemnities. From London's perspective, the settlement represented a victory of sorts for British diplomacy in its Asian quest to reduce the influence of other European states and thus enhance their own position.

8. See, for example, Arthur I. Bloomfield, *Patterns of Fluctuation in International Investment before 1914*, Princeton Studies in International Finance no. 21 (Princeton: Princeton University Department of Economics, 1968).

9. Lindert, *Key Currencies and Gold*, 57. As gold reserves fell, the Bank of England would raise its discount (or interest) rate, an action that would produce a needed capital inflow to Britain, thus bolstering the Bank of England's gold and foreign exchange reserves. Thus the discount rate was used by the Bank of England to ensure the convertibility of sterling. For the classic nineteenth-century portrayal of the Bank of England and financial markets, see Walter Bagehot, *Lombard Street* (Fairford, UK: Echo Library, 1873, 2005).

10. Ibid., 57.

11. Arthur I. Bloomfield, *Short-Term Capital Movements under the Pre-1914 Gold Standard*, Princeton Studies in International Finance no. 11 (Princeton: Princeton University Department of Economics, 1963), 96–97.

12. The unsettling effect of czarist Russian deposits that could be withdrawn without notice is discussed in Lindert, *Key Currencies and Gold*, 29–31.

13. See Arthur I. Bloomfield, *Monetary Policy under the International Gold Standard* (New York: Federal Reserve Bank, 1959), 57. Help from the West was forthcoming following Russian losses in the war with Japan. A consortium of private French, British, and other European banks made the Russian government a loan for more than 2 billion francs in 1906 so as to stabilize Russian exchange. See Bloomfield, *Short-Term Capital Movements*, 84.

14. R. G. Hawtrey, *The Gold Standard in Theory and Practice*, 5th ed. (London: Long-

man's, Green and Co., 1927, 1947), 71.

15. deCecco, *Money and Empire*, 43.

16. Ibid., 43–44.

17. Since Britain was an important source of manufactures in the newly industrializing Continental states, gold was an increasingly popular medium. Moreover, the French public had demonstrated a proclivity toward gold hoarding. Nevertheless, the French interests in favor of bimetallism were the Bank of France and various private banking interests, notably the House of Rothschild and the Comptoir d'Escompte. One reason offered for this opposition was the profit made through arbitrage. Nevertheless, the idea of gold monometallism had gained in legitimacy. See Walter T. K. Nugent, *Money and American Society* (New York: Free Press, 1968), 70–71; and deCecco, *Money and Empire*, 43–44.

18. deCecco, *Money and Empire*, 44.

19. Expenditures on building a railroad and for other development projects as well as financing a war with Austria were reasons for the inflationary monetary policy. See ibid., 46.

20. See Charles P. Kindleberger, *A Financial History of Western Europe* (London: George Allen and Unwin, 1984), 58–59; deCecco, *Money and Empire*, 46–47; and Nugent, *Money and American Society*, 118.

21. Nugent states that "coinage unification among the German states would be a preliminary to political unification." Since the "policymakers of Prussia knew that German coinage unification would not come on the basis of silver, or with any existing unit, including the Prussian [silver] thaler," it was argued that there would have to "be a wholly new gold coin." See Nugent, *Money and American Society*, 121.

22. Hawtrey, *The Gold Standard in Theory and Practice*, 73–74.

23. Ibid., 74.

24. Kindleberger, *A Financial History of Western Europe*, 59.

25. Ibid., 29.

26. Ibid., 60.

27. Bloomfield remarks that "although a considerable measure of success appears to have been achieved in the years just before World War I, the mark acceptance never attained the status of the sterling bill as an instrument of trade financing." See Bloomfield, *Short-Term Capital Movements*, 37.

28. For one thing, "the possession of sterling balances was the surest means of getting gold when wanted." See Lindert, *Key Currencies and Gold*, 34.

29. There is also evidence of collaboration in the opposite direction. In 1898, for example, "the Bank of England and the Bank of France are reported to have given aid to certain German banks . . . , thus easing pressures in the Berlin market." See Bloomfield, *Monetary Policy under the International Gold Standard*, 57.

30. See the discussion in Bloomfield, *Short-Term Capital Movements*, 25–27.

31. Ibid., 25.

32. Ibid.

33. For a detailed narrative of this conference, see Nugent, *Money and American Society,* 67–90.

34. Ibid., 79.

35. Ibid., 85.

36. Ibid., 87.

37. Ibid., 89.

38. deCecco, *Money and Empire,* 47–48.

39. Nugent, *Money and American Society,* 255.

40. deCecco, *Money and Empire,* 48.

41. Indeed, the Bank of France was not particularly pleased by the fact that it was left holding unredeemable Italian silver. See ibid., 49.

42. Ibid., 50. Principal defenders of silver at the conference were the United States, Austria-Hungary, and Russia.

43. Bloomfield, *Short-Term Capital Movements,* 33.

44. Edward Hallett Carr, *Nationalism and After* (London: Macmillan and Co., 1945), 14–15.

CHAPTER 2

1. D. E. Moggridge, *British Monetary Policy, 1924–1941* (Cambridge: Cambridge University Press, 1972), 19.

2. William Adams Brown, Jr., *The International Gold Standard Reinterpreted , 1914–1934* (New York: National Bureau of Economic Research, 1940) , 13.

3. Ibid., 14.

4. See, for example, Milton Friedman and Anna Jacobson Schwartz, *A Monetary History of the United States,* 1867–1960 (Princeton: Princeton University Press, 1963), 192.

5. Brown, *The International Gold Standard Reinterpreted,* 53.

6. See Paul Einzig, *World Finance, 1914–1935* (New York: Macmillan, 1935), 30–31.

7. See Brown, *The International Gold Standard Reinterpreted,* 22–23.

8. Ibid., 23.

9. For British rates, see David K. Sheppard, *The Growth and Role of UK Financial Institutions* (London: Methuen and Co., 1971), 190. American rates are in Friedman and Schwartz, *A Monetary History of the United States,* 214.

10. Of course, factors other than interest rates—such as confidence in the future exchange value of a given currency—also entered into the calculations of would-be depositors.

11. Brown, *The International Gold Standard Reinterpreted,* 69–70.

12. Ibid., 62–63.

13. Ibid., 93.

14. Einzig comments that "with the aid of paying special deposit rates, the British authorities managed to attract considerable funds from neutral countries, notwithstanding the exchange risk." See Einzig, *World Finance*, 37.

15. Brown, *The International Gold Standard Reinterpreted*, 94.

16. Prices paid varied between 77s. 9d. and 77s. 10.5d. per ounce of gold. See ibid., 31, 40–41.

17. Moreover, even when Britain extended credits to the dominions, these funds were to be spent within the United Kingdom. See ibid., 73.

18. See Einzig, *World Finance*, 38.

19. For example, several joint stock banks sent £20 million to London in August 1915. See Brown, *The International Gold Standard Reinterpreted*, 41–42.

20. Ibid., 58, 61.

21. Ibid., 41, 55–56.

22. At gold parity this amounted to just under $100 million. See ibid., 43–44.

23. Switzerland also received silver in lieu of gold from the other members of the Latin Monetary Union—namely, France and Italy. Ibid., 107.

24. Ibid., 47.

25. Ibid., 73.

26. Brown, *The International Gold Standard Reinterpreted*, 103.

27. Ibid., 62. British, French, and American collaboration during the war produced relative stability in the exchange rates of the three major Allied currencies. After fluctuating between a high of $7 in 1914 and a low of $4.50 in 1915, London stabilized the pound at $4.76 and 7/16 cent in January 1916, a figure two percentage points lower than the pre-1914 value of sterling. Early in the war the French franc was at a premium, but it was kept from going higher by official intervention involving French purchase of both sterling and the dollar. The situation changed, however, and the French franc hit a low of 16.74 cents in April 1916 from a pre-1914 value of 19.30 cents. The franc climbed back to 17.51 cents in 1917 and reached 18.37 cents in 1918. See Friedman and Schwartz, *A Monetary History of the United States*, 200; and Einzig, *World Finance*, 41.

28. U.S. net cash advances during the war to Great Britain, France, and Italy amounted, respectively, to $4.196 billion, $2.966 billion, and $1.631 billion. The source is *Annual Report of the Secretary of the Treasury* (1920), as cited in Brown, *The International Gold Standard Reinterpreted*, 74. In the two years following the Armistice the United States advanced an additional $2.2 billion to its allies. See Friedman and Schwartz, *A Monetary History of the United States*, 216.

29. Similar loans were granted by Spain to France and the United States. See Brown, *The International Gold Standard Reinterpreted*, 67–68.

30. Ibid., 67.

31. Ibid., 83, 96.

32. Ibid., 137.

33. Ibid., 138.

34. E. J. Hobsbawm, *Industry and Empire* (Baltimore, MD: Penguin Books, 1968, 1969), 152.

35. Bureau of the Census, *Historical Statistics of the United States, 1789–1945*, Series M-l, 1949, 242, as cited by Friedman and Schwartz, *A Monetary History of the United States*, 199.

36. Brown, *The International Gold Standard Reinterpreted*, 65.

37. See Charles P. Kindleberger, *The Formation of Financial Centers*, Princeton Studies in International Finance no. 36 (Princeton: Princeton University Department of Economics, 1974), 61.

38. Brown, *The International Gold Standard Reinterpreted*, 153.

39. Ibid.

40. Although Britain pursued a policy that inhibited the export of gold during the war by various means, the country had not "formally abandoned the gold standard" until "immediately after the war," when a legal embargo was placed on gold exports. From this time until 1925 the value of sterling was allowed to fluctuate. See Donald Winch, *Economics and Policy* (New York: Walker and Co., 1969), 77.

41. The fluctuations of sterling from March 1919 through December 1933 are contained in Brown, *The International Gold Standard Reinterpreted*, 231.

CHAPTER 3

1. The Genoa Conference included representatives from Britain, France, Italy, Germany, Russia, and other countries. In monetary affairs it was preceded by work at the International Financial Conference in Brussels in September 1920 and, more immediately, by meetings at Cannes in January 1922. See J. Saxon Mills, *The Genoa Conference* (London: Hutchinson and Co., c. 1923), 9, 11, 370. Compare William Adams Brown, Jr., *The International Gold Standard Reinterpreted* (New York: National Bureau of Economic Research and AMS Press, 1940, 1970), 341–46.

2. See Stephen V. O. Clarke, *Central Bank Cooperation* (New York: Federal Reserve Bank, 1967), 223.

3. British leadership was clearly evident before the Genoa Conference convened. Indeed, several weeks before the opening day, the British called a meeting of Allied "experts" in London, a gathering that produced "a long report dealing" with subjects to be discussed at the conference. See Mills, *The Genoa Conference*, 82.

4. Donald Winch, *Economics and Policy* (London: Hodder and Stoughton, 1969), 85; and Susan Strange, *Sterling and British Policy* (Oxford: Oxford University Press, 1971). 50–53. Compare the more recent commentary on Norman's central banking role in Liaquat Ahamed, *Lords of Finance* (New York: Penguin Press, 2009), ch. 2.

5. See Winch, *Economics and Policy*, 70. Compare *First Interim Report of the Committee on Currency*, as reprinted in *Select Statutes, Documents and Reports Relating to British*

Banking, 1832–1928, ed. T. E. Gregory (Oxford: Oxford University Press, 1929).

6. See Brown, *The International Gold Standard Reinterpreted*, 166.

7. Ibid., 168.

8. Mills, *The Genoa Conference*, 14.

9. Ibid., 12–13.

10. Clarke, *Central Bank Cooperation*, 34.

11. Ibid., 33.

12. Quotations from these resolutions below may be found in Mills, *The Genoa Conference*, 360–68.

13. Compare Gustav Cassell, *The Downfall of the Gold Standard* (London: Frank Cass and Co., 1936, 1966), 27.

14. Hawtrey remarks that "in saying that all countries must avoid inflationary finance and stabilize their currencies, and that stabilization meant stabilization in relation to gold, the Conference was merely repeating what had been said often enough before." See R. G. Hawtrey, *The Gold Standard in Theory and Practice*, 5th ed. (London: Longman's, Green and Co., 1927, 1947), 97. Compare Brown, *The International Gold Standard Reinterpreted*, 387.

15. Susan Strange comments that this "new form of international organization" proposed by the British "would have operated to maintain a stable international system but also would have restricted the freedom of action of the participating states." Accordingly, "the Americans resisted, with the result that [these] Genoa proposals were still-born." See Strange, *Sterling and British Policy*, 53.

16. On the "gestation and birth" of the BIS, see Gianni Toniolo and Piet Clement, *Central Bank Cooperation at the Bank for International Settlements, 1930–1973* (Cambridge: Cambridge University Press, 2005), ch. 2. Compare the earlier treatment of this tale in Roger Auboin, *The Bank for International Settlements, 1930–1955*, Princeton Studies in International Finance no. 22 (Princeton: Princeton University Department of Economics, 1955). For the British (that is, Norman's) role, see Strange, *Sterling and British Policy*, 50.

17. Clarke, *Central Bank Cooperation*, 40.

18. Ibid., 38.

19. Ibid., 38–39.

20. He states that there was an "hiatus created in the interwar period by British inability to serve as a lender of last resort for Europe and U.S. unwillingness . . . to take over the task." See Charles P. Kindleberger, *The Formation of Financial Centers*, Princeton Studies in International Finance no. 36 (Princeton: Princeton University Department of Economics, 1974), 61.

21. See Paul Einzig, *World Finance, 1914–1935* (New York: Macmillan, 1935), 152.

22. Ibid., 84.

23. Clarke, *Central Bank Cooperation*, 222.

24. Einzig, *World Finance*, 96.

25. Clarke, *Central Bank Cooperation*, 222.

26. John Maynard Keynes, *The Economic Consequences of the Peace* (New York: Harcourt, Brace and Howe, 1920), 111–12.

27. See Clarke, *Central Bank Cooperation*, 45.

28. Central banking interests were, however, granted some representation, most notably in the persons of Owen D. Young and Sir Robert Kindersly, who were then on the boards of directors of the New York Federal Reserve Bank and the Bank of England, respectively. See ibid., 46.

29. Ibid., 49.

30. Ibid., 62.

31. Ibid., 69.

32. Einzig, *World Finance*, 87.

33. Ibid., 84.

34. Clarke, *Central Bank Cooperation*, 58.

35. Ibid.

36. Winch, *Economics and Policy*, 83.

37. Sweden returned to gold in March 1924, and Hungary stabilized in the summer of the same year. Various Latin American currencies had stabilized in terms of dollars, and Poland attempted to do the same in 1924. Holland, Switzerland, Australia, South Africa, and various other countries were seen as planning to return to gold as soon as possible. In this context, the American central banker, Benjamin Strong, wrote his British counterpart, Montagu Norman, that "the question uppermost in my mind is whether sterling is not now rather far behind in the progression." See Clarke, *Central Bank Cooperation*, 80. Compare Brown, *The International Gold Standard Reinterpreted*, 323.

38. Brown, *The International Gold Standard Reinterpreted*, 27–29.

39. Hawtrey, *The Gold Standard in Theory and Practice*; Brown, *The International Gold Standard Reinterpreted*, 95.

40. Brown, *The International Gold Standard Reinterpreted*, 37 and 39.

41. Einzig, *Word Finance*, 48.

42. See the discussion in Karl W. Deutsch, *The Nerves of Government* (New York: Free Press, 1963, 1966), 167–71.

43. Winch, *Economics and Policy*, 86.

44. See Edward I. Friedland, "Introduction to the Concept of Rationality in Political Science" (Morristown, NJ: General Learning Press, 1974), 8.

45. Mannheim argued that "the sociology of knowledge is concerned not so much with distortions due to a deliberate effort to deceive as with the varying ways in which objects present themselves to the subject according to the difference in social settings." See Karl Mannheim, *Ideology and Utopia* (New York: Harcourt, Brace, and World, 1929,

1936), 265.

46. House of Commons Debates, May 4, 1925, c. 670, as cited by Winch, *Economics and Policy*, 84.

47. John Maynard Keynes, "The Economic Consequences of Mr. Churchill" (1925), in Keynes, *Essays in Persuasion* (New York: Harcourt, Brace, and Co., 1932), 248–49.

48. Ibid., 248–50.

49. Ibid., 250–51.

50. Ibid., 262.

51. Edward Friedland observes: "The values and perceptions of reality . . . in all decision situations are a function of the social environment." See Friedland, "Introduction to the Concept of Rationality in Political Science," 10. For his part, Karl Mannheim argues that "there is implicit in the word 'ideology' the insight that in certain situations the collective unconscious of certain groups obscures the real condition of society." See Mannheim, *Ideology and Utopia*, 265.

52. The minister is quoted in D. F. Moggridge, *The Return to Gold, 1925: The Formulation of Policy and Its Critics* (Cambridge: Cambridge University Press, 1969), 9. Compare Charles P. Kindleberger, *The World in Depression* (Berkeley: University of California Press, 1973), 47.

53. Clarke, *Central Bank Cooperation*, 105.

54. Ibid., 107.

55. Ibid.

CHAPTER 4

1. See Charles P. Kindleberger, *The World in Depression, 1929–1939* (Berkeley: University of California Press, 1973), 28, 213, 291–92 et passim.

2. Ibid., 259.

3. Kindleberger refers to "Germany's monopsony position as an important market for the goods of southeastern Europe," and he notes that "these countries" sold "their foodstuffs and raw materials to Germany on clearing account, and that they were willing to wait some time to get manufactured goods in exchange, often at high prices." Ibid., 241.

4. See the account in Charles P. Kindleberger, *A Financial History of Western Europe* (London: George Allen and Unwin, 1984), 406.

5. Kindleberger provides details on Anglo-American bargaining on Lend-Lease. Ibid., 424–27.

6. See R. G. Hawtrey, *The Gold Standard in Theory and Practice*, 5th ed. (London: Longman's, Green and Co., 1927, 1947), 222.

7. See B. R. Mitchell, *Abstract of British Historical Statistics* (Cambridge: Cambridge University Press, 1962), 1001; and David K. Sheppard, *The Growth and Role of UK Financial Institutions* (London: Methuen and Co., 1971), 190.

8. See Robert Triffin, "Excerpts from 'Gold and the Dollar Crises,'" in *World Monetary*

Reform, ed. Herbert G. Grubel (Stanford: Stanford University Press, 1963), 70.

9. In January 1934 the American gold stock was $6.833 billion, but this climbed to $10.648 billion by July 1936. The French gold stock declined from $3.238 billion in March 1935 to $2.116 billion in June 1936 and $1.963 billion by September. See Hawtrey, *The Gold Standard in Theory and Practice*, 174 and 177. Conversions to dollar values were made at the official gold par of $0.03918 per franc.

10. Milton Friedman and Anna Jacobson Schwartz, *A Monetary History of the United States, 1867–1960* (Princeton: Princeton University Press, 1963), 509.

11. Ibid.

12. Ibid., 587.

13. The conversion rate used in these calculations is £1.0 = $4.00. See John Maynard Keynes, *How to Pay for the War* (New York: Harcourt, Brace and Company, 1940), 83.

14. Friedman and Schwartz, *A Monetary History of the United States, 1867–1960*, 509.

15. Ibid., 497.

16. Ibid., 259, 497.

17. Richard A. Lester, *International Aspects of Wartime Monetary Experience*, Princeton Studies in International Finance no. 3 (Princeton: Princeton University Department of Economics, 1944), 2. Compare Kindleberger, *A Financial History of Western Europe*, 406–9.

18. Vladimir Petrov, *Money and Conquest* (Baltimore: Johns Hopkins University Press, 1967), 16. See also Lester, *International Aspects of Wartime Monetary Experience*, 2–8, 16–17. Compare Frank A. Southard, Jr., *Some European Currency and Exchange Experiences*, Princeton Studies in International Finance no. 7 (Princeton: Princeton University Department of Economics, 1946).

19. Petrov, *Money and Conquest*, 27. See his ch. 2, 23–41, for a more complete account of what it meant to be "under German rule." For details on Allied wartime occupation monetary policy in North Africa, France, and Italy, see chs. 3 and 4, 42–106.

20. For example, in 1942 "free" China borrowed $50 million and £50 million from the United States and Britain, respectively. See Lester, *International Aspects of Wartime Monetary Experience*, 13. During World War II, the United States purchased the currency of (or made loans to) a number of countries including Argentina, Brazil, China, Cuba, Ecuador, Liberia, and Mexico. See Margaret G. Myers, *A Financial History of the United States* (New York: Columbia University Press, 1970), 362.

21. Lowell M. Pumphrey, "The Exchange Equalization Account of Great Britain, 1932–1939," *American Economic Review* 32 (1942): 811.

22. Paul Einzig, *The History of Foreign Exchange* (New York: St. Martin's Press, 1962), 291.

23. Ibid.

24. See the discussion in E. Victor Morgan, *A History of Money* (Baltimore: Penguin Books, 1965), 171–72; and Fred Hirsch, *Money International* (Garden City, NY: Double-

day and Co., 1969), 334–41.

25. See Gianni Toniolo and Piet Clement, *Central Bank Cooperation at the Bank for International Settlements, 1930–1973* (Cambridge: Cambridge University Press, 2005), 233.

26. Ibid., 233–35.

27. The role played in such transactions by the Paris office of the Chase Bank or of British banks that continued operations is not clear, but the fact that their doors stayed open—thus "trading with the enemy"—is indeed striking. See Charles Higham, *Trading with the Enemy* (New York: Barnes and Noble, 1983, 1995), 29.

28. Jacobsson joined the BIS in 1931, became head of the Economic and Monetary Department in 1946, and remained there until being appointed chairman of the Executive Board and managing director of the IMF (1956–63). Ibid., 231, 703.

29. Ibid., 227.

30. Ibid., 228–29.

31. Ibid., 227.

32. Norman actively promoted the idea of an "international bank" of this kind in the mid-to-late 1920s. See ibid., 30. Prior to the Nazi period, Norman had established a close friendship with his German counterpart, Hjalmar Schacht (Reichsbank president, 1924–30 and 1933–39), which contributed fuel to the fire later on his alleged pro-German sympathies. On the friendship, see Liaquat Ahamed, *Lords of Finance* (London: Penguin Press, 2009), esp. 488. Compare the more scathing commentary about Norman in Higham, *Trading with the Enemy*, 5. On the other hand, Norman also had close personal ties with Benjamin Strong (New York Federal Reserve Bank president, 1914–28) that were central to Anglo-American monetary cooperation at the time. See Richard Meyer, *Bankers' Diplomacy* (New York: Columbia University Press, 1970), 50–51, 69–75 et passim.

33. Richard N. Gardner, *Sterling-Dollar Diplomacy* (Oxford: Clarendon Press, 1956), 4. Gardner identifies at least three lessons: unpreparedness of the American delegation at Paris after World War I should not be repeated; great harm was done by the U.S. failure to join the League of Nations and, as a result, U.S. policy following World War II should be oriented toward participation in international organizations; and the inadequate handling of economic problems in the postwar settlements should not be repeated. See ibid., 4, 12.

34. J. Keith Horsefield, *The International Monetary Fund*, vol. I (Washington, DC: International Monetary Fund, 1969), 5.

35. John Morton Blum, *From the Morgenthau Diaries* (Boston: Houghton Mifflin, 1967), 229. Compare Gardner, *Sterling-Dollar Diplomacy*, 75–76.

36. Sir Roy Harrod, "Problems Perceived in the International Financial System," in *Bretton Woods Revisited*, ed. A. L. K. Acheson et al. (Toronto: University of Toronto Press, 1972), 7.

37. See Gardner, *Sterling-Dollar Diplomacy*, 31, 76.

38. In particular, Secretary of State Cordell Hull and his undersecretary, Sumner Welles, were outspoken free trade advocates. See ibid., 4, 12–22.

39. Horsefield, *The International Monetary Fund*, 5.

40. Gardner cites government leaders such as Clement Atlee and Ernest Bevin and such economists as Lionel Robbins, James Meade, Hubert Henderson, Dennis Robertson, and John Maynard Keynes for their commitment to restoring a liberal, postwar order of economic multilateralism or collaboration. Gardner also notes some exceptions to this general trend. See *Sterling-Dollar Diplomacy*, 25–26, 28–31.

41. Horsefield, *The International Monetary Fund*, 6.

42. Gardner, *Sterling-Dollar Diplomacy*, 56.

43. See UK Treasury, *Proposal for an International Clearing Union* (London, 1943), as cited by Gardner, ibid., 79. The same fear of deflation born of the interwar experience also influenced the early IMF leadership. See ibid., 290–91.

44. See the discussion in Gardner, *Sterling-Dollar Diplomacy*, 75–76.

45. John Maynard Keynes, *The End of Laissez-Faire* (London: Hogarth Press, 1926). An abbreviated version is in Keynes, *Essays in Persuasion* (New York: Harcourt, Brace, and Co., 1932), 312–38. On the rejection of laissez-faire liberalism, see also Karl Polanyi, *The Great Transformation* (Boston: Beacon Press, 1944, 1957), 135–62, 221–58; Joseph Schumpeter, *Capitalism, Socialism, and Democracy* (New York: Harper and Row, 1950, 1962); and Karl Mannheim, *Freedom, Power and Democratic Planning*, ed. Hans Gerth and Ernest K. Bramstedt (London: Routledge and Kegan Paul, 1950, 1951).

46. Keynes, *The End of Laissez-Faire*, 50.

47. "Proposals for an International Clearing Union," British Government Publication, Cmd. 6437 (London: H.M. Stationery Office, 1943), in *World Monetary Reform*, ed. Herbert G. Grubel (Stanford: Stanford University Press, 1963), 57. See also the discussion of the Keynes Plan in Horsefield, *The International Monetary Fund*, 14–21, 27–32, 48–53.

48. Horsefield, *The International Monetary Fund*, 58.

49. Ibid., 58–59.

50. Ibid., 59–60.

51. Ibid., 62.

52. By contrast, there were advocates of a liberal postwar order within American organized labor because liberalism was seen as capitalizing on the competitive advantage of U.S. exports, thus promoting job opportunities in the United States. For a discussion of illiberal sentiments expressed by such organizations as the American Bankers Association, the National Association of Manufacturers, the U.S. Chamber of Commerce, and the National Foreign Trade Council, see Gardner, *Sterling-Dollar Diplomacy*, 97–98, 131, 197.

53. The right favored protection and maintenance of imperial preferences, whereas the left sought "to insulate domestic programmes of planning and control" aimed at full

employment. See ibid., 32–39. The citation is on p. 39.

54. See ibid., 125, 144, 191, 196–97.

55. Ibid., 143.

56. For additional discussions of the Keynes and White plans and the resulting agreements at Bretton Woods, see Friedrich A. Lutz, *International Monetary Mechanisms*, Princeton Studies in International Finance no. 1 (Princeton: Princeton University Department of Economics, 1943); and Horsefield, *The International Monetary Fund*, vol. I, 3–118.

CHAPTER 5

1. Robert Solomon, *The International Monetary System, 1945–1976* (New York: Harper and Row, 1977), 19.

2. Solomon notes that "the gold and dollar reserves of Europe fell by one-fourth in this period." Ibid., 14.

3. For a chronology, see ibid., 339–40. The hard bargaining over the Anglo-American loan is described in Richard N. Gardner, *Sterling-Dollar Diplomacy* (Oxford: Clarendon Press, 1956), 188–207. The funds were not to be used merely to pay off sterling balances accrued during the war; the United States held the view that the sterling area countries should share the costs of the war with Britain and reduce sterling balance obligations without payment. (In this regard, the United States reduced its claims on Britain for Lend-Lease obligations from $20 billion to $650 million.) See ibid., 204–5, 209. Also, under U.S. pressure Britain made sterling convertible on July 15, 1947, but the attempt to defend a fixed exchange rate proved impossible and controls were put back into effect on August 20.

4. Solomon, *The International Monetary System*, 19.

5. Solomon observes that "of the $8.5 billion increase in world reserves in the years 1949–59, the United States provided $7 billion through the increase in its liabilities to foreign monetary authorities." Ibid., 31.

6. Between 1950 and 1957, the U.S. net gold exports amounted to $1.7 billion. The gold outflow then accelerated such that between 1958 and 1960 an additional $5.1 billion net was exported. Ibid., 37.

7. See Note 4, above.

8. The flow of gold-convertible dollars into the accounts of foreign central banks provided the needed increase in international liquidity that made convertibility of foreign currencies possible. In 1958 alone, international liquidity increased by $1 billion, about $700 million in new gold production, and $300 million in foreign exchange, mainly dollars. See Lawrence A. Veit and Rona S. Woodruff, *Handbook of International Finance* (New York: National Industrial Conference Board, 1967), 4.

9. Gross drawings from the IMF between 1947 and the end of 1959 amounted to just $3.4 billion. See Solomon, *The International Monetary System*, 30.

10. Ibid., 16.

11. Solomon notes that "the French franc was devalued by a total of 29 percent against the dollar" during the late 1950s financial crises that beset the country. In August 1957 the franc was devalued by 16.7 percent and in December 1958 by an additional 14.8 percent. See ibid., 24–25, 340–41.

12. See the discussion in ibid., 86–99.

13. Ibid., 151–65, 344–45.

14. Ibid., 341, 344–45.

15. Coordinating interest rate differentials, some countries raise and others lower interest rates. Owners of capital seeking higher returns (risk and other things equal) tend to move money from lower to higher interest rate countries, which increases or decreases the aggregate demand for the target currency and results in its appreciation or depreciation, respectively.

16. Interpretation of differential discount rates has to be tempered, of course, by recognition that capital flows are also sensitive to differential inflation rates. Thus a country with a relatively high rate of inflation may not attract foreign capital in spite of a relatively high discount rate.

17. The loss of purchasing power resulting from inflation may not be compensated sufficiently by the relatively higher interest rates to make purchases of securities profitable to foreign investors. This caveat is particularly relevant in the years since World War II, when inflation rates have varied considerably from country to country.

18. The Soviets are said to have given initial impetus to the establishment of the Eurodollar market by their reluctance to hold dollar deposits in New York, where they could conceivably have been blocked by U.S. government action. By maintaining gold-convertible, interest-earning dollar deposits in London, the Soviets perceived that they had improved their margin of safety against confiscation or freezing of their assets.

19. Veit and Woodruff, *Handbook of International Finance*, 23, 26.

20. The Group of Ten leading industrially developed countries included Belgium, Canada, France, Germany, Italy, Japan, the Netherlands, Sweden, the United Kingdom, and the United States, with Switzerland participating, in effect, as an associate member.

21. Members of the London Gold Pool included Belgium, France, Germany, Italy, the Netherlands, Switzerland, the United Kingdom, and the United States. Group of Ten members not formally participating were Canada, Japan, and Sweden.

22. WP3, which overlapped with the Group of Ten, included Canada, France, Germany, Italy, Japan, the Netherlands, Sweden, Switzerland, the United Kingdom, and the United States.

23. See Robert W. Cox, "Politics of Money and Trade," in *International Organization*, ed. Cox (London: Macmillan, 1969), esp. 43.

24. See an early discussion of this phenomenon in Robert W. Russell, "Transgovernmental Interaction in the International Monetary System, 1960–1972," *International*

Organization 17, no. 4 (Autumn 1973): 439. Collaboration by central bankers within the institutional setting provided since 1930 by the Bank for International Settlements is well documented in Gianni Toniolo and Piet Clement, *Central Bank Cooperation at the Bank for International Settlements, 1930–1973* (Cambridge: Cambridge University Press, 2005). Compare Claudio Borio, Gianni Toniolo, and Piet Clement, eds., *Past and Future of Central Bank Cooperation* (Cambridge: Cambridge University Press, 2008).

25. See International Monetary Fund, *Articles of Agreement*, Article I.

26. Susan Strange, "The Meaning of Multilateral Surveillance," in Cox, ed., *International Organization*, 245. Significantly, Article I of the I.M.F. Articles of Agreement (1944) holds that the organization should aim "to shorten the duration and lessen the degree of disequilibrium in the international balances of members."

27. For example, close transgovernmental links between American and Canadian monetary officials were not sufficient to overcome different national perspectives associated with balance-of-payments problems. See Gerald Wright and Maureen Appel Molot, "Capital Movements and Government Control," *International Organization* 28, no. 4 (Autumn 1974): esp. 683.

28. On the Gold Pool, see Toniolo and Clement, *Central Bank Cooperation at the Bank for International Settlements*, 356, 375–81, 410–23, as well as commentaries in Borio, Toniolo, and Clement, *Past and Future of Central Bank Cooperation*, 46–47, 88–90.

29. See the discussion in J. Keith Horsefield, *The International Monetary Fund, 1945–1965*, vol. I (Washington, DC: International Monetary Fund, 1969), 484–85.

30. Ibid., 485.

31. Before reaching the decision to establish the GAB, there was considerable debate among the parties as to the role of the IMF in the arrangement. The influential IMF managing director, Per Jacobsson, was instrumental in keeping the IMF from being totally excluded from the GAB as the French would have preferred. The IMF managing director retained the "right to activate the GAB, but the real decision lay with the Group of Ten, meeting with him but without other Fund members." See Susan Strange, "IMF," in *The Anatomy of Influence*, ed. Robert W. Cox and Harold K. Jacobsson (New Haven: Yale University Press, 1973), 263–97. Compare Horsefield, *The International Monetary Fund*, vol. I, 510–14.

32. Horsefield, *The International Monetary Fund*, vol. I, 483.

33. Ibid.

34. "Roosa bonds," named for Undersecretary of the Treasury Robert V. Roosa, were "dollar-denominated securities" sold by the U.S. Treasury "at special rates of interest to foreign monetary authorities." See Solomon, *The International Monetary System*, 40. For a discussion of various financial expedients, see the interview with Roosa conducted by Hirsch in Robert V. Roosa and Fred Hirsch, *Reserves, Reserve Currencies, and Vehicle Currencies*, Princeton Studies in International Finance no. 54 (Princeton: Princeton University Department of Economics, 1966).

35. For example, "[W]hen the Federal Reserve drew on another central bank, it normally used the proceeds to redeem dollars already held by that central bank," thus avoiding their being cashed in at the U.S. Treasury for gold. Following this modality, the foreign central bank substituted a claim on the Federal Reserve in its own currency for "uncovered dollar holdings." See Solomon, *The International Monetary System*, 41–42.

36. Horsefield, *The International Monetary Fund*, vol. I, 484.

37. See the table that summarizes British liabilities to the IMF and various central banks on a year-to-year basis in Susan Strange, *Sterling and British Policy* (London: Oxford University Press, 1971), 261.

38. Ibid., 278.

39. A total of sixty-one countries used IMF credit and forty-six did not.

40. See the discussion in Horsefield, *The International Monetary Fund*, vol. I, 531–36.

41. See "Compensatory Financing of Export Fluctuations," and *IMF Report* dated February 27, 1963, in ibid., vol. III, 442–57. The quotation is on p. 455. Drawings under the facility were "not normally [to] exceed 25 percent of the member's quota" and were, of course, to be in addition to the unquestioned "gold tranche" drawing.

42. See Decision no. 1477-(63–8), February 27, 1963, in ibid., vol. III, 239–40.

43. See "Compensatory Financing of Export Fluctuations," in ibid., vol. Ill, 492–94. Even with this liberalization, the less developed countries were still not satisfied with the restrictive nature of the compensatory-finance facility. Finally, after prolonged discussions it would be liberalized even further in 1976.

44. According to Solomon: "CRU would be held and used in a uniform ratio with gold; they would be created on the basis of *unanimous* decision by the participants. They would be distributed to participants in proportion to their gold reserves. . . . Since the distribution of CRU would be in proportion to gold holdings, countries would have an incentive to maximize their gold reserves by converting existing currency balances into gold. . . . The scheme was to be outside the IMF" and largely confined to members of the Group of Ten. See Solomon, *The International Monetary System*, 76–77. Compare Stephen D. Cohen, *International Monetary Reform, 1964–1969* (New York: Praeger, 1970), 32. To economist Edward Bernstein, the CRU, or Composite (or Collective) Reserve Unit could have a value equivalent to a gold dollar (1/35 ounce of gold), but would be composed of fifty American cents and varying amounts of other currencies. See Leland P. Yeager, *International Monetary Relations* (New York: Harper and Row, 1966), 474–75. Compare Horsefield, *The International Monetary Fund*, vol. I, 592.

45. The American position was articulated by Roosa, who was "chief architect of U.S. international monetary policy in the 1961–64 period." See the discussion in Cohen, *International Monetary Reform*, 43.

46. See the interview of Rueff conducted by Hirsch in Jacques Rueff and Fred Hirsch, *The Role and the Rule of Gold*, Princeton Studies in International Finance no. 47 (Princeton: Princeton University Department of Economics, 1965).

47. Ibid., 55–56. These are Cohen's, not Giscard's, words.

48. Ibid., 56.

49. See the discussion in Cohen, *International Monetary Reform*, 60–64. Compare Fred Hirsch, *An SDR Standard*, Princeton Studies in International Finance no. 99 (Princeton: Princeton University Department of Economics, 1973), 4–7.

50. Cohen, *International Monetary Reform*, 68.

51. Ibid., 125.

52. Ibid.

53. The negotiations are discussed in great detail in ibid., particularly ch. 5. Compare Solomon, *The International Monetary System*, ch. 8.

54. See "Outline of a Facility Based on Special Drawing Rights in the Fund," IMF press release, September 11, 1967, as reprinted in Cohen, *International Monetary Reform*, 179–86; and Horsefield, *The International Monetary Fund*, vol. III, 538–41, esp. V.4(b)(i).

55. See Cohen, *International Monetary Reform*, 149.

56. See "Outline of a Facility Based on Special Drawing Rights in the Fund," III.5.A., in ibid., 179–86.

57. See the amendments to the Articles of Agreement reprinted in Horsefield, *The International Monetary Fund*, vol. Ill, 521–34, esp. Art III.2/4, Art IV.7/8, Art V.7, Art XXIII.3, and XXIV.4(d). See also the discussion in Cohen, *International Monetary Reform*, 137–38, 141; and Joseph Gold, *Special Drawing Rights* (Washington, DC: IMF, 1970), 22–23. For an excellent defense of the thesis that SDRs represent a shift in monetary power from the United States toward Europe, see Eugene A. Birnbaum, "A Simple, Sound Way to Repair the Monetary System," *Fortune* 77, no. 6 (June 1, 1968): 115–17, 158–62.

58. See Horsefield, *The International Monetary Fund*, vol. I, 605–7. Compare Gold, *Special Drawing Rights*, 10.

59. The SDR was originally defined as equivalent to a gold-convertible dollar such that an ounce of gold was equal to SDR 35 or $35. It has since been changed in valuation to a set or basket of currencies. The typical pattern of transfers among participating countries is fairly simple. Countries in need of foreign exchange for international payments surrender SDRs to the IMF in exchange for the needed currency. The IMF issues the needed foreign exchange from its own reserves (in which case it retains the surrendered SDRs in its own account), or it requests another country to supply the needed currency in exchange for SDRs that are then added to that country's account. Such surplus countries, however, need not accept SDRs in exchange for their currency when their SDR holdings are three times the original allocation. In lieu of using the IMF as go-between, countries also retain the right to negotiate SDR transfers bilaterally.

CHAPTER 6

1. Between 1959 and 1971 the value of the dollar relative to other currencies appreciated by about 4.7 percent. See Alfred E. Eckes, Jr., *A Search for Solvency* (Austin: Univer-

sity of Texas Press, 1975), 257.

2. In 1971 the French did put such a two-tier regime into effect, distinguishing between the "commercial" franc and the "financial" franc. See Michael J. Brenner, *The Politics of International Monetary Reform* (Cambridge, MA: Ballinger Publishing Company, 1976), 29, 58.

3. Although the trade balance deteriorated during the 1960s, it remained in surplus until 1971. A very heavy drain on the overall balance, however, was military spending abroad. See the discussion in David P. Calleo and Benjamin M. Rowland, *America and the World Political Economy* (Bloomington: Indiana University Press, 1973), 97–99.

4. See Robert Triffin, "Excerpts from 'Gold and the Dollar Crises,'" in *World Monetary Reform*, ed. Herbert G. Grubel (Stanford: Stanford University Press, 1963), 15–54. The essay is a condensation of Triffin's *Gold and the Dollar Crisis* (New Haven: Yale University Press, 1961), which he updated in his *The World Money Maze* (New Haven: Yale University Press, 1966), 346–73. See also Maxwell Stamp, "The Stamp Plan—1962 Version," in *World Monetary Reform*, ed. Herbert G. Grubel (Stanford: Stanford University Press, 1963), 80–89.

5. See, for example, James E. Meade, "The Future of International Monetary Payments," in *World Monetary Reform*, ed. Grubel, 307–16.

6. All of this assumes that both supply and demand functions are elastic and thus vary freely with respect to the exchange rate—the price of a currency.

7. See Milton Friedman and Robert V. Roosa, *The Balance of Payments* (Washington, DC: American Enterprise for Public Policy Research, 1967), 49–50.

8. See Charles N. Stabler, "IMF Members Warned on Using Credit to Hide Domestic Economic Weaknesses," *Wall Street Journal*, October 5, 1976, 12.

9. See "Treasury Secretary Indicates U.S. Dollar to Continue to Float," *Wall Street Journal*, November 20, 1975, 4.

10. See Herbert Stein, "Fear of Floating," *Wall Street Journal*, June 30, 1975, 10. At the time (March 1973), Stein was still chairman of the Council of Economic Advisors. For an account of events occurring between 1971 and 1974, see John Williamson, *The Failure of World Monetary Reform, 1971–1974* (New York: New York University Press, 1977).

11. The quotations in this paragraph are taken from "World Monetary Reform," *Wall Street Journal*, June 16, 1975, 10.

12. This quotation and others in this paragraph are taken from "Treasury Secretary Simon Replies," a letter to the editor of the *Wall Street Journal*, June 16, 1975, 10.

13. See Milton Friedman, "Six Fallacies," and Gottfried Haberler, "Not That Simple," letters to the editor of the *Wall Street Journal*, June 30, 1975, 11.

14. According to Simon, even Secretary of State Henry Kissinger coordinated his public statements on such matters with the treasury secretary. See the Simon letter cited above in Note 11.

15. Incrementalism in devising new regime rules was acknowledged in Simon's letter to the *Wall Street Journal* cited above in Note 11. The secretary asserted that the Trea-

sury had been trying to "negotiate gradual improvements in international monetary arrangements." He specifically took issue with advocates of "a full, one-shot introduction of a comprehensive new system of rules," arguing that "a sudden adoption of a brave new international monetary world would, in practice, prove both impermanent and disruptive."

16. The complete text of the Rambouillet joint statement is contained in the *London Times*, November 18, 1975, 7.

17. See Simon's press statement of February 3–4, 1976.

18. See Tom deVries, "Jamaica, or the Non-Reform of the International Monetary System," *Foreign Affairs*, 54, 3 (April 1976), 589.

19. See the discussion of these arrangements in the *Wall Street Journal*, November 18 and November 20, 1975. Compare the *Financial Times*, London, December 20, 1975.

20. The Interim Committee was the functional successor to the Committee of Twenty and came into existence in the autumn of 1974. Its charter, as with the earlier Committee of Twenty, was international monetary reform.

21. Access to fund resources was increased to 145 percent of quota, pending approval of the amendment to increase quotas. See deVries, "Jamaica, or the Non-Reform of the International Monetary System," 599.

22. For details on the operation of the trust fund, see IMF, *Annual Report of the Executive Directors*, 111–17.

23. The sterling area ceased in 1979, "when Britain abolished exchange controls and moved to full currency convertibility." See Richard N. Cooper, "Almost a Century of Central Bank Cooperation," in *Past and Future of Central Bank Cooperation*, ed. Claudio Borio, Gianni Toniolo, and Piet Clement (Cambridge: Cambridge University Press, 2008), 84–85.

CHAPTER 7

1. See George F. Kennan, *Around the Cragged Hill* (New York: W. W. Norton, 1993), 203–4.

2. In 1961 the OEEC was renamed the Organization for Economic Cooperation and Development (OECD). The United States, Canada, and Japan became members of the new organization.

3. For a discussion of the Treaty of Rome as it relates to development of the monetary area, see Arthur I. Bloomfield, "The Historical Setting," in *European Monetary Unification and Its Meaning for the United States*, ed. Lawrence B. Krause and Walter S. Salant (Washington, DC: Brookings Institution, 1973), 1–3.

4. The Monetary Committee was established in 1958 by the Treaty of Rome (Article 105). The Committee of Governors of the Central Banks was established in April 1964 by the EEC Council.

5. The original six members were Germany, France, Italy, Belgium, the Netherlands, and Luxembourg.

6. For information on the two Barre plans, the Schiller plan, the Werner plan, and other considerations relating to European monetary integration, see Peter Coffey and John R. Presley, *European Monetary Integration* (London: Macmillan/St. Martin's Press, 1971); James C. Ingram, *The Case for European Monetary Integration*, Princeton Studies in International Finance no. 98 (Princeton: Princeton University Department of Economics, 1973); Giovanni Magnifico, *European Monetary Unification* (New York: John Wiley and Sons, 1973) and *European Monetary Unification for Balanced Growth*, Princeton Studies in International Finance no. 88 (Princeton: Princeton University Department of Economics, 1971); Donald R. Hodgman, *National Monetary Policies and International Cooperation* (Boston: Little Brown, 1974); and Krause and Salant, *European Monetary Unification and Its Meaning for the United States*.

7. Magnifico, *European Monetary Unification*, 2–4.

8. See Hodgman, *National Monetary Policies and International Cooperation*, 244.

9. Of this $2 billion, the German and French contributions were *30 percent* each, the Italian share was 20 percent, and the shares of Belgium and Luxembourg were 10 percent each. See Magnifico, *European Monetary Unification*, 5.

10. See Krause and Salant, *European Monetary Unification and Its Meaning for the United States*, 85–86, 106–7, 213–14.

11. A *central rate* is "a de facto substitute for a par value . . . whereas par values, under the IMF Articles of Agreement, had to be expressed in gold or in gold-convertible dollars," central rates can "be declared in gold, SDRs, or in a currency." See the glossary in Krause and Salant, *European Monetary Unification and Its Meaning for the United States*, 311.

12. See Joseph Kraft, *The Mexican Rescue* (New York: Group of Thirty, 1984), 39, as cited by Eric Helleiner, *States and the Reemergence of Global Finance* (Ithaca, NY: Cornell University Press, 1994), 177.

13. Ibid., 177–78.

14. For discussion of this coordinated, multilateral response, see Richard N. Cooper, "Almost a Century of Central Bank Cooperation," and Ethan B. Kapstein, "Architects of Stability? International Cooperation among Financial Advisors," in *Past and Future of Central Bank Cooperation*, ed. Laudio Borio, Gianni Toniolo, and Piet Clement (Cambridge: Cambridge University Press, 2008), 98–99, 129–30.

15. Opponents in the U.S. Congress were successful in derailing the Truman administration's plan for an International Trade Organization (ITO), which was to operate alongside the IMF and World Bank. Institutionally the fallback was the Geneva-based General Agreement on Tariffs and Trade (the GATT)—a series of conferences by which reductions in both tariff and nontariff barriers to trade were negotiated throughout the Cold War period.

16. See M. Yves Laulan, ed., *Banking, Money and Credit in Eastern Europe* (Brussels: NATO Information Service, 1973), 20.

17. The source of this observation is a conversation between the author and Michael

Gillette, an employee of the World Bank.

18. See Andrzej Korbonski, "COMECON," *International Conciliation*, no. 549 (September 1964): 37.

19. Apparently "only 1.5 percent of the total volume of intra-COMECON trade was paid for in this fashion." Ibid., 38. Part of the Gosbank, the Soviet Trade Bank (*Vnesh-torgbank*), was charged with coordinating and conducting foreign currency transactions. See U.S. Department of Commerce, *The Soviet Financial System,* International Population Statistics Reports, Series P-90, no. 23 (1968), 29. Compare Mikhail V. Condoide, *The Soviet Financial System* (Columbus: Ohio State University, 1951), 118–20.

20. Korbonski, "COMECON," 38–39.

21. Susan Strange, *Sterling and British Policy* (Oxford: Oxford University Press, 1971), 30.

22. Laulan, *Banking, Money and Credit in Eastern Europe,* 22.

23. One of the best sources on the history of creating the EMU is Harold James, *Making the European Monetary Union* (Boston: Harvard University Press/Belknap, 2012). More on the EMU is at the outset of Chapter One, above.

24. For a more detailed summary on the emergence of the euro and the European Central Bank, see Madeleine O. Hosli, *The Euro* (Boulder, CO: Lynne Rienner, 2005).

Bibliography

Acheson, A. L. K., J. F. Chant, and M. F. J. Prachowny. *Bretton Woods Revisited.* Toronto: University of Toronto Press, 1972.

Acheson, Dean. *Present at the Creation: My Years in the State Department.* New York: W. W. Norton, 1969.

Ahamed, Liaquat. *Lords of Finance: The Bankers Who Broke the World.* New York: Penguin, 2009.

Aliber, Robert Z. *The International Money Game.* New York: Basic, 1973.

————. *Stabilizing World Money Arrangements.* London: Trade Political Research Centre, 1979.

Allen, Larry. *The Global Financial System, 1750–2000.* London: Reaktion, 2001.

Allison, Graham T. *Essence of Decision.* Boston: Little Brown, 1971.

Argg, Victor E. *The Postwar International Money Crisis.* Boston: Allen and Unwin, 1981.

Aronson, Jonathan David. "The Impact of American Commercial Banks on the International Monetary System, 1958–1976." Unpublished Ph.D. dissertation, Stanford University, 1976.

————. *Money and Power: Banks and the World Monetary System.* Beverly Hills, CA: Sage, 1977.

Artus, Jacques R., and John H. Young. "Fixed and Flexible Exchange Rates: A Renewal of the Debate." *IMF Staff Papers* 26, no. 4 (December 1979).

Auboin, Roger. *The Bank for International Settlements.* Princeton Studies in International Finance no. 22. Princeton: Princeton University Department of Economics, 1955.

Axelrod, Robert. *Structure of Decision: The Cognitive Maps of Political Elites.* Princeton: Princeton University Press, 1976.

Bagehot, Walter. *Lombard Street: A Description of the Money Market.* Fairford, UK: Echo Library, 1873, 2005.

Bair, Sheila. *Bull by the Horns: Fighting to Save Main Street from Wall Street and Wall Street from Itself.* New York: Free Press, 2012.

Baker, Andrew. *The Group of Seven: Finance Ministries, Central Banks and Global Financial Governance.* London and New York: Routledge, 2006.

Barkin, J. Samuel. *Social Construction and the Logic of Money: Financial Predominance and International Economic Leadership.* Albany: State University of New York Press, 2003.

Barofsky, Neil. *Bailout: An Inside Account of How Washington Abandoned Main Street While Rescuing Wall Street.* New York: Free Press, 2012.

Bergsten, C. Fred. *The Dilemmas of the Dollar: The Economics and Politics of United States International Monetary Policy.* Council on Foreign Relations Book. New York: New York University Press, 1975; 2nd ed., Armonk, NY, and London: M. E. Sharpe, 1996.

Bird, Graham. *The International System and the Less Developed Country.* 2nd ed. London: Macmillan, 1982.

Black, Stanley. *International Money Markets and Flexible Exchange Rates.* Princeton Studies in International Finance no. 32. Princeton: Princeton University Department of Economics, 1973.

Block, Fred L. *The Origins of International Economic Disorder: A Study of United States International Monetary Policy from World War II to the Present.* Berkeley: University of California Press, 1978.

Bloomfield, Arthur I. "The Historical Setting." In *European Monetary Unification and Its Meaning for the United States.* Edited by Lawrence B. Krause and Walter S. Salant. Washington, DC: Brookings Institution, 1973.

———. *Monetary Policy under the International Gold Standard: 1880–1914.* New York: Federal Reserve Bank, 1959.

———. *Patterns of Fluctuation in International Investment before 1914.* Princeton Studies in International Finance no. 21. Princeton: Princeton University Department of Economics, 1968.

———. *Short-Term Capital Movements under the Pre-1914 Gold Standard.* Princeton Studies in International Finance no. 11. Princeton: Princeton University Department of Economics, 1963.

Blum, John Morton. *From the Morgenthau Diaries: Years of War, 1941–1945.* 3 vols. Boston: Houghton Mifflin, 1959, 1965, 1967.

———. *Roosevelt and Morgenthau: A Revision and Condensation from the Morgenthau Diaries.* Boston: Houghton Mifflin, 1970.

Borio, Claudio, Gianni Toniolo, and Piet Clement, eds. *Past and Future of Central Bank Cooperation.* Cambridge: Cambridge University Press, 2008.

Brenner, Michael D. *The Politics of International Monetary Reform: The Exchange Crisis.* Cambridge, MA: Ballinger, 1976.

Brett, E. A. *International Money and Capitalist Crisis: The Anatomy of Global Disintegration.* Boulder, CO: Westview, 1983.

Brown, Brendan. *The Dollar-Mark Axis: On Currency Power.* New York: St. Martin's, 1979.

Brown, William Adams, Jr. *The International Gold Standard Reinterpreted, 1914–1934.* 2 vols. New York: National Bureau of Economic Research, and AMS, 1970.

Bull, Hedley. *The Anarchical Society: A Study of Order in World Politics.* New York: Columbia University Press, 1977.

Buzan, Barry. "The Interdependence of Security and Economic Issues in the 'New World Order.'" In *Political Economy and the Changing World Order.* Edited by Richard Stubbs, and Geoffrey R. D. Underhill. New York: St. Martin's, 1994, 89–102.

Calleo, David P. "The Historiography of the Interwar Period: Reconsiderations." In *Balance of Power or Hegemony: The Interwar Monetary System.* Edited by Benjamin M. Rowland. New York: New York University Press, 1976.

———, ed. *Money and the Coming World Order.* New York: New York University Press, 1976.

Calleo, David P., and Benjamin M. Rowland. *America and the World Political Economy.* Bloomington: Indiana University Press, 1973.

Carr, Edward Hallett. *Nationalism and After.* London: Macmillan, 1945.

———. *Conditions of Peace.* New York: Macmillan, 1947.

Carter, Ashton B., William J. Perry, and John D. Steinbruner. *A New Concept of Cooperative Security.* Brookings Occasional Papers. Washington, DC: Brookings Institution, 1992.

Cassell, Gustav. *The Downfall of the Gold Standard.* London: Frank Cass, 1936, 1966.

CED. *The Dollar and the World Monetary System.* New York: Committee for Economic Development, 1966.

Cerny, Philip G. "Gridlock and Decline: Financial Internationalization, Banking Politics, and the American Political Process." In *Political Economy and the Changing World Order.* Edited by Richard Stubbs and Geoffrey R. D. Underhill. New York: St. Martin's, 1994, 425–38.

Chick, Victoria. *Transnational Enterprises and the Evolution of the International Monetary System.* Sydney, Australia: Faculty of Economics, University of Sydney, 1976.

Clarke, Stephen V. O. *Central Bank Cooperation: 1924–1931.* New York: Federal Reserve Bank, 1967.

Clendenning, E. Wayne. *The Euro-dollar Market.* Oxford: Clarendon, 1970.

Cline, William R. *International Monetary Reform and the Developing Countries.* Washington, DC: Brookings Institution, 1976.

———. *International Debt: Systemic Risk and Policy Response.* Washington, DC: Institute for International Economics/MIT Press, 1984.

Coffey, Peter, and John R. Presley. *European Monetary Integration.* London: Macmillan/St. Martin's, 1971.

Cohen, Stephen D. *International Monetary Reform, 1964–1969: The Political Dimension.* New York: Praeger, 1970.

———. "The System Responds to Exchange Rate and Trade Balance Disequilibria." In *The Making of United States International Economic Policy.* Edited by Stephen D. Cohen. 4th ed. Westport, CT, and London: Praeger, 1994.

Coleman, William D., and Tony Porter. "Regulating International Banking and Securities." In *Political Economy and the Changing World Order.* Edited by Richard Stubbs and Geoffrey R. D. Underhill. New York: St. Martin's, 1994, 190–203.

Commonwealth Secretariat. *Towards a New Bretton Woods: Challenges to the World Financial and Trading System.* London: Cartermill International (September 1983).

Conan, A. R. *The Rationale of the Sterling Area.* London: Macmillan, 1961.

Condoide, Mikhail V. *The Soviet Financial System: Its Development and Relations with the Western World.* Columbus: Ohio State University, 1951.

Cooper, Richard N. "An Analysis of Currency Devaluation in Developing Countries." In *International Trade and Money: The Geneva Essays.* Edited by Michael B. Connolly and Alexander K. Swoboda. Toronto: University of Toronto Press, 1973, 167–96.

———. "Prolegomena to the Choice of an International Monetary System." *International Organization* 29, no. 1 (Winter 1975).

Cox, Robert W. "Politics of Money and Trade." In *International Organization: World Politics.* Edited by Robert W. Cox. London: Macmillan, 1969.

Coyne, Deborah M. R. *Monetary and Financial Reform: The North-South Controversy.* Ottawa: North-South Institute, 1984.

Dam, Kenneth W. *The Rules of the Game: Reform and Evolution in the International Monetary System.* Chicago: University of Chicago Press, 1982.

Davidson, Paul. *International Money and the Real World.* New York: Wiley, 1982.

Deane, Marjorie. *Economic Cooperation from the Inside.* New York: Group of Thirty, 1984.

deCecco, Marcello. *Money and Empire: The International Gold Standard, 1890–1914.* Oxford: Basil Blackwell, 1974.

deGoede, Marieke. *Virtue, Fortune and Faith: A Genealogy of Finance.* Minneapolis: University of Minnesota Press, 2005.

Del Mar, Alexander. *History of Monetary Systems.* London: Effingham Wilson, Royal Exchange, 1895; and New York: Augustus M. Kelley, 1969.

Deutsch, Karl W. *The Nerves of Government.* New York: Free Press, 1963, 1966.

deVegh, Imre. *The Pound Sterling: A Study of the Balance of Payments of the Sterling Area.* New York: Scudder, Stevens, and Clark, 1939.

deVries, Tom. "Jamaica, or the Non-Reform of the International Monetary System." *Foreign Affairs* 54, no. 3 (April 1976).

Dombrowski, Peter. *Policy Responses to the Globalization of American Banking.* Pittsburgh: University of Pittsburgh Press, 1996.

———, ed. *Guns and Butter: The Political Economy of National Security.* Boulder, CO: Lynne Rienner, 2005.

Donn, Albert I. *World War II Prisoner of War Scrip of the United States.* Iola, WI: Krause, 1970.

Eckes, Alfred E., Jr. *A Search for Solvency: Bretton Woods and the International Monetary System, 1941–1971.* Austin: University of Texas Press, 1975.

Eichengreen, Barry. *Golden Fetters?: The Gold Standard and the Great Depression, 1919–1939.* New York: Oxford University Press, 1992.

———. *Globalizing Capital: A History of the International Monetary System.* Princeton: Princeton University Press, 1996.

———. *The European Economy since 1945: Coordinated Capitalism and Beyond.* Princeton: Princeton University Press, 2007.

———. *Exorbitant Privilege: The Rise and Fall of the Dollar and the Future of the International Monetary System.* Oxford: Oxford University Press, 2011.

Einzig, Paul. *World Finance, 1914–1935.* New York: Macmillan, 1935.

———. *The History of Foreign Exchange.* New York: St. Martin's, 1962.

Everest, Allan Seymour. *Morgenthau, the New Deal and Silver: A Story of Pressure Politics.* New York: Da Capo, 1973.

Fagan, Stuart I. *Central American Economic Integration: The Politics of Unequal Benefits.* Berkeley: University of California Institute of International Studies, 1970.

Ferguson, Niall. *The Ascent of Money: A Financial History of the World.* New York: Penguin, 2008.

Ford, A. G. *The Gold Standard, 1890–1914: Britain and Argentina.* Oxford: Clarendon, 1962.

Frances, Stewart. *International Financial Cooperation: A Framework for Change.* Boulder, CO: Westview, 1982.

Frankel, Jeffrey A. *The Yen/Dollar Agreement: Liberalizing Japanese Capital Markets.* Policy Analyses in International Economics no. 9. Washington, DC: Institute for International Economics, 1984.

Franks, Edward Carr. *Flexible vs. Fixed Exchange Rates and International Monetary Stability.* Santa Monica, CA: RAND Paper P-6093, December 1977.

Friedland, Edward I. *Introduction to the Concept of Rationality in Political Science.* Morristown, NJ: General Learning, 1974.

Friedman, Milton. "Six Fallacies." *Wall Street Journal.* June 30, 1975.

Friedman, Milton, and Robert V. Roosa. *The Balance of Payments: Free versus Fixed Exchange Rates.* Washington, DC: American Enterprise Institute for Public Policy Research, 1967.

Friedman, Milton, and Anna Jacobson Schwartz. *A Monetary History of the United States, 1867–1960.* Study by the National Bureau of Economic Research. Princeton: Princeton University Press, 1963.

———. *Monetary Statistics of the United States: Estimates, Sources, Methods.* Study by the National Bureau of Economic Research. New York: Columbia University Press, 1970.

Frolich, Norman, Joe A. Oppenheimer, and Oran R. Young. *Political Leadership and Collective Goods.* Princeton: Princeton University Press, 1971.

Galbraith, John Kenneth. *Money: Whence It Came, Where It Went.* Boston: Houghton-Mifflin, 1975.

Gardner, Richard N. *Sterling-Dollar Diplomacy: Anglo-American Collaboration in the Reconstruction of Multilateral Trade.* Oxford: Clarendon, 1956.

Geltz, Theodore H. *The International Balance of Payments and the Military Services.* Air War College thesis no. 2472. Montgomery, AL: Air War College, 1964.

Gilbert, Charles. *American Financing of World War I.* Westport, CT: Greenwood, 1970.

Gilbert, Milton. *Quest for World Monetary Order: The Gold-Dollar System and Its Aftermath.* New York: Wiley, 1980.

Gilpin, Robert. *U.S. Power and the Multinational Corporation: The Political Economy of Foreign Direct Investment.* New York: Basic, 1975.

———. "Economic Interdependence and National Security in Historical Perspective." In *Economic Issues and National Security.* Edited by Klaus Knorr and Frank N. Trager. Lawrence: Allen Press (Regents Press of Kansas), 1977, 19–66.

———. *The Political Economy of International Relations.* Princeton: Princeton University Press, 1987.

———. *The Challenge of Global Capitalism: The World Economy in the 21st Century.* Princeton: Princeton University Press, 2000.

———. *Global Political Economy.* Princeton: Princeton University Press, 2001.

Gold, Joseph. *Special Drawing Rights.* Washington, DC: International Monetary Fund, 1970.

———. *The Stand-by Arrangements of the International Monetary Fund.* Washington, DC: International Monetary Fund, 1970.

———. *Order in International Finances: The Promotion of the IMF Stand-by Arrangement and the Drafting of Private Loan Agreements.* Washington, DC: International Monetary Fund, 1982.

Goode, Richard. *Economic Assistance to Developing Countries through the IMF.* Studies in International Economics. Washington, DC: Brookings Institution, 1985.

Gowa, Joanne. *Closing the Gold Window: Domestic Politics and the End of Bretton Woods.* Ithaca, NY: Cornell University Press, 1983.

Greider, William. *Secrets of the Temple: How the Federal Reserve Runs the Country.* New York: Simon and Schuster, 1987.

Griffith-Jones, Stephany. *International Finance and Latin America.* New York: St. Martin's, 1984.

Grubel, Herbert G., ed. *World Monetary Reform: Plans and Issues.* Stanford: Stanford University Press, 1963.

Guitián, Manuel. *The Unique Nature of the Responsibilities of the International Monetary Fund.* Pamphlet Series no. 46. Washington, DC: International Monetary Fund, 1992.

Haas, Peter M., ed. *Knowledge, Power, and International Policy Coordination.* Columbia: University of South Carolina Press, 1992.

Haberler, Gottfried. *A Survey of International Trade.* Special Papers in Economics no. 1. Princeton: Princeton University Department of Economics, 1961.

Habermas, Jürgen. *The Crisis of the European Union: A Response.* Cambridge, UK: Polity, 2011, 2012.

Hall, Rodney Bruce. *Central Banking as Global Governance: Constructing Financial Credibility.* Cambridge: Cambridge University Press, 2008.

Hamelink, Cees J. *Finance and Information: A Study of Converging Interests.* Norwood, NJ: Ablex, 1983.

Harrod, Roy F. *The Pound Sterling.* Princeton Studies in International Finance no. 13. Princeton: Princeton University Department of Economics, 1952.

———. "Problems Perceived in the International Financial System." In *Bretton Woods Revisited.* Edited by A. L. K. Acheson et al. Toronto: University of Toronto Press, 1972.

Hawtrey, R. G. *The Gold Standard in Theory and Practice.* 5th ed. London: Longman's, Green, 1927, 1947.

Helleiner, Eric. "From Bretton Woods to Global Finance: A World Turned Upside Down." In *Political Economy and the Changing World Order.* Edited by Richard Stubbs and Geoffrey R. D. Underhill. New York: St. Martin's, 1994, 163–75.

———. *States and the Reemergence of Global Finance: From Bretton Woods to the 1990s.* Ithaca, NY: Cornell University Press, 1994.

Helleiner, Eric, and Jonathan Kirshner, eds. *The Future of the Dollar.* Ithaca, NY: Cornell University, 2009.

Heller, E. Robert. *International Trade: Theory and Empirical Evidence.* Englewood Cliffs, NJ: Prentice Hall, 1968.

Hieronymi, Otto, ed. *Globalization and Reform of the International Banking and Monetary System.* New York: Palgrave, 2009.

Higham, Charles. *Trading with the Enemy: The NAZI-American Money Plot, 1933–1949.* New York: Barnes and Noble, 1983.

Hinshaw, Randall, ed. *Global Monetary Anarchy: Perspectives on Restoring Stability.* Beverly Hills, CA, and London: Sage, 1981.

Hirsch, Fred. *Money International.* Garden City, NY: Doubleday, 1969.

———. *An SDR Standard: Impetus, Elements, and Impediments.* Princeton Studies in International Finance no. 99. Princeton: Princeton University Department of Economics, 1973.

Hirschman, Albert O. *The Passions and the Interests: Political Arguments for Capitalism before Its Triumph.* Princeton: Princeton University Press, 1977.

Hobsbawm, E. J. *Industry and Empire.* Baltimore, MD: Penguin, 1968, 1969.

Hodgman, Donald R. *National Monetary Policies and International Cooperation.* Boston: Little Brown, 1974.

Hodgson, James Goodwin. *Cancellation of International War Debts.* New York: H. W. Wilson, 1932.

Hogan, Edward B. *The Gold Problem and US National Interests.* Air War College Research Report no. 3618. Montgomery, AL: Air War College, 1968.

Holtrop, M. W. "Central Banking and Economic Integration." Lecture. Stockholm: Per Jacobson Foundation, 1968.

Horsefield, J. Keith, ed. *The International Monetary Fund, 1945–1965: Twenty Years of International Monetary Cooperation.* 3 vols. Washington, DC: International Monetary Fund, 1969.

Hosli, Madeleine O. *The Euro: A Concise Introduction to European Monetary Integration.* Boulder: Lynne Rienner, 2005.

Ikenberry, G. John. "A World Economy Restored: Expert Consensus and the Anglo-American Postwar Settlement." In *Knowledge, Power, and International Policy Coordination.* Edited by Peter M. Haas. Columbia: University of South Carolina Press, 1992, 265–87.

———. *Liberal Leviathan: The Origins, Crisis, and Transformation of the American World Order.* Princeton: Princeton University Press, 2011.

Ingram, James C. *The Case for European Monetary Integration.* Princeton Studies in International Finance no. 98. Princeton: Princeton University Department of Economics, 1973.

Inouye, Junnosuke. *Problems of the Japanese Exchange: 1914–1926.* London: Macmillan, 1931.

Jacobsson, Per. "The Role of Money in a Dynamic Economy." Arthur K. Salomon lecture. New York: New York University Graduate School of Business Administration, 1963.

James, Harold. *Making the European Monetary Union.* Cambridge: Harvard University Press/ Belknap, 2012.

Jèze, Gaston, and Henri Truchy. *The War Finance of France.* New Haven: Yale University Press, 1927.

Kane, Daniel R. *The Eurodollar Market and the Years of Crisis.* New York: St. Martin's, 1983.

Kapstein, Ethan Barnaby. "Between Power and Purpose: Central Bankers and the Politics of Regulatory Convergence." In *Knowledge, Power, and International Policy Coordination.* Edited by Peter M. Haas. Columbia: University of South Carolina Press, 1992, 265–87.

———. *The Political Economy of National Security: A Global Perspective.* New York: McGraw-Hill, 1992.

Kapur, Devesh. "The IMF: A Cure or a Curse." *Foreign Policy* 3 (Summer 1998): 114–29.

Kelly, Janet. "International Monetary Systems and National Security." In *Economic Issues and National Security.* Edited by Klaus Knorr and Frank N. Trager. Lawrence: Allen Press (Regents Press of Kansas), 1977, 231–58.

Kenen, Peter B. *The Role of the Dollar as an International Currency.* New York: Group of Thirty, 1983.

———. *Managing Exchange Rates.* Royal Institute of International Affairs, Chatham House Papers. London and New York: Routledge, 1988.

Kennan, George F. *Around the Cragged Hill: A Personal and Political Philosophy.* New York: W. W. Norton, 1993.

Keohane, Robert O., and Joseph S. Nye. *Power and Interdependence: World Politics in Transition.* Boston: Little Brown, 1977.

———, eds. *Transnational Relations and World Politics.* Cambridge: Harvard University Press, 1970, 1971.

Keynes, John Maynard. *The Economic Consequences of the Peace.* New York: Harcourt, Brace and Howe, 1920.

———. *The End of Laissez-Faire.* London: Hogarth, 1926.

———. "The British Balance of Payments: 1925–1927." *Economic Journal* (December 1927).

———. "The Economic Consequences of Mr. Churchill." In Keynes, *Essays in Persuasion.* New York: Harcourt, Brace, 1932.

———. *Essays in Persuasion.* New York: Harcourt, Brace, 1932.

———. *The General Theory of Employment, Interest and Money.* New York: Harcourt Brace Jovanovich, 1935, 1953.

———. *How to Pay for the War: A Radical Plan for the Chancellor of the Exchequer.* New York: Harcourt, Brace, 1940.

Kindleberger, Charles P. *Foreign Trade and the National Economy.* New Haven: Yale University Press, 1962.

———. *Power and Money: The Politics of International Economics and the Economics of International Politics.* New York: Basic, 1970.

———. *The Formation of Financial Centers: A Study in Comparative Economic History.* Princeton Studies in International Finance no. 36. Princeton: Princeton University Department of Economics, 1974.

———. *The World in Depression, 1929–1939.* Berkeley: University of California Press, 1973.

———. "Systems of International Economic Organization." In *Money and the Coming World Order.* Edited by David P. Calleo. New York: New York University Press, 1976.

———. *A Financial History of Western Europe.* London: George Allen and Unwin, 1984.

Kirshner, Jonathan. *Currency and Coercion: The Political Economy of International Monetary Power.* Princeton: Princeton University Press, 1995, 1997.

Knorr, Klaus. *Power and Wealth: The Political Economy of International Power.* New York: Basic, 1973.

———. "Economic Interdependence and National Security." In *Economic Issues and National Security.* Edited by Klaus Knorr and Frank N. Trager. Lawrence: Allen Press (Regents Press of Kansas), 1977, 1–18.

———. "International Economic Leverage and Its Uses." In *Economic Issues and National Security.* Edited by Klaus Knorr and Frank N. Trager. Lawrence: Allen Press (Regents Press of Kansas), 1977, 99–126.

———. "Military Strength: Economic and Non-Economic Bases." In *Economic Issues and National Security.* Edited by Klaus Knorr and Frank N. Trager. Lawrence: Allen Press (Regents Press of Kansas), 1977, 183–99.

Kobayashi, Ushisaburo. *War and Armament Loans of Japan.* New York: Oxford University Press, 1922.

Kooker, Judith L. "French Financial Diplomacy: The Interwar Years." In *Balance of Power or Hegemony: The Interwar Monetary System.* Edited by Benjamin M. Rowland. New York: New York University Press, 1976.

Kraft, Joseph. *The Mexican Rescue.* New York: Group of Thirty, 1984.

Krause, Lawrence B., and Walter S. Salant, eds. *European Monetary Unification and Its Meaning for the United States.* Washington, DC: Brookings Institution, 1973.

Kris, Miroslav A. *Gold: Barbarous Relic or Useful Instrument?* Princeton Studies in International Finance no. 60. Princeton: Princeton University Department of Economics, 1967.

Krugman, Paul. *The Return of Depression Economics and the Crisis of 2008.* New York: W. W. Norton, 1999, 2009.

Lane, Frederic C. *Venice: A Maritime Republic.* Baltimore, MD: Johns Hopkins University Press, 1973.

Laulan, M. Yves, ed. *Banking, Money and Credit in Eastern Europe.* Brussels: NATO Information Service, 1973.

Leive, David M. *International Regulatory Regimes.* Lexington, MA: Lexington, 1976.

Lester, Richard A. *International Aspects of Wartime Monetary Experience.* Princeton Studies in International Finance no. 3. Princeton: Princeton University Department of Economics, 1944.

Lewis, Michael. *Boomerang: Travels in the New Third World.* New York: W. W. Norton, 2011.

Lindert, Peter H. *Key Currencies and Gold, 1900–1913.* Princeton Studies in International Finance no. 24. Princeton: Princeton University Department of Economics, 1969.

Lipson, Charles. "Bankers' Dilemmas: Private Cooperation in Rescheduling Private Debts." In *Cooperation under Anarchy.* Edited by Kenneth A. Oye. Princeton: Princeton University Press, 1986, 200–225.

Llewellyn, David T. *International Financial Integration and the Limits of Sovereignty.* New York: Macmillan, 1980.

Lomax, David F., and P. T. G. Gutmann. *The Euromarkets and International Financial Policies.* New York: Wiley, 1981.

Lutz, Friedrich A. *International Monetary Mechanisms: The Keynes and White Proposals.* Princeton Studies in International Finance no. 1. Princeton: Princeton University Department of Economics, 1943.

Macesich, George. *The International Monetary Economy and the Third World.* New York: Praeger, 1981.

———. *World Banking and Finance: Cooperation vs. Conflict.* New York: Praeger, 1984.

Machlup, Fritz. *Remaking the International Monetary System: The Rio Agreement and Beyond.* Baltimore, MD: Johns Hopkins University Press, 1968.

MacKenzie, Donald. *An Engine, Not a Camera: How Financial Models Shape Markets.* Cambridge: MIT Press, 2006.

Magnifico, Giovanni. *European Monetary Unification for Balanced Growth.* Princeton Studies in International Finance no. 88. Princeton: Princeton University Department of Economics, 1971.

———. *European Monetary Unification.* New York: John Wiley and Sons, 1973.

Mannheim, Karl. *Ideology and Utopia.* New York: Harcourt, Brace, and World, 1929, 1936.

———. *Freedom, Power and Democratic Planning.* Edited by Hans Gerth and Ernest K. Bramstedt. London: Routledge and Kegan Paul, 1950, 1951.

Mastanduno, Michael. "Economics and Security in Statecraft and Scholarship." *International Organization* 52 (1998): 825–54.

Mattione, Richard P. *OPEC's Investments and the International Financial System.* Washington, DC: Brookings, 1985.

Maullin, Richard L. *The Colombia-IMF Disagreement of November-December 1966: An Interpretation of Its Place in Colombian Politics.* Santa Monica, CA: RAND Memorandum RM-5314-RC, June 1967.

McCormick, Bruce. "The Smithsonian Agreement: The Road to the 'Greatest Monetary Achievement in the History of the World.'" Unpublished paper (photocopy). University of California, Berkeley. 1975.

McKinnon, Ronald I. *Private and Official International Money: The Case for the Dollar.* Princeton Studies in International Finance no. 74. Princeton: Princeton University Department of Economics, 1969.

———. *An International Standard for Monetary Stabilization.* Policy Analyses in International Economics no. 8. Washington, DC: Institute for International Economics, 1984.

McNeil, William C. *American Money and the Weimar Republic: Economics and Politics on the Eve of the Great Depression.* New York: Columbia University Press, 1986.

Mead, Walter Russell. *God and Gold: Britain, America, and the Making of the Modern World.* New York: Random House/Vintage, 2007.

Meade, James E. *The Belgium-Luxembourg Economic Union, 1921–1939.* Princeton: Princeton Studies in International Finance no. 25. Princeton: Princeton University Department of Economics, March 1956.

———. "The Future of International Monetary Payments." In *World Monetary Reform: Plans and Issues.* Edited by Herbert G. Grubel. Stanford: Stanford University Press, 1963.

Meier, Gerald M. *Problems of a World Monetary Order.* New York: Oxford University Press, 1982.

Mendelson, M. S. *Commercial Banks and the Restructuring of Cross-Border Debt.* New York: Group of Thirty, 1983.

Metzger, Laure. *American Loans in the Postwar Period.* Washington, DC: Foundations for Foreign Affairs, 1948.

Metzger, Stanley D. *Lowering Nontariff Barriers.* Washington, DC: Brookings Institution, 1974.

Meyer, Richard Hemmig. *Banker's Diplomacy: Monetary Stabilization in the Twenties.* New York: Columbia University Press, 1970.

Michelson, Alexander M., Paul N. Apostol, and Michael W. Bernatzky. *Russian Public Finance during the War.* New Haven: Yale University Press, 1928.

Mills, J. Saxon. *The Genoa Conference.* London: Hutchinson, c. 1923.

Missiroli, Antonio. *Euros for ESDP: Financing EU Operations.* Paris: Institute for Security Studies, European Union, Occasional Paper no. 45, June 2003.

Mitchell, B. R. *Abstract of British Historical Statistics*. Cambridge: Cambridge University Press, 1962.

Moffitt, Michael. *The World's Money: International Banking from Bretton Woods to the Brink of Solvency*. New York: Simon and Schuster, 1982.

Moggridge, D. E. *The Return to Gold, 1925: The Formulation of Policy and Its Critics*. Cambridge: Cambridge University Press, 1969.

———. *British Monetary Policy, 1924–1931: The Norman Conquest of $4.867*. Cambridge: Cambridge University Press, 1972.

Moncarz, Raul. "Monetary Aspects of the Central American Common Market." *Journal of Common Market Studies* 12, no. 2 (December 1973).

Monroe, W. F. *International Monetary Reconstruction*. Lexington, MA: Lexington, 1974.

Morgan, E. Victor. *A History of Money*. Baltimore, MD: Penguin, 1965.

Morgan-Webb, Sir Charles. *The Money Revolution*. New York: Economic Forum, 1935.

———. *The Rise and Fall of the Gold Standard*. New York: Macmillan Company, 1934.

Morrell, James. *The Future of the Dollar and the World Reserve System*. London and Boston: Butterworths, 1981.

Moulton, Harold G., and Leo Pasvolsky. *World War Debt Settlements*. New York: Macmillan, 1929.

———. *War Debts and World Prosperity*. Brookings Institution Study. New York: Century, 1932.

Myers, Margaret G. *A Financial History of the United States*. New York: Columbia University Press, 1970.

New, Noah C. *Effect of Military Expenditures on Gold Outflow*. Air War College Research Report no. 3662. Montgomery, AL: Air War College, 1968.

Newcomer, Mabel. *Central and Local Finance in Germany and England*. New York: Columbia University Press, 1937.

Norrlof, Carla. *America's Global Advantage: US Hegemony and International Cooperation*. Cambridge: Cambridge University Press, 2010.

Noyes, Alexander D. *The War Period of American Finance, 1908–1925*. New York: G. P. Putnam, 1974.

Nugent, Walter T. K. *Money and American Society: 1865–1880*. New York: Free Press, 1968.

Nurkse, Ragnar. *Conditions of International Monetary Equilibrium*. Princeton Studies in International Finance no. 4. Princeton: Princeton University Department of Economics, 1945.

Nussbaum, Arthur. *A History of the Dollar*. New York: Columbia University Press, 1957.

Odell, John S. *U.S. International Monetary Policy: Markets, Power, and Ideas as Sources of Change*. Princeton: Princeton University Press, 1982.

Offer, Avnar. *The First World War: An Agrarian Interpretation*. Oxford: Clarendon, 1989.

Oye, Kenneth A. *Eagle Entangled*. Edited by Donald Rothchild and Robert J. Lieber. New York: Longman, 1979.

———. "The Sterling-Dollar-Franc Triangle: Monetary Diplomacy, 1929–1937." In *Cooperation under Anarchy.* Edited by Oye. Princeton: Princeton University Press, 1986, 173–99.

———. *Economic Discrimination and Political Exchange: World Political Economy in the 1930s and 1980s.* Princeton: Princeton University Press, 1992.

Parboni, Riccardo. *The Dollar and Its Rivals: Recession, Inflation, and International Finance.* Translated by Jon Rothschild. London: NLB, 1981.

Paris, James Daniel. *Monetary Policies of the United States, 1932–1938.* New York: Columbia University Press, 1938.

Payer, Cheryl. *The Debt Trap: The International Monetary Fund and the Third World.* New York: Monthly Review Press, 1974.

Petrov, Vladimir. *Money and Conquest: Allied Occupation Currencies in World War II.* Baltimore, MD: Johns Hopkins University Press, 1967.

Piaget, Jean. *Structuralism.* Translated and edited by Chaninah Maschler. New York: Basic, 1970.

Pierce, David G., and David M. Shaw. *Monetary Economics: Theory, Evidence, and Policy.* London: Butterworth, 1974.

Polanyi, Karl. *The Great Transformation.* Boston: Beacon, 1957.

Poniachek, Harvey A. *Monetary Independence and Flexible Exchange Rates.* Boston: Lexington, 1979.

Pumphrey, Lowell M. "The Exchange Equalization Account of Great Britain, 1932–1939." *American Economic Review* 32 (1942).

Reed, Howard Curtis. *The Preeminence of International Financial Centers.* New York: Praeger, 1986.

Rees, David. *Harry Dexter White: A Study in Paradox.* New York: Coward, McCann and Geoghegan, 1973.

Reinhart, Carmen M., and Kenneth S. Rogoff. *This Time Is Different: Eight Centuries of Financial Folly.* Princeton: Princeton University Press, 2009.

Rickards, James. *Currency Wars: The Making of the Next Global Crisis.* New York: Portfolio/Penguin, 2011.

Robson, P., ed. *International Economic Integration.* Middlesex: Penguin, 1971, 1972.

Rolfe, Sidney E., and James Burtle. *The Great Wheel: The World Monetary System, a Reinterpretation.* New York: Quadrangle/New York Times , 1973.

Roosa, Robert V., and Fred Hirsch. *Reserves, Reserve Currencies, and Vehicle Currencies: An Argument.* Princeton Studies in International Finance no. 54. Princeton: Princeton University Department of Economics, 1966.

Rowland, Benjamin M., ed. *Balance of Power or Hegemony: The Interwar Monetary System.* New York: New York University Press, 1976.

Rueff, Jacques, and Fred Hirsch. *The Role and the Rule of Gold: An Argument.* Princeton Studies in International Finance no. 47. Princeton: Princeton University Department of Economics, 1965.

Rundell, Walter, Jr. *Black Market Money: The Collapse of U.S. Currency Control in World War II.* Baton Rouge: Louisiana State University Press, 1964.

Russell, Robert W. "Transgovernmental Interaction in the International Monetary System, 1960–1972." *International Organization* 17, no. 4 (Autumn 1973).

Rutlader, James. *Allied Military Currency: Issues of Military Payment Certificates from World War II to Date.* Kansas City, MO: Bill Johnson Creative Printers, 1968.

Sachs, Jeffrey. "Beyond Bretton Woods: A New Blueprint." In *Readings in International Political Economy.* Edited by David N. Balaam and Michael Veseth. Upper Saddle River, NJ: Prentice Hall, 1996.

Samuelson, Paul A. *Economics.* 9th ed. New York: McGraw-Hill, 1955, 1973.

Sayers, R. S. *History of the Second World War: Financial Policy, 1939–45.* London: H.M. Stationery Office and Longman's, Green, 1956.

Schmitter, Philippe C. *Autonomy or Dependence as Regional Integration Outcomes: Central America.* Berkeley: University of California Institute of International Studies, 1972.

Schumpeter, Joseph. *Capitalism, Socialism, and Democracy.* New York: Harper and Row, 1950, 1962.

Semmel, Bernard. *The Rise of Free Trade Imperialism: Classical Political Economy, the Empire of Free Trade and Imperialism, 1750–1850.* Cambridge: Cambridge University Press, 1970.

Sheppard, David K. *The Growth and Role of UK Financial Institutions: 1880–1962.* London: Methuen, 1971.

[Simon, William.] "Treasury Secretary Simon Replies." *Wall Street Journal.* June 16, 1975.

Skidelvsky, Robert J. A. "Retreat from Leadership: The Evolution of British Economic Foreign Policy, 1870–1939." In *Balance of Power or Hegemony: The Interwar Monetary System.* Edited by Benjamin M. Rowland. New York: New York University Press, 1976.

Sobol, Dorothy M. *Europe Confronts the Dollar: The Creation of the SDR, 1963–69.* New York: Garland, 1982.

Solomon, Robert. *The International Monetary System 1945–1976: An Insider's View.* New York: Harper and Row, 1977; rev. ed.: *The International Monetary System 1945–1981.* New York: Harper and Row, 1982.

Southard, Frank A., Jr. *Some European Currency and Exchange Experiences.* Princeton Studies in International Finance no. 7. Princeton: Princeton University Department of Economics, 1946.

Southard, Frank A., Jr., and William McChesney Martin [former chairman, Federal Reserve Board]. *The International Monetary System in Transition.* Washington, DC: Atlantic Council, May 1980.

Spero, Joan Edelman, and Jeffrey A. Hart. *The Politics of International Economic Relations.* Belmont, CA: Thomson/Wadsworth, 2003.

Stamp, Maxwell. "The Stamp Plan—1962 Version." In *World Monetary Reform: Plans and Issues.* Edited by Herbert G. Grubel. Stanford: Stanford University Press, 1962.

Stein, Herbert. "Fear of Floating." *Wall Street Journal.* June 30, 1975.

Stevenson, Jonathan. *Preventing Conflict: The Role of the Bretton Woods Institutions.* Adelphi Paper no. 336. London: International Institute for Strategic Studies, 2000.

Stiglitz, Joseph E. *Globalization and Its Discontents.* New York: W. W. Norton, 2002, 2003.

Stonehill, Arthur I. *Internationalizing the Cost of Capital.* New York: Wiley, 1982.

Strange, Susan. "The Meaning of Multilateral Surveillance." In *International Organization: World Politics.* Edited by Robert W. Cox. London: Macmillan, 1969.

———. *Sterling and British Policy: A Political Study of an International Currency in Decline.* Oxford: Oxford University Press, 1971.

———. "IMF: Monetary Managers." In *The Anatomy of Influence: Decision-Making in International Organization.* Edited by Robert W. Cox and Harold K. Jacobsson. New Haven: Yale University Press, 1973.

———. *International Monetary Relations.* London and New York: Oxford University Press, 1976.

Toniolo, Gianni, and Piet Clement. *Central Bank Cooperation at the Bank for International Settlements, 1930–1973.* Cambridge: Cambridge University Press, 2005.

Tosini, Paula A. *Leaning against the Wind: A Standard for Managed Floating.* Princeton Studies in International Finance no. 126. Princeton: Princeton University Department of Economics, December 1977.

Toy, Raymond S., and Bob Meyer. *World War II Axis Military Currency.* Tucson, AZ: Monitor Offset Printing, 1967.

Triffin, Robert. "Excerpts from 'Gold and the Dollar Crises.'" In *World Monetary Reform: Plans and Issues.* Edited by Herbert G. Grubel. Stanford: Stanford University Press, 1963.

———. *The Evolution of the International Monetary System: Historical Reappraisal and Future Perspectives.* Princeton Studies in International Finance no. 12. Princeton: Princeton University Department of Economics, 1964.

———. "The American Response to the European Monetary System." In *The European Monetary System: Its Promise and Prospects.* Edited by Philip H. Trezise. Washington, DC: Brookings Institution, 1979.

———. *Gold and the Dollar Crisis.* New Haven: Yale University Press, 1961.

———. *The World Money Maze.* New Haven: Yale University Press, 1966.

Ulbrich, Holley H. *International Trade and Finance: Theory and Policy.* Englewood Cliffs, NJ: Prentice-Hall, 1983.

Van Der Flier, M. J. *War Finances in the Netherlands up to 1918.* Oxford: Clarendon, 1923.

Veit, Lawrence A., and Rona S. Woodruff. *Handbook of International Finance, 1958–1966.* New York: National Industrial Conference Board, 1967.

Versluysen, Eugène. *The Political Economy of International Finance.* New York: St. Martin's, 1981.

Webb, Michael C. *The Political Economy of Policy Coordination.* Ithaca, NY: Cornell University Press, 1995.

Williams, David. "London and the 1931 Financial Crisis." *Economic History Review* 15 (April 1963).

Williamson, John. *The Failure of World Monetary Reform, 1971–1974.* New York: New York University Press, 1977.

———. *The Exchange Rate System.* Policy Analyses in International Economics no. 5. Washington, DC: Institute for International Economics, 1983.

Winch, Donald. *Economics and Policy: A Historical Study.* London: Hodder and Stoughton, 1969; New York: Walker and Company, 1969.

Wonnacott, Paul. *The Floating Canadian Dollar: Exchange Flexibility and Monetary Independence.* Washington, DC: American Enterprise Institute for Public Policy Research, 1972.

Wright, Gerald, and Maureen Appel Molot. "Capital Movements and Government Control." *International Organization* 28, no. 4 (Autumn 1974).

Yeager, Leland P. *International Monetary Relations: Theory, History, and Policy.* New York: Harper and Row, 1966.

Young, John Parke. *Central American Monetary Union.* Washington, DC: U.S. Agency for International Development, 1962.

Zimmerman, Hubert. *Money and Security: Troops, Monetary Policy, and West Germany's Relations with the U.S. and Britain, 1950–1971.* Cambridge: Cambridge University Press, 2002.

Zwass, Adam. *Monetary Cooperation between East and West.* White Plains, NY: International Arts and Sciences, 1975.

DOCUMENTS

Bank for International Settlements. *Annual Report.* Various years.

International Monetary Fund. *Annual Report.* Washington, DC. Various years.

International Monetary Fund. *Articles of Agreement.* 1944.

International Monetary Fund. *International Financial Statistics.* Washington, DC. Various issues.

International Monetary Fund. *Multilateral Surveillance.* Washington, DC: Independent Evaluation of the Office of the IMF, 2006.

League of Nations. Economic and Financial Section. *Statistical Yearbook.* Geneva. Various issues.

League of Nations. Economic, Financial and Transit Department. *The Course and Control of Inflation: A Review of Monetary Experience in Europe after World War I.* 1946.

United Kingdom. *First Interim Report of the Committee on Currency.* Reprinted in *Select Statutes, Documents and Reports Relating to British Banking, 1832–1928.* Edited by T. E. Gregory. Oxford: Oxford University Press, 1929.

United Kingdom. British Government Publication, *Proposals for an International Clearing Union.* Reprinted in *World Monetary Reform: Plans and Issues.* Edited by Herbert G. Grubel. Stanford: Stanford University Press, 1963.

United States. Department of Commerce. Bureau of the Census. *Historical Statistics of the United States: Colonial Times to 1970.* Washington, DC. 1975.

United States. Department of Commerce. International Population Statistics Reports. Series P-90, no. 23. *The Soviet Financial System: Structure, Operation, and Statistics*. 1968.

United States. Federal Reserve System. *Federal Reserve Bulletin*. 1932–37. January issues.

United States. Tariff Commission. *Report to the Committee on Finance, U.S. Senate, Subcommittee on International Trade*. Tariff Commission Publication no. 665. Washington, DC.

Index

149; financial crises, 140–41, 142–43; IMF and, 106–8, 127, 128–29, 183n43
Liberal economic policies: Genoa Conference, 56; laissez-faire, 8, 85, 117–18, 121–22, 123; loss of faith in, 85, 86; supporters after World War II, 85, 103, 179n40, 179n52
Liquidity: in banking crises, 149–50; IMF provision of, 90, 92, 108; importance, 33; international, 33; in managed flexibility regime, 129; in post-World War II period, 85, 86, 87, 89, 100–103, 102 (table), 113, 180n8; reform efforts to increase, 116–18
Lloyd George, David, 55, 56
London: Eurodollar market, 100–101, 144, 181n18; as financial center, 43, 46–47, 48, 52, 59, 65–66, 70, 100–101; gold market, 104; Soviet banks, 144; stock exchange, 47; World Economic Conference (1933), 85. *See also* Britain
London Gold Pool, 103, 104, 181n21
López Portillo, José, 132, 141
Louvre accords, 142
Low-income countries, *see* Less developed countries

Managed flexibility regime: advantages for United States, 125, 130–31, 159; collaborative management, 8, 119, 122–23, 124–25, 126–30, 149; criticism of, 122–24; currency market interventions, 22; "dirty" float, 8, 118, 122; discount rates, 126, 127 (table); euro in, 9; financial crises, 140–43; negotiations, 115–16, 121–22, 124–25; U.S. policies, 21–22, 23
Mark, *see* German mark
Marshall Plan, 90, 95–96, 133, 180n3
McKenna, Reginald, 62
McKittrick, Thomas, 82–83
Mexico: monetary crisis (1982), 140–41; peso crisis (1995), 142–43
Military currencies, 80
Military spending, *see* Defense spending

Monetary leadership: by Britain, 40, 55, 57, 58–60, 62, 64–65, 173n3; by United States, 89, 90–91, 95
Monetary policy: British, 69; European coordination, 4–5, 9, 31, 134–36, 137, 145; floating exchange rates and, 159; IMF conditions, 140–41; of United States, 4, 17, 140
Money, social construction of, 2, 34, 70. *See also* Currencies
Morgan, J. P., 59
Morgenthau, Henry, 82, 83, 86, 93
Multilateralism: economic, 24–25; economic security and, 33–34; in Europe, 132–33; in European Union, 29–31; institutionalized, 23–24, 33, 103, 132–33, 150, 151; norms, 151, 155; security organizations, 23–24; trade liberalization, 143, 187n15. *See also* Cooperative security

Narodny Bank, 144
National security, *see* Security; U.S. national security policy
NATO (North Atlantic Treaty Organization): Afghanistan war, 147, 148; economic arrangements and, 134; establishment, 23–24, 95, 133; European dependence on, 140; French withdrawal, 104, 109; members, 14, 167n19; U.S. defense spending and, 113, 119
Netherlands: exchange rates, 97; finance during World War I, 46, 47, 51–52, 157
New York, as financial center, 48, 53, 59
New York Federal Reserve Bank: BIS and, 82; discount rates, 60, 60 (table), 77, 77 (table), 98 (table), 99, 126. *See also* Strong, Benjamin
New York Stock Exchange (NYSE): crash (1929), 53–54, 75; hypothetical attack on, xiii–xiv
Nixon, Richard M., 21, 113, 115, 116, 138
Nonbelligerents, *see* Netherlands; Switzerland